BLACKWARDS

ALSO BY RON CHRISTIE

Acting White

Black in the White House

BLACKWARDS

|||||||||||||||||||||||||||||||||||||||||||||||||

HOW BLACK LEADERSHIP IS RETURNING
AMERICA TO THE DAYS OF
SEPARATE BUT EQUAL

RON CHRISTIE

THOMAS DUNNE BOOKS ST. MARTIN'S PRESS

NEW YORK

THOMAS DUNNE BOOKS.
An imprint of St. Martin's Press.

www.thomasdunnebooks.com
www.stmartins.com

Design by Steven Seighman

Library of Congress Cataloging-in-Publication Data

Christie, Ron, 1969–
    Blackwards : how Black leadership is returning America to the days of separate but equal / Ron Christie. — 1st ed.
            p. cm.
    Includes bibliographical references and index.
    ISBN 978-0-312-59147-2 (hardcover)
    ISBN 978-1-250-01352-1 (e-book)
    1. African Americans—History—1964– 2. African Americans—Civil rights—a History. 3. African Americans—Social conditions—2009–
4. African Americans—Politics and government. 5. African American leadership. 6. United States—Race relations—History. 7. United States—Social conditions—21st century. 8. United States—Politics and government—2009– I. Title.
    E185.615.C577 2012
    323.1196'073—dc23
                                                                    2012024019

First Edition: September 2012

10 9 8 7 6 5 4 3 2 1

CONTENTS

||||||||||||||||||||||||||||||||||||||||||||||||||||||

Our task is that of making ourselves individuals . . .
We create the race by creating ourselves and then to our
great astonishment we will have created something far more
important: we will have created a culture.
—Ralph Ellison, *Invisible Man*

BLACKWARDS

||||||||||||||||||||||||||||||||||||||||||||||||||||||

PROLOGUE

||||||||||||||||||||||||||||||||||||||||||||||||||||||||

QUIETLY, WITH LITTLE FANFARE, A PLAN THAT CAN DESTROY AMERICA IS
unfolding that threatens the very existence of the republic that was
founded some 225 years ago. From the inception of this nation, historians and early observers of the American landscape have commented
on the unique attributes of what it means to be an American. Our
cultural and political identity drew its strength from the ability of the
earliest residents of America to cast aside their ties to their previous
countries of origin to proclaim America—with its diversity of ethnic,
racial, and religious composition—as their new home. *E Pluribus
Unum*—"Out of Many, One"—was the motto affixed to the seal of
the United States of America created by founding father Charles
Thomson in 1782. As renowned historian Arthur M. Schlesinger Jr.
would note of this historic phrase:

> The United States had a brilliant solution for the inherent fra-
> gility, the inherent combustibility, of a multicultural society:
> the creation of a brand-new national identity by individuals
> who, in forsaking old loyalties and joining to make new lives,
> melted away ethnic differences—a national identity that ab-
> sorbs and transcends the diverse ethnicities that come to our

shore, ethnicities that enrich and reshape the common culture in the very act of entering into it.[1]

Astute observers such as John Stuart Mill, Hector St. John de Crèvecoeur, and Alexis de Tocqueville would note that our strength as a nation drew from our diversity and our diversity was the source of our strength. While far from perfect, America would struggle with issues of race, class, and culture for much of its 225-year history.

Slowly, quietly, deliberately in the years following World War II, the fabric that has held America together has begun to fray. The ties that bound us together before now threaten to tear us apart today. National pride and recognition of the special privilege of what it means to be a citizen of the United States have devolved into calls for lax immigration policies and granting amnesty to those who have arrived at our shores illegally.

Worst of all, the cries for multiculturalism and diversity sensitivity have balkanized America as never before. Calls for special rights based on one's race or ethnic origin, rather than equal rights, have driven people to self-identify based on their group rather than national affiliation.

It shouldn't be this way: the euphoria surrounding Barack Obama's election to the presidency led many to believe that America had finally— unthinkably—become a postracial society. So much had changed since Dr. Martin Luther King Jr. stood in the symbolic shadow of President Abraham Lincoln some forty-five years earlier to proclaim his dream to millions of Americans—a world in which the jangled discord of the turbulent country would be transformed into a beautiful symphony of brotherhood—a world in which Americans young and old would be judged by the content of their character rather than the color of their skin.

Indeed, with the subsequent election of Obama in 2008 many Americans asked whether the new president had also fulfilled King's vision—a vision articulated in a speech from 1959 in which King declared: "As I stand here and look out upon the thousands of Negro faces, and the thousands of white faces, intermingling like the waters of a river, I see only one face—the face of the future."[2]

And yet, once the elation of Obama's historic election had ebbed over time, tensions between black and whites, which had been bubbling in the melting pot that is America, have now bubbled over and into plain view as never before. The evolution of the civil rights movement led to the successful integration and assimilation into American society blacks had sought to achieve for more than one hundred years following the Emancipation Proclamation. Yet, over the decades, the hard-fought progress for equality began to erode rather than strengthen over time. The black power movement, moral relativism, the rise of affirmative action programs, and the monolithic voices that claimed the mantle of black leadership in the country began to sow seeds of discontent that would bloom into a full-blown backlash decades later, nearly concurrent with Barack Obama's historic election to the White House.

Rather than embrace Dr. King's call to come together as a nation and accept our fellow citizens as individuals we have become more polarized and paralyzed on issues of race than ever before. How could this possibly have occurred? *Blackwards* will examine this unique cultural phenomenon through a critically unfiltered lens. How did the affirmative action movement devolve from a program designed to provide blacks with a level playing field for college and employment opportunities into a new social narrative on college campuses and in our culture at large by which even the mildest criticism of blacks is equated to racism? This new "freedom" of speech—the ability for blacks to criticize others while decrying even the mildest form of criticism of themselves as racist has led to a backlash from which we must break free as a society.

Most important, *Blackwards* will reveal how the monolithic political, academic, and cultural straitjackets have smothered diversity of thought across the country. Rather than move the country forward in the wake of the election of the nation's first African American president, they have seemingly put the country back on a slippery downslope

in which the loyalty of being part of an ethnic and cultural group—
African American—is valued more than being an American citizen
who happens to be black.

The corresponding result of this disturbing phenomena is that an
elite group of so-called black leaders has emerged who purport to
speak with one voice for African Americans today. Their vehement
push for a "black agenda" accepts a refusal to view the world in which
blacks are entitled to special, rather than equal, rights based on skin
color has polarized race relations in the United States to levels not seen
in decades.

While a group of dissidents has emerged in recent years to challenge the status quo of what purports to be mainstream thinking in
the black community—new leaders who would walk us back from the
strident, at times militant tones that have helped create racial acrimony in America—their task is a formidable one. While 2012 GOP
presidential contender Herman Cain was excoriated for lamenting
that blacks today are "tethered to the plantation" and "brainwashed"
for voting in lockstep with the Democratic Party in numbers that hover
around 90 percent of the vote, Cain was roundly criticized for offering
his views rather than praised for questioning such fealty to one political party over another.

Unerringly, those blacks that dare stray from the socially and politically accepted status quo established by the elite are branded as
traitors, sellouts to their race, and are swiftly retaliated against and
isolated in the court of public opinion. It is beyond ironic that the
progress made by the brave pioneers of the civil rights era for blacks to
be treated equally based on the content of their character and ability is
now in danger of retreating to a new era of segregation in America—
this time championed by black "leaders" themselves who wrap their
actions in the cloak of the civil rights era but instead seek to usher in a
new era in which progress is judged by blacks receiving special rather
than equal treatment before the law and society at large.

In this vein, the America that is now supposed to be "postracial" in
the era ushered in by President Obama's election in 2008, many of our
fellow citizens find themselves under assault and branded as racists for

expressing legitimate political opposition to the president's policies; on the eve of the 2012 presidential election, many prominent black leaders have explicitly called for voters to support the president *because* of his race.

Will America continue to retreat to the cultural norms of an era in which individuals were judged on their skin color rather than their merit as individuals? Are the segregated days loathed in the days prior to and the decades following the *Brown v. Board of Education* in the rearview mirror of American history or have we reversed course ourselves once again in a country divided along barriers of color—this time erected by the proponents of special, rather than equal, rights for blacks? *Blackwards* will answer these vexing questions while charting a positive course forward to reclaim the promise of our cherished motto as citizens of the United States of America: *E Pluribus Unum*—"Out of Many, One."

I. THE GENESIS OF HEADING BLACKWARDS

‖‖‖

When Did America Stray from Equality Under the Law to a Push for Special, Rather than Equal, Rights?

BEFORE WE BEGIN OUR INQUIRY INTO WHY CERTAIN BLACK LEADERS would seek to lead America back to the days of separate, rather than equal rights for African Americans, we must first grapple with a difficult threshold question: What does it mean to be an American citizen today? This question is perhaps more vexing now in the twenty-first century than in the early days of American history, even taking into account that it was only in the latter half of the nineteenth century that blacks were guaranteed citizenship rights and the protections afforded under the Constitution.

In the infamous *Dred Scott* Supreme Court decision of 1857, the chief justice of the United States offered his rather stark assessment of the rights and liberties of African Americans in the United States in general as well as his particular belief that blacks were not American citizens—whether they were born on American soil or brought to the country involuntarily through slavery. In the relevant section of the opinion, Chief Justice Roger Taney asserted:

> The words "people of the United States" and "citizens" are synonymous terms, and mean the same thing. They both describe the political body who, according to our republican institutions, form the sovereignty, and who hold the power and conduct the

Government through their representatives. They are what we familiarly call the "sovereign people," and every citizen is one of this people, and a constituent member of this sovereignty.

The question before us is, whether the class of persons described in the plea [black people] . . . compose a portion of this people, and are constituent members of this sovereignty? We think they are not, and that they are not included, and were not intended to be included, under the word "citizens" in the Constitution, and can therefore claim none of the rights and privileges which that instrument provides for and secures to citizens of the United States. On the contrary, they were at that time considered as a subordinate . . . and inferior class of beings, who had been subjugated by the dominant race, and, whether emancipated or not, yet remained subject to their authority, and had no rights or privileges but such as those who held the power and the Government might choose to grant them.[1]

Only in the aftermath of the Civil War would Congress act to clarify the legal status of blacks to preserve both their legal status as citizens as well as their liberties and protections under the Constitution while explicitly rejecting the *Dred Scott* decision—one which constitutional and legal scholars consider the worst decision ever rendered by the Supreme Court.[2]

First Congress formally abolished slavery by adopting the Thirteenth Amendment to the Constitution on December 6, 1865. Next Congress passed the Civil Rights Act of 1866, making it federal law that everyone born in the United States and not subject to any foreign power was an American citizen without regard to his or her race, color, or previous condition of either slavery or involuntary servitude. Finally, Congress adopted the Fourteenth Amendment on July 9, 1868, to explicitly overrule the *Dred Scott* decision by declaring: "All persons born or naturalized in the United States, and subject to the jurisdiction thereof, are citizens of the United States and of the State wherein they reside."[3]

Congress took this explicit step of including what came to be known as the Citizenship Clause within the Fourteenth Amendment to quell efforts by opponents who sought to invalidate the Civil Rights Act of 1866 as being unconstitutional. The journey to full equality as citizens of the United States for blacks and other people of color began in the years following the Civil War; some would argue this struggle persists to the present day.

The civil rights era remains one of the brightest reminders of the fulfillment of the promises enshrined in the Declaration of Independence that all men and women are equal and that as American citizens they are guaranteed the rights of life, liberty, and the pursuit of happiness. Utilizing the power of words rather than the threat of violence, leaders and supporters of the civil rights movement sought to rebuild an American society in which its citizens were to be treated equally without regard to the color of their skin, ethnicity, or country of origin. And yet, after fighting for so long to be free from the chains of slavery and the oppression endured decade by decade via separate and inherently unequal treatment before the law, a new form of self-segregation began in the days following the civil rights era that has emerged as a potential threat to the stability of our societal fabric today—the desire by some to identify themselves as members of a particular racial and/or ethnic group rather than treasuring the privileges, rights, and responsibilities of being an individual American citizen.

Noted historian and Pulitzer Prize winner Arthur M. Schlesinger Jr. likened this new trend that gathered momentum in the 1970s and the 1980s as the "cult of ethnicity," an abandonment of the vision of America as a melting pot of opportunity in which people set aside their racial or ethnic allegiance to honor their special status of being American citizens. Elaborating on this troubling phenomenon, Schlesinger noted:

But pressed too far, the cult of ethnicity has had bad consequences, too. The new ethnic gospel rejects the unifying vision of individuals from all nations melted into a new race. Its underlying philosophy is that America is not a nation of individuals at all but a nation of groups, that ethnicity is the defining experience for Americans, that ethnic ties are permanent and indelible, and that division into ethnic communities establishes the structure of American society and the basic meaning of American history.[4]

Before delving into the substance of Schlesinger's remarks, it should be noted that far from being a conservative or rightward-leaning commentator, Schlesinger's political ideology was decidedly liberal. For one, Schlesinger had served as a special assistant to President John F. Kennedy from 1961 to 1963 and he wrote a definitive account of the Kennedy presidency entitled *A Thousand Days,* for which he received his second Pulitzer Prize in 1968. Instead, Schlesinger's opinion can be said to have been wrought from his front-row seat to power in politics in Washington, D.C., as well as his vocation as an author and social critic—his concern over an evolving "cult of ethnicity" was one that was informed from decades of observation of the American psyche.

To this end, I concur with Schlesinger's assessment—that a cult of ethnicity has manifested itself in the manner in which people of color in general, and blacks in particular, have identified themselves over the past quarter century. The "Negro" from the 1950s and 1960s later gave way to the nomenclature of "black" as the black power movement took hold in the 1970s. Singer/songwriter James Brown's song, "Say It Loud—I'm Black and I'm Proud," released in 1968, was a popular anthem of the black power movement during its epoch. This form of self-identification continued into the 1980s and 1990s but suddenly the term "black American" gave way to "African American"—a development, I believe, that has had more negative than positive developments.

Black Americans fought for more than a hundred years to be treated as equals by their fellow citizens, regardless of the color of their skin and/or ethnicity. And yet, as America has moved from the late days of the twentieth century into the twenty-first, there appears to be a disturbing new trend of self-identification based on race that runs counter to all of the blood, sweat, and tears the pioneers of the civil rights era had shed in their hope that one day Americans would be equal under the color of law without regard to the color of their skin or ethnicity—tying us all together in the phrase Dr. Martin Luther King Jr. once made famous: "a single garment of destiny." Instead, the relatively new push for diversity and multiculturalism sensitivity has led more to the garment of destiny—the essence of the fabric of the United States—to fray, rather than knit us more closely together as a society.

Why? Because I agree with Schlesinger's assessment that certain people of color are placing a premium first and foremost on their identification as members of a specific group rather than accepting the premise that American citizens are comprised of people from a myriad of races that come together to form one individual entity—that of being an American citizen. Furthermore, they seem to regard the term "American" as synonymous with being white rather than denoting an entire group of people brought together by their very diversity. Under this logic, America is not a nation comprised of individual citizens, but rather of people who belong to competing groups with differing goals, beliefs, and ideologies.

This is not a theoretical exercise or conjecture on my part—this is a conflicting reality which I encounter on a daily basis—a twenty-first century embodiment of W. E. B. DuBois's term "double consciousness," that is, caught between a self-conception of what it means to be an American as well as being a person of African descent. People in general and blacks in particular are often amazed that I subscribe to the former theory and cringe at my lack of desire to self-identify with the latter. Let me take a moment to explain.

Unequivocally I believe the United States of America is the greatest country on the face of the Earth. Each year, more people try to immigrate to the United States, both legally and illegally, than any other country on the globe. Our democratic principles enshrined in both the Declaration of Independence from English tyranny as well as the Constitution of the United States have served as our guiding moral compass, allowing Americans to live their lives among a democratic government of enumerated powers. Our elections and transitions to and from power are peaceful and conducted with the force of law through the ballot box rather than the force of arms that plague many Third World countries. Millions of people from around the world seek precious few slots to become American citizens every year.

And yet, as I cherish my American citizenship as well as the solidarity shared by millions of my fellow native Californians, I am repeatedly criticized for identifying myself as an American as opposed to an "African American." Many of my detractors accuse me of being ashamed of my heritage or seeking to deny my African roots. To them I say I can trace my roots to a former slave plantation just outside of Valdosta, Georgia, that is owned by my family members to this very day. Generations ago, the same plantation was worked by my relatives, relatives who toiled under the whip and inhumane system of slavery. I am very well aware of my roots, both African and American, and I treasure rather than shun them both.

At the same time, slavery ended with the Thirteenth Amendment in 1865 and the United States has compiled nearly 150 years of history since then. While the stain of slavery will forever be a dark legacy of our history, I daresay that I do not have any immediate ties to Africa—why then would I seek to identify myself with a continent comprised of some forty-seven sovereign nations when I am proud of the very nation I live in? Moreover, I marvel at those who believe I have denied my cultural heritage in favor of Anglocentric styles of culture, speech, and dress.

I yearn for someone to explain to me exactly what "African" culture is said to comprise when we would grapple with such a definition to explain American culture other than our rights and liberties that are enshrined in our Constitution. It is not without irony that many who question my "denial" of African culture and heritage cannot place a country in Africa correctly on the map; I often ask such detractors to locate Cameroon, Ghana, and Angola in geographical relationship to Tanzania, Ethiopia, or Mozambique. If my detractors don't know the history and culture or location of the continent they ascribe to have such strong ties to, how can they be taken seriously? Is it just that they seek to belong to a specific group, feel a special connection or kinship to others who are members of said group due to the color of their skin or ethnicity rather than evaluating their fellow citizens as individuals?

I believe this self-segregation and balkanization has taken race relations in America from a state of empowerment embodying Dr. King's ideals for a color-blind society to one of exclusion, where people are evaluated based on their skin color or ethnicity—explicitly rejecting the notion that America is comprised of numerous races that blend together to form a more perfect union of citizens. Accordingly, I assert that such calls for diversity and multiculturalism have helped drive us further apart rather than closer together both as a people and as a society.

Moving forward, then, how does one best describe the term "multiculturalism"? Does multiculturalism imply that America has made good on its promise to form a true melting pot of cultural and ethnic diversity that is blended together to represent the very best of American society? Or does the expression underscore the reality that 225 years following our founding, not only do we remain balkanized by race, but that the ancestors of some who were once cruelly oppressed due to the color of their skin now feel most comfortable with self-segregation and the further desire to identify with a culture that is not truly their own rather than embrace the special privilege it is to be a citizen of the United States of America?

While there is no universally accepted definition as to what constitutes multiculturalism today, I believe the *Stanford Encyclopedia of Philosophy* offers a revealing insight:

> Multiculturalism is a body of thought in political philosophy about the proper way to respond to cultural and religious diversity. Mere toleration of group differences is said to fall short of treating members of minority groups as equal citizens; recognition and positive accommodation of group differences are required through "group-differentiated rights," a term coined by Will Kymlicka (1995). Some group-differentiated rights are held by individual members of minority groups, as in the case of individuals who are granted exemptions from generally applicable laws in virtue of their religious beliefs or individuals who

seek language accommodations in schools or in voting. Other group-differentiated rights are held by the group qua group rather [than] by its members severally; such rights are properly called group rights, as in the case of indigenous groups and minority nations, who claim the right of self-determination. In the latter respect, multiculturalism is closely allied with nationalism.[5]

On its face, the term appears innocuous: multiculturalism adherents look for a proper manner to treat members of minority groups as full and equal citizens while seeking positive accommodation of group-differentiated rights. Upon closer reflection, how can basic toleration of one's fellow citizens fail to be sufficient when one is talking about a member of a minority group? I believe this is precisely the warning Arthur Schlesinger referred to when he feared a cult of ethnicity had appeared on the American social landscape that began to pervade our political and sociological landscapes. Suddenly, equal rights and toleration of our fellow citizens were no longer sufficient—now minority group members needed *special* recognition and positive identification of "group differences" to fully assimilate in American society?

For one, I do not believe for a moment that Dr. Martin Luther King and the brave pioneers of the civil rights era who fought tirelessly but peacefully for equal rights under the color of law in the 1950s and 1960s would have approved turning back the clock on the momentous direction they had set for the country by allowing ethnic minorities to be treated more favorably due to the color of their skin at the dawn of the twenty-first century. Recognizing that racism still exists in America and we have yet to fully actualize Dr. King's dream, pressing for special rights in the early twenty-first century as some form of cultural sensitivity when it took some 350 years for blacks to receive equal rights and opportunity after their arrival in chains on American soil is a distressing step blackwards for the assimilation of her citizens to full participation in the American dream.

While I pondered the wisdom proponents of multiculturalism sought to offer with an open mind, I grappled with what the terms "special recognition" and "positive identification" were supposed to mean, precisely. Is it the invention of a special holiday during the Christmas season for blacks (Kwanzaa) to identify their religious beliefs based on their ethnicity, rather than the tenets of their faith? I was shocked to discover that Kwanzaa is not a traditional religious-based holiday, but the creation of Maulana Karenga (born Ronald McKinley Everett), a former member of the United Slaves Organization—a black militant nationalist group. Karenga's original goal in creating Kwanzaa was to politicize Christmas as a Western holiday and offer black Americans a Pan-African equivalent.

Is it the creation of offices of multicultural affairs across our college and university campuses and the encouragement of self-segregation by dormitory, fraternity/sororities, and graduation ceremonies? While these questions will be considered in greater detail in chapter 2, I remain perplexed at how far we have regressed as a nation from the call to service offered by President John F. Kennedy in his inaugural address, when he charged his fellow citizens:

> Ask not what your country can do for you but what you can do for your country . . . Finally, whether you are citizens of America or citizens of the world, ask of us here the same high standards of strength and sacrifice which we ask of you. With a good conscience our only sure reward, with history the final judge of our deeds, let us go forth to lead the land we love, asking His blessing and His help, but knowing that here on earth God's work must truly be our own.[6]

Just fifty years removed from President Kennedy's call to serve a cause and a calling higher than ourselves by putting national rather than individual self-interests at the forefront, how can it possibly be that we now find many in America who advocate just the opposite? A new society predicated on special recognition and rights for a preferred, select class at the expense of their fellow citizens? Not only does this run counter to the message presented to the nation by the thirty-fifth president of the United States some fifty years ago, but also contrary to the vision of what the United States of America would be in the mind of one of our most influential Founding Fathers and first president of the United States over two hundred years ago.

In a letter to newly arrived immigrants from Ireland to New York City written in 1783, George Washington famously opined:

> The bosom of America is open to receive not only the Opulent and respectable Stranger, but the oppressed and persecuted of all Nations And Religions; whom we shall wellcome to a participation of all our rights and previleges, if by decency and propriety of conduct they appear to merit the enjoyment.[7]

Unfortunately, the push for group-differentiated rights has led to a deterioration of racial and ethnic relations in the United States rather than strengthening them. As we shall see in the chapters to follow, the drive for exclusive racial and ethnic dormitories and graduation ceremonies has fractured many of our college communities while black politicians in the era of Obama decry racism rather than their individual underlying transgressions as the source of their angst. Somehow, the president who was sworn in on the sweeping promise of hope and change soon gave way to political strife and a swift decline in his overall approval ratings.

Rather than focusing on the issues and the policies pursued during President Obama's term in office, many of his supporters instead blamed racism and alleged racist sentiments expressed by the Tea Party as the root of the president's decline in stature. During the summer of 2011, members of the Congressional Black Caucus asserted that African American lawmakers had been verbally harassed due to their ethnicity by Tea Party participants during a rally on Capitol Hill; yet no evidence emerged in the era of the cellular videophone in which incidents were captured on film. Nonetheless, Representative André Carson (D-IN), a senior member of the Congressional Black Caucus, would further charge, "Some [members of the Tea Party] would love to see us hanging from a tree."[8]

Has this type of behavior and mind-set put America on a blackwards path from which the country will struggle to recover? What of the Obama administration's embrace of members of certain ethnic groups possessing special, rather than equal, rights? The voter intimidation case from the 2008 election cycle in which members of the New Black Panther Party were filmed brandishing a weapon near a polling station in Philadelphia to threaten white voters was *dismissed* by the Obama Justice Department despite a nonpolitical review of the case by career civil servants. More disturbingly, these white civil servants would testify under oath before the United States Commission on Civil Rights that crimes allegedly committed against white victims were to be ignored by the Justice Department's Civil Rights Division while crimes allegedly committed against black victims were to be vigorously prosecuted.

For the present inquiry, however, I want to return to the notion of multiculturalism and the real threat the practice poses for the balkanization and fragmentation of American society. As discussed above, multiculturalism seeks to respond to cultural and religious diversity beyond mere toleration of those persons of color in the country at large. From 1619 to 1865, when the practice of slavery was finally outlawed, some 500,000 Africans were brought to America's shores against their will. Today blacks comprise 13.5 percent of the American population, some 41 million people in a country with 308 million residents.

Moreover, according to the Population Reference Bureau (PRB), growth in the Latino community as well as their increasing strength as a percentage of the overall U.S. population has grown dramatically in recent years. In a report issued in December 2010 following the release of data from the 2010 U.S. Census, the PRB noted:

Latinos are increasingly shaping the demographic makeup of the United States. While the U.S. population grew by 36 percent between 1980 and 2009, the Latino population more than tripled, increasing from 14.6 million to nearly 48.4 million. Latinos accounted for slightly more than 40 percent of the roughly 81 million people added to the U.S. population over the past 30 years. The influence of the Latino population will only grow in coming decades, and mostly through natural increase, not immigration.[9]

That blacks and Latinos continue to make strong increases in American demographics is a positive development. In fact, recent test results from the National Assessment of Educational Progress—the nation's report card for public school children—indicated that black and Latino students had steadily shown improvement from 2005 to 2009 when compared with their white student peers.[10]

On the other hand, while student achievement across racial lines may be improving in the classroom, the assimilation and intermingling among certain of the racial and ethnic groups that comprise the U.S. population appear to be deepening a schism rather than drawing us closer together as a society. Some social observers and politicians point to the rise of multiculturalism as the thread that is being pulled that has begun to unravel our society.

This is neither a political nor a narrow partisan observation; both conservative and moderate commentators have warned of the dangers posed by stressing multiculturalism rather than the unique societal framework of what it means to be an American citizen today. Sadly, these warnings have largely been ignored. Consider, for example, an essay and subsequent speech given by former Democratic governor Richard Lamm of Colorado entitled "I Have a Plan to Destroy America." The speech is a dire call to action and a warning that our acquiescence and acceptance of multiculturalism has led to an erosion of the uniqueness of what it means to be American; a cancer spreading throughout our body politic that will destroy us if left untreated. While we do not have the space to include the speech in its entirety here, there are several key excerpts that merit our review at this time.

"I have a secret plan to destroy America," Lamm begins.

If you believe, as many do, that America is too smug, too white bread, too self-satisfied, too rich, let's destroy America. . . . Here is my plan: We must first make America a bilingual-bicultural country. History shows, in my opinion, that no nation can survive the tension, conflict, and antagonism of two competing languages and cultures. It is a blessing for an individual to be bilingual; it is a curse for a society to be bilingual. . . .

I would then invent "multiculturalism" and encourage immigrants to maintain their own culture. I would make it an article of belief that all cultures are equal: that there are no cultural differences that are important. I would declare it as an article of faith that the black and Hispanic dropout rate is only due to prejudice and discrimination by the majority. Every other explanation is out-of-bounds. . . . I would replace the melting pot metaphor with a salad bowl metaphor. It is important to insure that we have various cultural subgroups living in America reinforcing their differences rather than Americans emphasizing their similarities. . . .

Having done all this, I would make our fastest-growing demographic group the least educated—I would add a second underclass, unassimilated, undereducated, and antagonistic to our population. I would have this second underclass have a 50 percent dropout rate from school.

I would then get the big foundations and big business to give these efforts lots of money. I would invest in ethnic identity, and I would establish the cult of victimology. I would get all minorities to think their lack of success was all the fault of the majority. I would start a grievance industry blaming all minority failure on the majority population.

I would celebrate "diversity." "Diversity" is a wonderfully seductive word. It stresses differences rather than commonalities. Diverse people worldwide are mostly engaged in hating each other—that is when they are not killing each other. . . . If we can put the emphasis on "pluribus," instead of the "unum," we can balkanize America as surely as Kosovo. . . .

Then I would place all of these subjects off-limits—make it taboo to talk about. I would find a word similar to "heretic" in the sixteenth century—that stopped discussion and paralyzed thinking. Words like "racist," "xenophobe" halt argument and discussion.[11]

Lamm aptly threads the needle when describing the dangers associated with permitting special, rather than equal, rights to be socially acceptable in American society today. Drawing upon roots planted during the time of slavery in which ethnic minorities were victimized by white oppressors, multiculturalism and diversity supporters today enjoy celebrating our differences rather than focusing upon the singular bond we hold in common: our American citizenship. Why celebrate one's American heritage when they can instead self-segregate by proclaiming themselves to be *African American*? As we shall see throughout the rest of our discussion in this book, most of the tenets of Lamm's secret plan to destroy America has already been implemented to disastrous effect—mostly in the name of multiculturalism, the need for vigorous affirmative action programs, and the push for a "black" agenda undertaken by "black" leaders in such fields as politics and academia in which blacks are entitled to special, rather than equal, treatment than the rest of their multiracial peers.

Accordingly, I believe this disturbing trend of celebrating diversity and multiculturalism has only accelerated rather than decreased in our colleges and universities. Can there be little doubt that students electing to isolate themselves from the larger society as a whole to remain in their cocoon and safety net of those of a similar race and/or ethnicity find it difficult to relate to their peers at work or play who are of another race? It seems that former governor Mario Cuomo's admonition has largely been ignored:

> Most Americans can understand both the need to recognize and encourage diversity as well as the need to ensure that such a broadened multicultural perspective leads to unity and an enriched sense of what being an American is, and not to a destructive factionalism that would tear us apart.[12]

What then, does it mean to be an American citizen in the twenty-first century? My concern is that we have allowed a sizable minority to set the tone for the majority by celebrating our differences rather than focusing upon our similarities. This factionalism and balkanization has led to more strain than harmony among our citizenry, based as it is on racial and ethnic ties rather than the one aspect that binds us together: our American citizenship.

While Latinos and other ethnic minorities have stressed calls for diversity and multiculturalism, I believe this phenomenon is most pervasive in the black, dare I say, African American community. I believe that calls for special, rather than equal, rights and hiding behind calls of racism and unequal treatment in the era of Obama have helped create a toxic climate that will spread unless we stop the stain that is spreading through our schools, offices, communities of worship, and political discourse. Perhaps President Franklin D. Roosevelt was prescient beyond his years when he noted what I believe is the essence of what it means to be an American citizen during a speech permitting Japanese Americans to serve in World War II delivered on February 1, 1943:

> The principle on which this country was founded and by which it has always been governed is that Americanism is a matter of the mind and heart; Americanism is not, and never was, a matter of race and ancestry. A good American is one who is loyal to this country and to our creed of liberty and democracy.[13]

If we fail to heed Roosevelt's call for loyalty to our country that is present both in our hearts and minds rather than viewing the world through the prism of race and ethnicity, the negative momentum blackwards that has begun may soon be too difficult to stop. One need only look at the present situation in Great Britain to envision what our future here in America might look like if we continue to permit ethnic and group identification rather than cultural intermingling brought together by the strong bond of citizenship.

Perhaps British Prime Minister David Cameron's speech in 2011 regarding multiculturalism embraced by many today should give them reason for pause and deliberation to reflect on what such efforts are doing to the American society. Are they bringing us together, or are they driving us apart, citizens united only with those who look and speak like us rather than embracing a true multicultural society whose unbreakable bond is the oath and obligations brought by being an American citizen? After spending many years on this experiment in Great Britain, consider the following remarks of Prime Minister Cameron in early February 2011:

> Under the doctrine of state multiculturalism, we have encouraged different cultures to live separate lives, apart from each other and apart from the mainstream. We've failed to provide a vision of society to which they feel they want to belong. We've even tolerated these segregated communities behaving in ways that run completely counter to our values.
>
> So, when a white person holds objectionable views, racist views for instance, we rightly condemn them. But when equally unacceptable views or practices come from someone who isn't white, we've been too cautious, frankly even fearful—to stand up to them . . . This hands-off tolerance has only served to reinforce the sense that not enough is shared.[14]

Is this not the path down which America has traveled in recent years—away from a truly color-blind society and toward one in which the behavior of some will be tolerated at the expense of others due to the color of their skin? The subsequent creation and rise in power of the Congressional Black Caucus in the United States Congress has served as an outlet for comments and views that, expressed by anyone other than black people, would be branded as racist. We shall discuss both the impact of the Congressional Black Caucus and whether it has helped contribute to the racial backlash presently underway in America today.

For the present, however, I believe the noted commentator Noam Chomsky was prescient on this point when he noted the following:

The smart way to keep people passive and obedient is to strictly limit the spectrum of acceptable opinion, but allow very lively debate within that spectrum—even encourage the more critical and dissident views. That gives people the sense that there's freethinking going on, while all the time the presuppositions of the system are being reinforced by the limits put on the range of the debate.[15]

As we shall see in the pages that follow, this is precisely the danger posed by efforts to impose multiculturalism, diversity, and societal norms that will only exacerbate and inflame relations between racial and ethnic groups in America rather than bringing us together. By sharply limiting the scope of acceptable debate to promote political correctness at the expense of honest political discussion we have set upon a sharp departure from the freedoms of speech and debate enshrined within our Bill of Rights. This limitation, rather than enhancement, of debate and discussion has taken place in our classrooms, offices, and even places of worship. This is a trend and tide that must be turned before the United States moves further down the path of subgroups and subcultures rather than remaining a country brought together by stressing the strengths of our diversity rather than emphasizing our differences.

Fortunately, there is a way forward and there is still time to prevent our society from the balkanization and resentments that have become entrenched in other countries that have embraced the cult of ethnicity described by Arthur Schlesinger in which the needs of particular ethnic groups and minorities are favored at the expense of the needs and beliefs of the mainstream of society. Should we continue on our present course I believe there will be increasing rather than decreasing instances of racial intolerance in our country, so long as people seek to self-identify by ethnicity and skin color rather than basking in our treasured status as American citizens. The backlash brewing could be easily quelled by abandoning the doctrine and demands imposed by multiculturalism. Consider the closing words of Prime Minister Cameron's speech on the topic:

We must build stronger societies and stronger identities at home. Frankly, we need a lot less of the passive tolerance of recent years and a much more active, muscular liberalism. A passively tolerant society says to its citizens, as long as you obey the law we will just leave you alone. It stands neutral between different values. But I believe a genuinely liberal country does much more; it believes in certain values and actively promotes them. Freedom of speech, freedom of worship, democracy, the rule of law, equal rights regardless of race, sex, or sexuality. It says to its citizens, this is what defines us as a society: to belong here is to believe in these things. Now, each of us in our own countries, I believe, must be unambiguous and hard-nosed about this defense of our liberty.[16]

Prime Minister Cameron's admonition for the harm multiculturalism has caused Great Britain should serve as a wake-up call to those in America seeking to unify, rather than divide, their fellow citizens along lines of race and ethnicity. We must push for equal rather than special rights, regardless of the color of one's skin. By promoting the values of freedom of speech and expression under the law rather than silencing the views of the majority to appease a vocal minority, America will pull closer together rather than splinter and fragment as a society. A strong move in this direction, as we shall see in chapter 2, would be to judge persons on their individual merit rather than the color of their skin for advancement in school and in the workplace. The time has come to end, rather than mend, the practice of affirmative action.

2. AFFIRMATIVE ACTION

||||||||||||||||||||||||||||||||||||||||||||||||||||||

How the Vision for True Equality Under the Law Has Retreated to the Days of Separate and Unequal Treatment in American Society

MANY HAVE DEBATED THE EFFICACY OF AFFIRMATIVE ACTION OVER THE decades with passion and compassion whether in support or against the practice. In *Acting White: The Curious History of a Racial Slur,* I discussed the origins of affirmative action and whether the program had strayed from the original concept envisioned by President Kennedy when he created the program in 1961—encouraging equal opportunity for employment in the federal government in the 1960s. The system that Kennedy advocated called for a color-blind program based on merit rather than the color of one's skin—a concept which I, as a free market conservative and Republican, embrace.

Our present inquiry will focus on whether the modern construct of affirmative action operating in America today has created a rift in race relations, that is, a resentment of those who participate in such programs as being the recipients of special, rather than equal, treatment under the color of law. Or, have the efforts to achieve parity through affirmative action driven a wedge rather than bring Americans together regardless of the color of their skin and/or ethnicity?

No one can question the need to create a level and equal playing field for people of color following the inequities wrought by slavery in the nineteenth century as well as state-sanctioned discrimination codified by the *Plessy v. Ferguson* ruling by the Supreme Court in 1896, which encouraged the creation and enforcement of Jim Crow laws for more than fifty years. Following its *Brown v. Board of Education* decision in 1954, the Supreme Court overturned *Plessy* and overruled the separate but equal doctrine that had amounted to state-sponsored discrimination based on the color of one's skin.

As a Republican and a student of the push for equal rather than separate rights, I was pleased to note that the origins of modern-day affirmative action can be traced to President Kennedy and Executive Order 10925, which he signed on March 6, 1961, to create the President's Committee on Equal Employment Opportunity. The goal and focus of the committee was to:

> Scrutinize and study employment practices of the Government of the United States, and to consider and recommend additional *affirmative* steps [emphasis added] which should be taken by executive department and agencies to realize more fully the national policy of nondiscrimination within the executive branch of government.[1]

Beyond this initial review toward achieving the president's goal of non-discrimination within the executive branch of government, Kennedy also sought for government contractors to

> not discriminate against any employee or applicant for employment because of race, creed, color, or national origin. The contractor will take affirmative action to ensure that applicants are employed, and that employees are treated during employment, without regard to their race, creed, color, or national origin.[2]

It is important to emphasize once more at this juncture what President Kennedy had asked his administration to do in regards to government sanctioned affirmative action in 1961 versus the system that is largely operating today, some fifty years later. At the outset, the president sought to ensure that affirmative steps would be taken to stamp out discrimination while directing federal contractors to take affirmative action to ensure all employees were hired without regard to the color of their skin. In a famous address on civil rights delivered on June 11, 1963, President Kennedy declared:

> I shall ask the Congress of the United States to act, to make a commitment it has not fully made in this century to the proposition that race has no place in American life or law. The Federal judiciary has upheld that proposition in a series of forthright cases. The Executive Branch has adopted that proposition in the conduct of its affairs, including the employment of Federal personnel, the use of Federal facilities, and the sale of federally financed housing.[3]

How did America move so far afield from Kennedy's proposition that race should have no place in American life or law such that it is the accepted belief today by many in the African American community that our life and laws should be *defined* by race? Rather than decreasing the invocation of race, nearly fifty years following Kennedy's remarks affirmative action programs permeate the federal, state, and local governments as well as private companies and institutions of higher learning. Are such efforts to atone for the sins of the past relevant in the early twenty-first century or are they creating recriminations and accusations of special, rather than equal, treatment that will drive us apart as a nation?

Perhaps Dr. Martin Luther King was omniscient on this very issue when he discussed the resistance held by some whites to embrace the importance as well as the mission of the civil rights movement in the 1960s. In a speech entitled "Impasse in race relations," delivered in late 1967, shortly before his death, Dr. King opined [that] "the white backlash declared true equality could never be a reality in the United States," [and he felt that] "mass civil disobedience as a new stage of struggle can transmute the deep rage of the ghetto into a constructive and creative force."[4] I interpret these remarks to suggest that true equality could only be achieved both in Dr. King's day as well as in our contemporary society by focusing constructively on the one thing that has bound us together regardless of our race or ethnicity: our status as American citizens. Equal rights under color of law is the very promise and value enshrined in the second paragraph of the Declaration of Independence itself, in which Thomas Jefferson touched upon the self-evident truth that all men are created equal.

To be fair, the climate in the 1960s was far more hostile toward people of color to actualize the self-evident truths that all men and women were created equal with the unalienable rights to live their lives, enjoy liberty, and pursue happiness without governmental interference.

Cognizant of the emotional and political realities he was facing at the time, Dr. King masterfully cultivated a coalition of concerned citizens who believed all should be treated equally under the law regardless of the color of their skin. King's leadership and perseverance in steering America toward a color-blind society eventually led to passage of the Civil Rights Act of 1964 and the slow but steady dismantling of the barriers that had kept blacks from achieving true equality.

President Kennedy, Dr. King, and millions of Americans followed the path set by the Declaration of Independence to break the chains of racial segregation that had manacled the nation since the days of slavery: they had determined that contemporary laws and practices were destructive to the self-evident truth that all men are created equal, and that blacks were denied true liberty and happiness under the law because of the color of their skin.

By abolishing judicially imposed inequality with the *Brown v. Board of Education* decision in 1954 followed by passage of the Civil Rights Act of 1964 a decade later, citizens had worked hard to put aside their racial and ethnic differences to ensure that all Americans would be treated equally under the law—and that the force of law would deter those who sought to circumvent these protections.

As a Republican and a conservative, I would be remiss not to acknowledge the criticism of those who suggest President Kennedy's remarks on civil rights in general and his specific comment that race has no place in American life or law were prompted more by political consideration rather than true conviction. At the same time, I believe both President Kennedy and Dr. King would have agreed that race had no place in American law or life in the 1960s or ever—they sought a color-blind society in which the government treated everyone equally as *Americans* rather than as people of a certain race or ethnicity deserving of special, rather than equal, rights.

How, then, did the affirmative action programs designed in the 1960s to treat Americans equally under the law bring us to where we are today: a mind-set among many in the United States that focuses on our differences—differences in skin color and ethnicity rather than our shared citizenship as Americans that is destructive to our nation, and serves no greater purpose other than being a wedge that will drive us apart rather than bring us together?

I believe the first strong seeds of discontent with affirmative action and diversity programs were planted by the *Regents of the University of California v. Bakke* Supreme Court decision in 1978, in which the High Court held that the University of California could properly consider race as a criterion in the admissions process as long as doing so did not amount to establishing a fixed quota system. Inadvertently, rather than limiting the use of race as a factor for admissions committees across the country, the *Bakke* decision only ruled out the use of a fixed quota system for minority student enrollment while allowing the consideration of a candidate's racial ethnicity as part of a systemic plan to increase diversity on campuses across the country.

The net result of this decision explicitly *sanctioned* the use of a student's race in the admissions process rather than heed President Kennedy's call that race had no place in American life or law. If the modern affirmative action program is truly about improving the lives of those who have been disenfranchised by society, why isn't the program targeted specifically at those at the lower end of the socioeconomic strata rather than using racial characteristics to provide special, rather than equal, treatment before the law? As such, with the passage of time, the *Bakke* decision would open the floodgates rather than close the spigot to the affirmative action programs that would spring up around the country—programs in which the federal government fully sanctioned the use of race for hiring and admissions decisions.

While the move to sanction certain forms of affirmative action was hailed by program supporters, there was also a growing number of dissenters who believed such efforts created an unequal playing field tilted toward members of certain racial or ethnic groups came at the expense of others. As noted in *The African American Experience: Black History and Culture,* edited by Kai Wright:

> Throughout the 1980s and 1990s the backlash to affirmative action swelled. By the close of the twentieth century, the future of both federal and state level programs, in the public as well as the private sector, was in question.[5]

I believe the feeling that some citizens were being given special rights, rather than equal rights, at the expense of others led to a judicial as well as political backlash in the 1990s. However well intentioned, some people bristled at the notion that blacks and ethnic minorities should be given special treatment in the procurement of federal contracts due to the government classifying them as being socially or economically disadvantaged.

First, the Supreme Court grappled with such a case in *Adarand Constructors, Inc. v. Pena* (515 U.S. 200) in 1995, in which a construction company had claimed that the federal government's practice of providing a financial incentive for general contractors to hire subcontractors that were controlled by "socially and economically distressed individuals" had run afoul of the equal protection component of the Fifth Amendment's due process clause. Adarand Constructors, Inc. was particularly distressed since the Small Business Administration had interpreted the phrase "socially and economically distressed individuals" to include racial and ethnic minorities. While the court largely concerned itself with the manner in which race-based cases should be analyzed by federal courts, Justice Clarence Thomas issued his own blistering concurrence to the majority opinion, authored by then justice Sandra Day O'Connor, regarding the federal government's injection of race into its hiring policies and procedures. In part, Justice Thomas noted:

> Government cannot make us equal; it can only recognize, respect, and protect us as equal before the law. That these programs

may have been motivated, in part, by good intentions cannot provide refuge from the principle under our Constitution, the government may not make distinctions on the basis of race. As far as the Constitution is concerned, it is irrelevant whether a government's racial classifications are drawn by those who wish to oppress a race or by those who have a sincere desire to help those thought to be disadvantaged. There can be no doubt that the paternalism that appears to lie at the heart of this program is at war with the principle of inherent equality that underlies and infuses our Constitution.[6]

Most important, Justice Thomas understood that the utilization of race by the federal government had the unintended effect of creating a backlash against those ethnic and racial minorities the programs had been designed to help. To this point Justice Thomas observed:

But there can be no doubt that racial paternalism and its unintended consequences can be as poisonous and pernicious as any other form of discrimination. So-called "benign" discrimination teaches many that because of chronic and apparently immutable handicaps, minorities cannot compete with them without their patronizing indulgence. Inevitably, such programs engender attitudes of superiority or, alternatively, provoke resentment among those who believe they have been wronged by the government's use of race. These programs stamp minorities with a badge of inferiority and may cause them to develop dependencies or to adopt an attitude that they are "entitled" to preferences . . . In my mind, government-sponsored racial discrimination based on benign prejudice is just as noxious as discrimination inspired by malicious prejudice. In each case, it is racial discrimination, plain and simple.[7]

President Kennedy's original commitment to eliminate race as a factor in American life and law had veered tragically in the opposite direction as America headed toward the end of the twentieth century. Rather than promote a system that treated all Americans as individual citizens, the federal government had instead created a system of winners and losers based on the racial and ethnic disposition of members of that particular group. Efforts to promote affirmative action and multiculturalism had become more prominent while efforts to treat Americans as individual citizens regardless of the color of their skin had been diminished as a new wave of political correctness spread across the United States at the dawn of the twenty-first century. As Justice Thomas eloquently noted above, ethnic minorities were not only marked with a badge of inferiority due to affirmative action and other set-aside programs, they could fuel and provoke resentment among those who felt they had been unfairly discriminated against by the government's infusion of race.

The highest court in the land was not alone in adjudicating affirmative action cases in which one party sought judicial protection from programs based on racial and/or ethnic identity rather than equal treatment under the law. While the Supreme Court had dealt with a case dealing with affirmative action racial set-aside programs in 1995, the Fifth Circuit Court of Appeals was asked to rule on a delicate case in 1996 involving four white students who alleged that they had been discriminated against for admission to the University of Texas Law School to fulfill diversity requirements.

Specifically, *Hopwood v. Texas* 78 F.3d 932 (1996) questioned whether the equal protection rights of the four white students had been infringed upon in seating a law school class of at least 10 percent Latino and 5 percent black students—students whose grade point averages and Law School Admission Test (LSAT) scores were inferior to those of the white students that had been rejected. In rejecting the University of Texas Law School's state-sanctioned discrimination of one group of students at the hands of another to seat a more diverse student body, the Fifth Circuit Court first noted that:

> Within the general principles of the Fourteenth Amendment, the use of race in admissions for diversity in higher education contradicts, rather than furthers, the aims of equal protection. Diversity fosters, rather than minimizes, the use of race. It

treats minorities as a group, rather than as individuals. It may further remedial purposes but, just as likely, may promote improper racial stereotypes, thus fueling racial hostility.[8]

However well intentioned, the court reasoned that actions taken on behalf of the government to marginalize members of certain racial or ethnic groups at the expense of others were not only unconstitutional, but also likely to fuel rather than quell racial hostility. Just as important, the circuit court went on to hold: "Finally, the use of race to achieve diversity undercuts the ultimate goal of the Fourteenth Amendment: the end of racially motivated state action."[9]

The aforementioned judicial decisions and the debates they generated in the middle part of the 1990s only heightened the political sensitivity surrounding whether the government should favor one race for hiring or admissions decisions at the expense of another through affirmative action programs. Ideological battle lines were formed and proponents and opponents of affirmative action were vigorous in holding their respective positions on the issue.

Rather than coming together on issues of race at the dawn of the twenty-first century, America instead found itself deeply divided on the issue of affirmative action in general and in the midst of a balkanization within the country on racial and ethnic lines not seen since the 1960s. Discontent was growing across the country, and one state moved boldly, some would say in a controversial manner, to eradicate affirmative action and quota-based programs as permissible under their state constitution.

On November 5, 1996, California voters flexed their muscles and became the first state in the union to eliminate affirmative action and quota-based systems in government-sponsored activities. As briefly touched upon in *Acting White*, the California Civil Rights Initiative (better known as Proposition 209) was championed by Ward Connerly, a black regent of the University of California, who was convinced that affirmative action programs as administered by the University of California and other state and local entities were tantamount to racial discrimination.

After nearly a year of legal challenges, the California Constitution was amended to reflect the views of the voters to eliminate affirmative action and quota-based programs:

CALIFORNIA CONSTITUTION
ARTICLE 1 DECLARATION OF RIGHTS

SEC. 31. (a) The State shall not discriminate against, or grant preferential treatment to, any individual or group on the basis of race, sex, color, ethnicity, or national origin in the operation of public employment, public education, or public contracting.[10]

While the debate surrounding affirmative action in California was animated prior to adoption of Proposition 209, the state became increasingly divided along racial and ethnic lines in the days that followed, a conflict that persists to the present day, some sixteen years later. While proponents had hoped passage of the measure would eradicate dissension based on the color of their skin among citizens of California, in many ways just the opposite has occurred.

First, many minority students within the University of California system were angered by the board of regents' vote to eliminate affirmative action and quota-based programs based on racial or ethnic identity in July 1995. When it became apparent that Proposition 209 would pass, students moved swiftly to mobilize and vocalize their displeasure. With passage of Proposition 209 on November 5, 2006, students took to the streets to protest and condemn the measure just adopted at the ballot box. According to published reports at the time, on November 6th hundreds of students at the San Francisco State University boycotted classes to take to the streets in protest.[11] Also that day across the San Francisco Bay students at the University of California (Berkeley) had staged a series of protests in opposition to Proposition 209.

In the days immediately following passage of Proposition 209, students across the University of California system fanned out to protest.

On November 8, 1996, nearly one hundred demonstrators organized by Hispanic students from the University of California (Irvine) marched to city hall in Los Angeles in unison against the new law to stamp out affirmative action–based programs in the state. According to one participant:

> "This is a message for all those who promoted 209," declared Isabel Silas, a Black student activist from Pitzer College in Claremont. She told the crowd, "we are not going to go away. We are going to fight."[12]

Indeed, the fight over affirmative action in California and across the United States continues to the present day. To this end, I believe that it is those who seek special, rather than equal, treatment in our society today who are deepening schisms and inspiring a backlash against those who strive to improve conditions for economically disadvantaged blacks and other persons of color.

It is not without irony that Proposition 209 was fully implemented in California after nearly a year of court challenges on August 28, 1997—the thirty-fourth anniversary of Dr. King's iconic "I have a dream" speech. Never one to miss the spotlight of opportunity, the Reverend Jesse Jackson Sr. led a protest march in San Francisco, where he and like-minded supporters took up the fight against those who had peacefully voted to eliminate racially based preferences in the state of California. While Reverend Jackson's march across the Golden Gate Bridge and through the streets of San Francisco was widely viewed as peaceful, the rhetoric he and his supporters articulated that day harkened back to a darker, earlier period in American history when black citizens were denied even the most basic human, let alone equal, rights.

In a *Jet* magazine article chronicling Reverend Jackson's march both to commemorate Dr. King's "I have a dream" speech while condemning the adoption and subsequent court challenges to Proposition 209, Jackson declared to the approximately nine thousand people gathered to hear him that:

In this country there are those who are dreamers and those who are dream-busters . . . The dreamers need to outlast the dream-busters. We must pursue the dream of an inclusive society . . . We deserve an America where all of us are welcome under one tent.[13]

At first glance, Reverend Jackson's words could be taken to be in *support* of rather than opposition to the Proposition 209 initiative. Objectively speaking, was it not the dream of President Kennedy to remove race from American law and life? Was it also not the dream of Dr. King's iconic speech and underlying philosophy to allow individuals to be judged on their individual character rather than their skin color? Wouldn't the pursuit of a policy to bar racial classifications and special rights for people based on their race or ethnic origin make America a more inclusive society? Conversely, would not conferring special rights and privileges on people based on their group identity status rather than individual merit and/or accomplishment lead those marginalized by such efforts to resent those who gained at their expense?

For his contribution to the marches and demonstrations held that day, then San Francisco mayor and former speaker of the California Assembly Willie Brown likened passage of Proposition 209 to Jim Crow laws imposed to inhibit the progress of blacks decades prior. "This same kind of march was held years ago when Southern bigots were doing the same thing," intoned Mayor Brown.[14] However well intentioned, I believe the calls by Reverend Jackson for equality and inclusion for some rather than all Americans and the insinuation that those for a truly color-blind society were somehow in favor of reinstituting Jim Crow laws have led directly to a backlash against ethnic minorities in America today. Allow me a moment to explain.

Consider, for example, a debate held between noted black scholar Dr. Michael Eric Dyson and former University of California regent Ward Connerly on the topic of affirmative action held before thousands at the Blacks in Government (BIG) conference in Washington, D.C., in August 1998. Both leaders characterize their support or opposition to affirmative action and then delve into the notion that curbing the practice would "roll back the clock" to the Jim Crow–era discrimination against blacks in America.

Dr. Dyson, an ardent supporter of affirmative action, initially declared:

> Race and class continue to gang up on African people in America to deprive them systematically, and to exclude them in very powerful ways. To marginalize them, yes—but not by bringing them into American society, or into the larger circle of American privilege, but by continuing to deny them the legal and moral access that their talents certainly merit.
>
> So for me, as a background, affirmative action has been quite successful, first, because it recognizes the government has worked against African-American people and other minorities, especially Latinos, Native Americans, and, of course, to a certain degree, Asian-American brothers and sisters.[15]

When given the opportunity for rebuttal to Dyson's remarks, Ward Connerly offered the following to refute the sense that affirmative action was beneficial and bringing the country together rather than driving it apart:

> This is about our government, and whether our government should be allowed to treat some of us differently. And when you strip through that very powerful, very eloquent statement, Dr. Dyson is saying yes. He's saying it's okay for our government to treat some of us differently. He's saying there are aesthetic reasons and all kinds of reasons that may be compelling to you, but they're not compelling to me. . . . It is not compelling for my government to say that it is going to treat me differently than it treats somebody else. What that is essentially saying is that we're going to give our government the power to discriminate. I thought we said we didn't want to do that.[16]

What is striking is the prism through which both men viewed America at the end of the twentieth century. Dr. Dyson's word choice here is particularly revealing: he spoke of a country where *African people in America* were ganged up on and treated in a hostile manner strictly due to their race or ethnicity. These African Americans, Latinos, Native Americans, and Asian Americans had not been brought into the mainstream culture of American society, in Dr. Dyson's view. In this vein, the government was an active participant in marginalizing the ability of people of color to succeed in America both past and present—a scenario where people of color are on the outside of mainstream society looking in.

Conversely, Mr. Connerly spoke of *our government* in his remarks. Not a government for some people, but the government of the United States acting on behalf of and for all the people of the United States. More concretely, Connerly sought to have a government that is color-blind, a government that refuses to pick winners and losers based on their ethnic identity, but one in which all Americans are treated equally under the color of law. Otherwise, a legal and governmental system in which some are given special, rather than equal, rights under the color of law could create a backlash—a backlash that has arisen when one set of Americans sees the government actively seeking to marginalize one *group* of people due to their racial or ethnic identity while the other side sees the government's proper role as an arbiter, in which all citizens are treated equally as *individuals*.

The dichotomy between those who view affirmative action as a protection of special rights against a government that has oppressed ethnic minorities due to their race and/or ethnic origin versus those who believe the proper role of government is to treat citizens equally without regard to the color of their skin is particularly illustrative when discussing whether the elimination of affirmative action would lead to the reintroduction of Jim Crow codes in America. Recall that two years prior to the Dyson-Connerly debate then mayor of San Francisco Willie Brown likened the march against Proposition 209 to the marches that had taken place to protest Jim Crow. Brown's view was not a singular line of thinking; both Dr. Dyson and Mr. Connerly were given the opportunity to address the issue during the question-and-answer segment of their debate.

> PROGRAM PARTICIPANT QUESTIONER: Many times it has been said that history repeats itself. The mood of white America today toward affirmative action is the same as in the period following the Civil War . . . Given the mood of the country today, do you think it's possible we could return to Jim Crow laws?[17]

Consider carefully Dr. Dyson's and Mr. Connerly's respective responses. First, Dr. Dyson opined:

> Yes, we can get back to a kind of Jim Crow situation *only* if those of us who are privileged, those of us who have resources—M.B.A.s, Ph.D.'s and so on, law degrees and doctors—only if we refuse (a) to recognize our moral responsibility and culpability to the least of these within our community, and (b) to make sure that we're not only concerned about race, but we're concerned about class. Because "them niggers" and "them spics" and them so-calleds is us! Right? And we are them. That's why we've got to constantly fight against not only racism from the outside, but classism and economic inequality from within. Otherwise, we will revisit Southern apartheid.[18]

To which Mr. Connerly forcefully rebutted:

> I think it is ludicrous for us to sit here thinking that we're going to allow our nation to go back to the era of Jim Crow. We're not helpless. The people in this room, you occupy prominent positions in government. We're decision makers . . . I mean that idea to me is the most mind-boggling idea I've ever heard. No we're not going to let that happen. That isn't even in the realm of possibility. So my answer to you, whether you agree or

not—I really don't care, I really don't give a damn—my belief
is no. No. It's not going to happen. No.[19]

The phraseology here is important, as I believe it encapsulates much of
why affirmative action remains a subject of division rather than healing
in the country today—a source of friction against those in favor of special, rather than equal, rights based on the color of their skin rather
than the color of law. While we specifically discussed the question of
whether the evolving practice of multiculturalism and diversity were
working to create a backlash in the previous chapter, the language utilized by Dr. Dyson and Mr. Connerly is particularly instructive.

For his part, Dyson was adamant (as was former San Francisco
mayor Willie Brown) in the belief that not only was there a sufficient
number of white people willing to restore the barriers imposed by Jim
Crow laws in the 1950s and 1960s to shut blacks out of society but that
the black "elite" would be willing to stand by and let such an atrocity
occur. While I have great respect for Dr. Dyson and we have had the
opportunity to work with each other and become friends over the years,
I am stunned not only by his belief that America is capable of sliding
back to a Jim Crow era without affirmative action plans in place, but
that there are other prominent, intelligent, and well-regarded people of
color who share his belief. Have not many of the barriers been lowered,
opportunities to advance been presented, and one given the opportunity
to pursue the American dream to become the first black president of the
United States, all because of a new sentiment of inclusiveness in America? Haven't the days for marches ended, and hasn't the time come to
roll up our sleeves to address issues of educating our children in elementary and high school so that affirmative action programs will be unnec-
essary for the college years and beyond? Most important, to avoid the
balkanization of citizens in America along lines of race and ethnicity, we
must find ways to come together as a singular and cohesive society comprised of diverse citizens; I believe affirmative action takes the country
on a backward rather than forward path in this regard.

This position is not merely my opinion—an amicus curiae brief filed
before the United States Supreme Court in 2011 by three members of

the United States Commission on Civil Rights warned of the destructive nature of affirmative action on increasing the number of black students in our colleges and universities as well as the American workforce. First, the commissioners noted that the unintended consequence of lowering admissions standards for minority students to promote diversity was to *reduce* the number of qualified minority students attending colleges and universities across the country. Here, commissioners Peter Kirsanow, Todd Gaziano, and Gail Heriot wrote convincingly:

> How can it be that affirmative action reduces the number of minority professionals? One of the consequences of widespread race-preferential policies is that minority students end up distributed among colleges and universities in very different patterns from their white and Asian counterparts. When the highest schools on the academic ladder relax their admissions policies in order to admit more under-represented minority students, schools one rung down must do likewise if they are to have minority students too. The problem is thus passed on to the schools another rung down, which respond similarly. As a result, under-represented minority students are overwhelmingly at the bottom of the distribution of entering academic credentials at most selective schools.[20]

In other words, rather than achieve the touted benefits of affirmative action to increase representation of blacks and other persons of color, it had the unintended effect of *reducing* minority representation at selective higher education institutions.

Moreover, the commissioners continued their analysis by noting that the impact on African American employees in the workplace was devastating, given that many students admitted to elite colleges and universities through affirmative action programs are unable to compete with their peers in school, self-segregate in study and support groups, and are not equipped to perform academically to put them in a position to obtain a job following their college years. This is by no means to suggest that these are inferior or bad students. To the contrary, the commissioners sought to illustrate that enrolling students in elite colleges and universities for the sake of diversity had the unintended impact of *reducing* the number of minority students who were able to perform academically at a certain level.

SO WHERE ARE WE TODAY AND HOW CAN WE BEST MOVE FORWARD RATHER THAN BLACKWARDS?

The arguments and the tensions created by wide discussion of affirmative action programs in general, and the Proposition 209 initiative adopted in California in particular, roiled the cauldron that is American society in ways we have not seen in more than forty years. The end of the twentieth century—a century in which blacks were emancipated from the separate but equal chains that had bound them to second-class citizenship—found America at the beginning of the twenty-first century grappling with difficult issues of race and equality.

Whereas the doors of opportunity had been locked and access to the schoolhouse had been barred some fifty years ago, I believe proponents of government-sanctioned affirmative action today are taking us blackwards, rather than advancing people of color with the insistence that they are incapable or unwilling to move forward without a crutch provided by the government. This is the same crutch to which I referred in *Acting White* that brands black children with an "I" for inferior by their classmates, who remain suspicious of whether students of color were admitted due to their qualifications or through an affirmative action and/or quota based program.

Although the California State Supreme Court upheld the legality of Proposition 209 in two subsequent challenges—the most recent challenge having occurred in August 2010—opponents have vowed to carry on their fight to the highest court in the land for what they believe is an entitlement that should remain in place for ethnic minorities to receive special, rather than equal, rights.

Finally, it will be interesting to watch how citizens in the individual states react once the Supreme Court considers and ultimately rules on litigation brought in favor or opposed to affirmative action. For example, when the Supreme Court upheld the use of race in admissions at the University of Michigan Law School in 2003, citizens of the state successfully amended their constitution in 2006, in direct response to the action taken by the high court, to treat all residents of the state of Michigan equally both under the law as well as before the government of the citizens themselves.

So how can we move forward together as a nation united based on our citizenship and shared heritage rather than advocating for special, rather than equal, rights based on skin color and/or ethnicity? I believe President Kennedy had articulated the proper vision for affirmative action some fifty years ago—a program he believed was necessary to ensure people were not discriminated under the law based on the color of their skin. To this end, Kennedy articulated a philosophy that was as cogent then as it is today: the government must ensure that race has no place in American law or life in the United States of America. However well intentioned the efforts to level the playing field have been over the decades, I believe efforts to promote and provide special rights based on one's race or ethnic origin have served two destructive purposes. First, they have added fuel to the fire of suspicion that burns when a certain group of citizens believe that the right to be treated as an equal citizen under the law has been abrogated when individuals of a particular ethnic group or race are treated differently. This in turn, I believe, has led to a backlash not only against affirmative action programs by many in the country today, but has also reinforced a stereotype that blacks are unable or unwilling to compete without preferential treatment—that they are fundamentally inferior based on their race, rather than being assessed and evaluated individually as American citizens.

If history is our guide as a predicate of future activity regarding the eradication of affirmative action programs at the federal level in the United States, the prospect of eliminating such programs is bleak. Despite the pronouncement of then justice Sandra Day O'Connor in the *Grutter v. Bollinger* decision in which the Supreme Court upheld the use of racial classifications at the University of Michigan Law

School for certain limited purposes, it is clear the practice not only will persist in the short term but will be sanctioned by the government in the decades to come. To this end, she wrote:

> [T]he Equal Protection Clause does not prohibit the Law School's narrowly tailored use of race in admissions decisions to further a compelling interest in obtaining the educational benefits that flow from a diverse student body.[21]

But perhaps the most famous phrase from this opinion is the one that gives me pause to believe special interest groups, if not federal government officials themselves, will fail to heed President Kennedy's call to eliminate race from American law and life. O'Connor's optimistic assessment in her opinion offers a prediction I believe will ultimately never occur and only lead to greater anxiety and animosity in race relations in the United States so long as we confer special, rather than equal, rights based on skin color:

> It has been twenty-five years since Justice [Lewis F.] Powell first approved the use of race to further an interesting student body diversity in the context of public higher education. Since that time, the number of minority applicants with high grades and test scores has indeed increased. We expect that twenty-five years from now, the use of racial preferences will no longer be necessary to further the interest approved today.[22]

That the Supreme Court would sanction race-based discrimination under the law is unconscionable in its own right. That it would do so when the eradication of race-based affirmative action programs at the state level has *boosted* rather than decreased the number of minority students is particularly disturbing.

Before we close our inquiry into the effects of affirmative action as a promotion of diversity and multicultural efforts that I believe ultimately emphasize rather than celebrate our differences, I want to point out a recent article from the *Los Angeles Times* that proves the point

Ward Connerly and supporters of Proposition 209 made nearly sixteen years ago in California. Despite the heated rhetoric that Proposition 209 would "turn back the clock" or bar minority students at the door of opportunity, passage of this "controversial" ballot initiative, there are *more* rather than fewer minorities admitted to college in the University of California system once race was no longer utilized as a preference for admission.

On July 10, 2010, authors David A. Lehrer and Joe R. Hicks wrote a piece entitled, "UC Proves Prop. 209's Point: Admissions Records Show That Minorities Don't Need Affirmative Action." In the relevant section the authors specifically noted:

Here are the facts: The number of minority admissions to the University of California for this fall [2010]—without the benefit of preferences—exceeds that of 1996, in absolute numbers and, more important, as a percentage of all "admits." The numbers are, in almost every category, quite staggering. Latino students have gone from 15.4% (5,744 students) of freshman undergraduate admissions in 1996 to 23% (14,081) in 2010 (a 145% increase). Asian students have gone from 29.8% (11,085) of the freshman admits to 37.47% (22,877). Native American admits have declined slightly, from 0.9% to 0.8%, but their absolute number increased, from 360 to 531. African American admits have gone from 4% (1,628) to 4.2% (2,624), a modest gain in percentage but nearly a 50% increase in numbers of freshmen admitted.

The only major category that declined in percentage terms was whites, who went from 44% (16,465) of the freshmen admits to 34% (20,807).[23]

Trained as a lawyer, I tend to let the facts speak for themselves. For all of the emotional calls that removing affirmative action programs at the state level would "turn back the clock" or reimpose Jim Crow–era sanctions on people of color, students in the state of California have shown that they are up to the challenge to compete regardless of the color of their skin or ethnicity. Only by regarding one another as citizens of these United States bound together by our common bond as Americans will we break away from the special, rather than equal, treatment sought by those who seek to identify us as members of differing racial and ethnic groups. Only then will we achieve the vision articulated by President Kennedy so long ago and personified by Dr. Martin Luther King's "I have a dream" speech, which he delivered in 1963. The best affirmative action we can take together as a country to unify as citizens rather than cause a backlash based on the skin color of those seeking special, rather than equal, rights? I close with the beginning of Justice Thomas's dissent opinion in the *Grutter v. Bollinger* decision—if only the justice's detractors could overcome his conservative eloquence as an *individual* jurist without seeking to identify him as a member of an ethnic or racial *group*. Here, Justice Thomas remarked:

Frederick Douglass, speaking to a group of abolitionists almost 140 years ago, delivered a message lost on today's majority:

> [I]n regard to the colored people, there is always more that is benevolent, I perceive, than just, manifested toward us. What I ask for the negro is not benevolence, not pity, not sympathy, but simply justice. The American people have always been anxious to know what they shall do with us. . . . I have had but one answer from the beginning. Do nothing with us! Your doing with us has already played the mischief with us. Do nothing with us! If the apples will not remain on the tree of their own strength, if they are worm eaten at the core, if they are early ripe and disposed to fall, let them fall! . . . And if the negro cannot stand on his own legs, let him fall also. All I ask is, give him a chance to stand on his own legs! Let him alone! . . . [Y]our interference is doing him positive injury.[24]

We can overcome the acrimony and ill will caused by the promotion of affirmative action programs by ensuring that all Americans regardless of the color of their skin are given an affirmative opportunity to succeed in our society. In my view, true affirmative action must be taken as early as elementary school to ensure those children that are most at risk academically are provided with the tools they need to excel—tutors, mentoring, and summer instruction programs. For those parents whose children attend underperforming schools and are shuffled from grade to grade without demonstrable academic progress, charter and magnet schools must be made available as an escape hatch to parachute away from a failing school and into a more positive environment for learning. Rather than face the stigma and sting of being accused of "taking" a seat in college or position in the workplace based on affirmative action and diversity, this flare up of racial tension will ease when all of our children—regardless of their skin color—are given an equal opportunity to learn, compete, and become productive members of our American society.

Unfortunately, recent events indicate affirmative action has already created a recoil across America for the continued push for special, rather than equal, rights. In September 2003, Southern Methodist University (SMU) officials stepped in to halt a student bake sale designed to protest affirmative action in which different prices were charged for different items based on the race and gender of the potential buyer. According to the *Beaumont Enterprise* report, white males were charged one dollar per cookie while the price would drop to 75 cents for a white woman, 50 cents for Hispanics, and 25 cents for blacks. The sale had been organized by a conservative group at SMU to visibly demonstrate the inequity of affirmative action by contrasting differing admissions standards to different prices for the same baked product at the sale.

Predictably, the sale was halted after forty-five minutes when a crowd of students had gathered around the sale display stand and a black student lodged a complaint with SMU officials, claiming the sale could create a potentially unsafe situation for students.[25] Sadly, the incident is an illustrative reminder of why affirmative action has created a sense of entitlement for some and resentment for others: being given special treatment based solely on the color of one's skin should not be permitted in the United States today to right past wrongs. I believe the SMU students were merely trying to bring light to a sensitive issue in a provocative manner—is the practice of setting different standards for admission based on skin color any less provocative and/or offensive?

As might be expected, SMU was not the only school in 2003 to conduct a bake sale in opposition to affirmative action. In Texas, students at the University of Texas at Austin and Texas A&M were allowed to conduct similar bake sales as protected, thus permissible, free speech activities.

The original affirmative action protest bake sale can be traced to February 2003, when students at the University of California (Los Angeles) conducted a sale similar to the one described above at Southern Methodist University. The UCLA sale was soon followed by similar events sponsored by college Republican chapters at the University of California (Berkeley), the University of New Mexico, the University of Richmond, the University of Michigan, Northwestern University, and the Illinois State University. Far from being isolated occurrences, these student-led bake sales demonstrated a fact that has seemed lost on politically correct university officials and multicultural adherents both then and now: treating people as individuals without regard to the color of their skin fosters true equality, whereas providing special rights or treatment for the same only fosters resentment and mistrust. This simple fact would be borne out one year later when university students in Rhode Island escalated their protest against affirmative action beyond mere bake sales in a more provocative attempt to garner attention.

In February 2004, the college Republican chapter at Roger Williams University in Bristol, Rhode Island, thought of ways they could protest the practice of affirmative action admissions and diversity practices underway on their campus. The students came up with the idea of creating a scholarship fund that would collect and disperse money for white students only, as a provocative way to register their displeasure of dispensing special treatment and/or rights based on the color of one's skin. According to CNN, applicants for the scholarship "must be of Caucasian descent, have high honors, write an essay, and show an impressive list of accomplishments."[26]

I do not condone scholarships for white students any more than I do for those targeting students of color. At the same time, I can understand the frustration of those who believe one group of people is being given special, rather than equal, rights due solely to the color of their skin. Unfortunately, the bake sales at college campuses in the early 2000s were not isolated student protests against affirmative action—I believe the acrimony surrounding affirmative action continues to grow rather than subside. For example, in February 2011, students at the University of Texas at San Marcos also called for the creation of a whites-only scholarship to provide assistance to what proponents called an "underrepresented group."

Published reports noted that students at the University of Texas at San Marcos formed the Former Majority Association for Equality to organize for the scholarships—a nine-member board of directors containing one black, three women, and one Hispanic student.[27] Students were hoping to dispense $1,000 scholarships to five students during the spring 2012 semester to qualified applicants with a 3.0 grade point average and being "at least 25 percent Caucasian."[28] What I found particularly interesting as the University of Texas students sought to gain attention for their disapproval of affirmative action programs was the composition of the board of directors itself. It would be easy to label the "whites-only scholarship" program as the fringe thinking of a group of white students; it is much harder to dismiss the fact that five of the nine members of the board are from what have been traditionally identified as "underrepresented" groups.

I believe the next true battle for civil rights will be for *equal* rather than *special* rights for all of our American children. If we persist in seeking diversity rather than equality in all aspects of our society, we will perpetuate myths, stereotypes, and suspicions of black inferiority rather than confronting the hard reality that we are failing our students and condemning them to failure in life.

HEADING BLACKWARDS ON CAMPUS?

Before we leave the destructive manner in which affirmative action has segregated students and those in the workforce at the demand by some for special, rather than equal, rights due to race, I want to touch briefly on an equally destructive practice that is prevalent at many of our colleges and universities today. Every fall across America, millions of students arrive at institutions of higher learning to challenge themselves, their fellow students, and members of the faculty at large. College is supposed to be a time to explore and embrace diversity of thought, culture, and perspective. In the not too distant past, members of the 101st Airborne Division and the National Guard were activated to ensure that black students could take their seats in schools across the South that were opposed to their presences due to integration.

Sadly, I believe a new form of segregation has spread across the collegiate landscape over the last quarter century—this time encouraged and perpetuated by black students and faculty members themselves. The calls for integration have given way to demands for all-black fraternities, sororities, and dormitories under the banner of multiculturalism. Is it right for blacks to demand specific facilities and accommodations based on the color of their skin when their white peers would be accused of racism for doing the same? Is this not the notion that history is repeating itself—advocates of the *Plessy v. Ferguson* decision, in which the doctrine of *separate but equal* accommodations for whites and blacks was the rule of law in the United States for more than fifty years—a reality in which the conditions were truly separate and the treatment under the law was decidedly unequal. And yet, in the era of a supposed postracial America ushered in by President Obama's election, black intellectual, political, and academic leaders sanction such segregation based on skin color and ethnicity rather than embracing equal rights for all American citizens under the color of law. How can it be that those who purport to speak for African American citizens today implicitly advocate policies in which citizens are treated differently based on the color of their skin when Dr. Martin Luther King and countless brave leaders rejected such incongruity? On the surface, it would appear that current supporters of such a practice are taking us back to the days of separate and differing treatment under the law, rather than judging each American citizen as an individual equally under the color of law today.

While there is not much empirical data to demonstrate whether the call for separate dorms, Greek life, and housing has yet caused turmoil at America's institutions of higher learning, Stanford University's Hoover Institution fellow John Bunzel wrote a captivating book on the subject, *Race Relations on Campus: Stanford Students Speak*, in 1992. Dr. Bunzel conducted a series of in-depth personal interviews with 54 Stanford undergraduate students during the 1988–89 academic calendar year to discuss relations between white and black students on campus. Of the 54 students interviewed, 20 were white and 24 were black.[29] Beyond the personal interviews conducted by Bunzel, he also distributed a nine-page questionnaire to half of the senior class of 1989—some 862 students.

One of the more interesting findings Bunzel discovered was that increasing the number of minority students at Stanford had led to more, rather than fewer, incidents of racism. To this regard he noted:

> But there is a great irony. While the increased numbers of minority students have generated a new era of race relations at Stanford, there have been more, not fewer, racial problems. Although students are regularly told by University officials of the importance of such concepts as "pluralism," "multiculturalism," and "appreciation of differences"—as the UCMI reports, "incoming students now hear these themes articulated during freshman orientation and repeatedly through their undergraduate years"—the dynamics of the critical mass have led to an accumulation of underlying tensions and racial incidents, as well as frequent disagreements between white and minority students about whether the interracial environment that has emerged on campus is friendly or hostile.[30]

As an undergraduate at Haverford College, located just outside of Philadelphia, during the time this survey was conducted, I can relate to the views expressed above on a personal basis. Haverford prides itself on both the diversity of the student body as well as on fostering a strong sense of community. Yet during my time as an undergraduate, there was a pervasive sense, both during my freshman orientation as well as my remaining four years on campus, that such conversations on multiculturalism and inclusiveness tended to stifle, rather than add to, meaningful discussions on race for fear of one being labeled politically incorrect. We spent so much time talking about how multicultural, diverse, and inclusive we were and perhaps not as much time just immersing ourselves in the college experience and enjoying each other as individuals rather than being members of this race or that ethnicity.

To this end, I was very interested to note that in Bunzel's study regarding race relations at Stanford, similar to my experience at Haverford, there was no singular definition students—white or black—could agree upon in regards to what constituted racism, but that blacks often felt that it was more institutionalized, rather than being able to point to a specific racist incident they had encountered. Here Bunzel noted:

> But Stanford, it is equally clear, is both much more and much less than a microcosm of American society. Most of the black students who said they had personally encountered racist behavior at the University . . . were hard-pressed to describe what it was like or how it worked—because, as many of them said, the racism they confronted, although it pervaded the whole campus, was subtle and could not be effectively explained to others.[31]

Then as now, the self-segregation of some blacks at Stanford, Haverford College, and many of our colleges and universities today is one of my gravest concerns about the push for multiculturalism. For me, Haverford was and remains a wonderfully inclusive and tight-knit community where people of all races felt free to mingle, socialize, and date based on the individuality of the people involved rather than the color of their skin. At the same time, I worried about the impact that the self-segregation of many blacks through their living in the Black Cultural Center or sitting at separate tables in the dining hall would have upon our collective unity as a college community. If the entire point of going to college was the opportunity to interact and meet people of differing races, I found the notion of separate dorms or special tables to be self-defeating and leading to more misunderstandings about race rather than coming together as a diverse student body comprising a community.

Put another way, why would we strive for inclusiveness in the classroom and on the athletic fields on our college campuses, yet permit separate and distinct theme houses for dormitories, separate graduation ceremonies, and other special accommodations when in every other aspect of campus life equality is stressed at the expense of equal rights? I am concerned that the exclusivity, rather than inclusivity based on demanding special, rather than equal, rights based on skin color will only contribute to a racial backlash (whether conscious or not) by whites that feel they are being castigated for being racist and noninclusive.

Finally, consider a thought-provoking article written by Michael Meyers, former assistant national director of the NAACP and presently the president and executive director of the New York Civil Rights Coalition. A few years back Meyers wrote an op-ed in *The Washington Post* entitled "Stop the Black-Only Treatment" in which he discussed with great anxiety the rise of "special" programs for minority students that provide separate counseling, mentoring, tutoring, residences, and instruction based strictly on the color of their skin.[32] Unlike the survey conducted by Dr. Bunzel during the late 1980s or my personal experience at Haverford College through 1991, Meyers spoke of a new fad called Black Male Initiatives (BMIs) that became popular in the first six years of the twenty-first century—government-funded and university-sponsored projects in several states, including Kansas, Georgia, Ohio, New York, and Pennsylvania.[33] What is particularly distressing about these initiatives is that they label all black men as being "at risk" and devote special programs and counseling to assist their development. The New York Civil Rights Coalition lodged a complaint against the City University of New York about these special programs and to this end, Meyers noted:

Until recently, when the New York Civil Rights Coalition filed a complaint against the City University of New York, these programs were unassailable. But more and more they are being shown to feature new variants of an old prejudice. This has included stereotyping all black male students as "at risk," and for example, running special classes only for black men at CUNY's Medgar Evers College. This special instruction focused on black men's alleged deficiencies and their need to act more responsibly in order to reclaim their traditional patriarchal roles in the black community and of the so-called black race.[34]

I can't think of a more destructive program or set of government-funded and university-sponsored initiatives to drive a wedge between fellow students based exclusively on race. What are the characteristics of being "at risk"? Why wouldn't disadvantaged white or Latino students qualify for such a program unless it is a perpetuation of the cult of ethnicity in which many blacks welcome, rather than condemn, self-segregation?

Meyers would also powerfully observe that:

Many black leaders in and outside of academia seem to have no objection to the figurative black-only signs over certain doorways at America's colleges. Not surprisingly, this racial identity ferment—aka self determination—is proudly endorsed by white liberals disturbed by the dwindling numbers of black men on campus . . . Hence college presidents are listening to their black students and to officials for diversity and affirmative action or minority affairs, and they are setting up BMIs as a way to make life more comfortable for black students . . . When the college takes on such tasks it is only confirming and reinforcing pernicious racial stereotypes. The penchant to isolate, track, and segregate black men is a deeply offensive and nasty American social habit, and programs that parrot and mirror such group prejudices are as crude as they are paternalistic.[35]

In all, my fear, as articulated by Mr. Meyers above, is that the push for racial exclusion and self-segregation perpetuates the cult of ethnicity discussed in chapter 1, in which people identify as being a member of a racial/ethnic group rather than individually taking pride in their status as an American citizen and part of the collective fabric of our unique society. The corresponding result, which we will discuss in chapter 3, has led to a call for a black agenda pursuing black rights on behalf of black leaders, which can only perpetuate the notion that people of color are entitled to special rights—leading America backwards by pursuing such special status and privilege in the twenty-first century. Such calls have moved away from the vision articulated by our Founding Fathers where we would set aside our self-identification by our ancestral roots and instead singularly identify as citizens of the United States of America. The pursuit of separate public policy agendas undertaken by leaders of a particular race, rather than seeking the best results and outcomes for America's citizens regardless of their color or racial identity, will not only lead to a backlash but also a self-segregation that will foster more racial resentment rather than harmony—a step backward, toward the divisive days encountered during the 1960s in America rather than a step forward to a place where one's individual perspective and content is valued more than the color of their skin.

3. SO-CALLED BLACK LEADERS TAKING AMERICA BLACKWARDS WHILE PURSUING A BLACK AGENDA

||||||||||||||||||||||||||||||||||||||||||||||||||

What is a leader today? Dictionary.com defines a leader as one with "a guiding or directing hand, as of an army, movement, or political group."[1] With that definition before us, is there such a thing as a black leader in the United States today? I do not ask the question rhetorically, but with all the sincerity and conviction I can muster. A disturbing trend has emerged in America in the era of Obama that I believe contributes to America being pulled further apart based on skin color rather than being united in solidarity of our collective citizenship. The problem? The ease with which certain black elected officials, civil rights leaders, and others have cloaked themselves in their racial and ethnic identity, while deriding those who wish to assess their leadership attributes based on skill and competence as being racist or racially motivated. In other words, their primary qualification for being given a position of public trust stems more from the color of their skin rather than seeking to improve the welfare of all Americans regardless of the color of their skin.

Unfortunately, this disturbing phenomenon is present at all levels of government in our American society today and is a practice that must be eradicated in order for American citizens to be evaluated and treated equally in society rather than one group demanding special, rather than equal, rights of their fellow citizens.

While there are several ostensible leadership groups we could discuss to demonstrate the use of race in a detrimental manner, I will limit my present inquiry to one organization in particular. This group, I believe, has taken racial grievances to the limit and should either disband or dramatically change their mission in the twenty-first century with the election of America's first president who also happens to be black. The institution in question is the Congressional Black Caucus.

The Congressional Black Caucus was formed in 1971 during the ninety-second session of Congress (1971–1972). Led by Congressman Charles Diggs (D-MI), the original thirteen members of the Congressional Black Caucus (hereinafter "CBC") boycotted President Richard Nixon's State of the Union address after repeated demands by the CBC to meet with the president were denied in which they sought to discuss issues of concern to benefit black Americans and other minority group members.

In a public relations coup for the newly formed group, President Nixon granted the CBC a meeting shortly after the State of the Union address in which they would outline their specific series of recommendations the government should undertake to ameliorate the conditions of blacks living in America. President Nixon met with the CBC on March 25, 1971, and on the day of the meeting, CBC chairman Diggs circulated a letter to his congressional colleagues outlining the priorities they would share with the president. As part of their opening statement, the CBC declared to President Nixon:

> We sought this meeting, Mr. President, out of a deep conviction that large numbers of citizens are being subjected to intense hardship, and denied their basic rights, and are suffering irreparable harm as a result of current policies . . .
>
> We would be less than honest, Mr. President, if we did not reflect a view widely shared among a majority of the citizens we represent. That view is that the representatives of this Administration, by word and deed, have at crucial points retreated from the national commitment to make Americans of all races and cultures equal in the eyes of their government—to make equal

the poor as well as the rich, urban and rural dwellers as well as those who live in the suburbs.

Our people are no longer asking for equality as a rhetorical promise. They are demanding from the national Administration and from elected officials without regard to party affiliation, the only kind of equality that ultimately has any meaning—equality of results. If we are in fact to be equal in this country, then the government must help us achieve these results . . . [2]

The CBC further emphasized priorities such as an end to racism, access to affordable housing, livable wages, fair and impartial administration of justice and the enforcement of civil rights protections, and affirmative action, among other key goals. In all, the CBC presented some sixty recommendations for the president and his administration's consideration.

While the CBC would receive a 115-page report from President Nixon in direct response to their specific policy recommendations, the members felt that Nixon had not taken seriously their request for specific legislative action despite Nixon's assertion that his administration would push for "[j]obs, income, and tangible benefits, the pledges that this society has made to the disadvantaged in the past decade."[3] The CBC would respond to Nixon's report with "A Report to the Nation" on June 3, 1971, expressing and detailing their disappointment with the White House response. The following year, CBC member Louis Stokes (D-OH) unveiled the Black Declaration of Independence and the Black Bill of Rights during the Democratic National Convention. The Black Declaration of Independence demanded that the Democratic Party and its eventual nominee would make racial equality a priority, while the Black Bill of Rights set forth a series of specific policy initiatives that eventual standard-bearer George McGovern would largely ignore.[4]

In the decades since its founding, the CBC would form a non-profit foundation for policy and educational initiatives with a mission where "[w]e envision a world in which the black community is free of all disparities and able to contribute fully to advancing the common good."[5] The foundation would also conduct an Annual Legislative Conference in which key policy leaders from Washington, D.C., and across the country would convene in the nation's capital to mingle and share ideas. Since its founding many corporations have been eager to contribute to the Congressional Black Caucus Foundation to demonstrate their commitment to diversity both to CBC members as well as the greater public as a whole.

Concurrent with activities undertaken by their foundation, CBC members would also press their colleagues in Congress as well as the occupant of the Oval Office to pay mind to their specific policy concerns. While I can fully understand the need for an informal caucus to meet with legislative leaders and those within the executive branch to strengthen the economy, ensure fair adjudication of the law and equal opportunity within the American society, I have always been troubled by the notion that there is a specific "black agenda" the nation must follow at the expense of others. Consistent with Arthur Schlesinger's warning about the creation of a cult of ethnicity discussed in chapter 1, I have always believed in the quote famously adopted by President Kennedy from the regional New England Chamber of Commerce, where he commented that a rising tide lifts all boats; could not the United States set a course in the best national interest that would benefit all of her citizens regardless of skin color?

Upon my arrival on Capitol Hill in 1991, I would question both the relevance of the CBC in the late twentieth century as well as of a corresponding staff group that had been established by black congressional aides called the Congressional Black Associates. For those not familiar with my background, I discussed in *Acting White* my concern of affiliating with groups while a student at Haverford College based strictly on skin color. My personal view was (and remains) that people should gravitate toward others based on shared values and mutual interests—not strictly based on skin color and/or ethnicity.

Eric Foster, a smart and gregarious staff member on my hall and a leader of the Congressional Black Associates as well as a good friend, repeatedly enjoined me to attend a meeting of the CBA. He stressed

that as one of the few black Republican aides in the House of Representatives during the middle 1990s, he felt my conservative ideology
would bring diversity and a different point of view to a monolithic
group of Democrat staff members. I agreed to attend and was stunned
by the less-than-welcome treatment I received when I walked through
the door. One participant asked me if I hadn't joined the group because I didn't like black people and yet another asked me why I had
sold out by joining the Republican Party.

Concluding that pressure on Capitol Hill was intense enough
without having to be attacked by fellow black staffers accusing me of
racism and self-loathing, I immediately wheeled around and departed
my lone Congressional Black Associates meeting—never to return
again. If these are the staff members who work for members of the
Congressional Black Caucus, I was disappointed that they could well
represent the viewpoints held by their respective members of Congress
for whom they worked.

Over the years, I would watch to see if the Congressional Black
Caucus honored their original commitment to fight for an end to racism, equal protection and rights for all under the law, and an unyield-
ing commitment to justice. The more I watched, however, the more
disappointed I became. There are three specific instances in which the
CBC did a great disservice to the philosophy espoused by the thirteen founding members in 1971 to become an organization focused
exclusively on race and ethnicity. The push for equality and justice
became a demand for special, rather than equal, rights under the
law—a cult of ethnicity mentality pursuing multiculturalism and diversity at the expense of our national cohesiveness—adding to the
present polarization along racial lines and racial identity that afflicts
our country today.

The first hint I had of their true agenda was the manner in which
the CBC fought to shield former Representative William Jefferson
from losing his seat on the powerful Ways and Means Committee as
ethics clouds swirled around the congressman in 2006. Unbeknownst
to Jefferson, the then charismatic congressman from New Orleans had
been under FBI surveillance to ascertain whether he had been trading

his services as a member of Congress in exchange for cash bribes and/
or gifts. Jefferson was ultimately convicted on 11 out of 16 counts alleging bribery, fraud, money laundering, and racketeering, and he became an unfortunate punch line on late night television program for
hiding a bribe he had received from the vice president of Nigeria—
$90,000 in cold cash—in his kitchen refrigerator. He was subse-
quently sentenced to serve thirteen years in federal prison.

In response to leader Nancy Pelosi's request to Jefferson that he
voluntarily relinquish his seat on the Ways and Means Committee,
the Congressional Black Caucus closed ranks around him and told the
minority leader that they would fight attempts to "involuntarily remove" Congressman Jefferson from his committee assignment. The
desire of the Democratic leader to remove an albatross from around
the neck of the Democratic Party clashed with the CBC's insistence to
protect one of their own in the midst of an ongoing government bribery investigation led to rising tensions between the two sides. Rather
than call for Jefferson's removal from the Ways and Means Committee, the CBC instead voted on June 6, 2006—the second such vote
inside of a three-week period—to stand united as a group opposed to
Jefferson's removal from his seat on the powerful tax-writing committee.

Less than a month prior to the Congressional Black Caucus votes
of solidarity in support of Congressman Jefferson, the FBI had raided
his home and congressional office in furtherance of their bribery investigation. Why, then, would the Congressional Black Caucus stand firmly
against the removal of a member of Congress under serious investigation by the Department of Justice for allegedly accepting bribes from
foreign leaders and engaging in a reckless pattern of unethical behavior? Because Congressman Jefferson was black, a fellow member of the
Congressional Black Caucus, and therefore entitled to special, rather
than equal, rights because he was black. Simple. End of story.

At the heart of the CBC opposition was the sense that Pelosi had
employed a racially tinged double standard to allow veteran congressman Alan Mollohan (D-WV), a white member, to remain at his post
during a federal investigation in which Mollohan was alleged to have

enriched himself through his position on the powerful Appropriations Committee, while Jefferson, a black member, was eventually ousted from his Ways and Means post. I believe the difference between the two members was actually quite simple: one member of Congress had been under direct surveillance by the FBI for allegations of bribery; the other member merely had charges lodged against him by the House Ethics Committee.

I do not believe race had any motivation behind Pelosi's treatment of Mollohan versus her call for Jefferson to step aside from his committee assignment, but that distinction made no difference to the membership of the CBC, who were convinced Jefferson had been wronged because of his race—the underlying $90,000 in bribe money found in his freezer notwithstanding. Curiously omitted by CBC members in their disdain with leader Pelosi for the manner in which she had pressed Congressman Jefferson to step down from the House Ways and Means Committee was the fact that at her urging, Congressman Mollohan had relinquished his gavel as chair of the Ethics Committee for the duration of its investigation. Ironically, despite the solidarity shown Congressman Jefferson due to the color of his skin by the CBC rather than the underlying facts and belief in his innocence, Congressman Jefferson ultimately stood trial and was convicted and sentenced to thirteen years in federal prison. As for now former Congressman Mollohan? After several years of investigating Mollohan's alleged involvement in illegal activities, the Public Integrity Section of the Department of Justice dropped all charges against him in January 2010, due to insufficient evidence of crimes having been committed.

Rather than seeking to remove Congressman Jefferson from his prominent committee assignment based on the color of his skin, the corrupt actions and activity had instead proven too much of a distraction for senior Democrats who sought to reclaim control of the House of Representatives from Republicans beset with ethical issues of their own. Pelosi sought to minimize whatever damage Jefferson might cause the party in reclaiming control of the House by removing him from his prominent position on the Ways and Means Committee to mitigate any damage the beleaguered congressman might cause his party in the upcoming November 2006 election.

Minority leader Pelosi was seeking to become Speaker Pelosi and the Democrats had promised to run the most ethically honest Congress in history should they be given control of the House. The country had been sickened and distraught once the corruption of lobbyist Jack Abramoff had fully come to public view that year. Taking no chances of being tarnished by a corruption scandal that primarily centered around Republican members of the House, Jefferson was subsequently removed from his post despite heated opposition by the CBC, and Nancy Pelosi was elected the first woman Speaker of the House in January 2007.

One would like to believe the William Jefferson controversy was an isolated incident, but it only exposed what would become the norm rather than the exception: the Congressional Black Caucus would close ranks behind black members accused of ethical or legal wrongdoing—despite the underlying charges of ethical or legal misconduct—based strictly and solely on the black color of skin of the alleged wrongdoer.

Unfortunately, our second example of Congressional Black Caucus involves many familiar aspects we have seen thus far with Representative William Jefferson as we turn to consider the ethical charges lodged against the dean of the New York congressional delegation, Representative Charles "Charlie" Rangel (D-NY), the flashy and charming chairman of the Ways and Means Committee from Harlem. The case, similar to the Jefferson matter, involves the color-based solidarity displayed by the Congressional Black Caucus to unify behind one of the members facing ethical allegations because he was black, rather than assess that individual's conduct to ascertain the proper course of action that should be taken.

In many respects, Rangel's story is the quintessential rags to riches story—a poor man rose from Harlem, bravely fought for his country in the Korean War, and returned home to subsequently upend the political career of Adam Clayton Powell on ethics charges. Rangel is one of the most popular members of the House of Representatives and there are few within the halls of Congress at the member, staff, or lobbyist level (myself included) who don't have a warm story to share about the man who was known for many years as "Mr. Chairman."

Unfortunately for Congressman Rangel, the House Ethics Committee began to look into serious allegations that Rangel had failed to properly pay his income taxes (while serving as the chairman of the tax-writing committee in the House) and failed to properly disclose rental income from property in the Dominican Republic. The Ethics Committee was also concerned that Representative Rangel had maintained several rent-controlled apartments in New York City, one of which was used for a campaign office, in violation of local housing ordinances, among other charges.

As the Ethics Committee stepped up its investigation of Rangel during the summer of 2010, Rangel would inject the race card into the remarkably detailed transgressions that had been lodged against him for his personal behavior by noting the following to *Politico* about a looming adjudicatory hearing before the House Ethics Committee:

> "I wish this thing never happened," Rangel said, referring to the host of ethics complaints against him. "I wish there was no Thursday but the situation being what it is, it's one step at a time. So compared to being lynched, I'd rather go through Thursday."[6]

Compared to a *lynching*? Of all of the words Rangel could have chosen to describe his self-inflicted political and ethical controversy, he chose to compare his situation to being hoisted upon a tree limb and murdered in a gruesome fashion by white supremacists used to instill fear in black communities during one of the darkest periods in American history. And the reaction of the Congressional Black Caucus, a group that once reminded President Nixon of its quest for equality, not as a rhetorical promise, but equality of results? Nothing. Nothing negative, that is. The Congressional Black Caucus would support Rangel as the House Ethics Committee would ultimately convene a trial and find Congressman Rangel had broken rules of the House of Representatives.[7] Meanwhile, the American people witnessed once again the tiresome excuse that an individual had been targeted for review of their ethical conduct based on the color of their skin rather than the actual conduct that member was alleged to have committed.

While Rangel would not face the judgment of his colleagues in the House until the looming November 2010 elections had passed, he did not shy away from wrapping himself in the cloak as a defender of the civil rights era during the August 2010 congressional recess, as Democrats scrambled to maintain their majority control of the House of Representatives. Speaking to a group of supporters in Harlem that August, Rangel's remarks to the assembled group were met with strong applause:

> All of you remember that this fight is never, ever going to end. I'm just one of the foot soldiers; just one of those [who] fought in the march so that one day our kids [will] be able to say, "Do you remember when there was bigotry and prejudice in this country? Do you remember when there wasn't fairness?"
>
> This is not Charlie Rangel's struggle. All over this country these things are happening.[8]

As I reread Rangel's impassioned entreaty to his supporters and admirers above, I was struck wondering if his remarks would have been better received in the summer of 1965 rather than the summer of 2010. I wondered how bigotry and prejudice and unfairness had anything to do with Rangel's present situation except other than the distinct possibility he felt it was unfair that his misdeeds were actually noticed by the House Ethics Committee that held him accountable for breaking the rules of the institution. Despite the claims he had been unfairly targeted or that he had simply forgotten to file necessary paperwork, and that his conduct was not criminal, the congressman was ultimately found to have been intentionally misleading in the manner in which he had reported income from his vacation property in the Dominican Republic, failed to properly file his federal income taxes, and attempted to endow a chair under his own name at the City College of New York improperly using official congressional letterhead, among other transgressions.

Instead, he regrettably sought to hide behind the cult of ethnicity to imply that he had somehow been aggrieved and was a victim of the entire ethics process rather than tacitly acknowledging that his actions and his actions alone had led to his present precarious predicament where the House of Representatives would ultimately render their judgment to either expel him from the House, censure him, or formally reprimand the congressman.

Sadly, the ethics investigation was not the first time in Representative Rangel's public service career in which he used the race card to gain perceived political advantage to silence his political detractors or opponents. Consider the following account from the *New York Sun* regarding a town hall meeting Rangel spoke at during 2005 with two fellow CBC members and Senator Hillary Rodham Clinton by his side:

> Comparing President Bush to the Birmingham, Ala., police commissioner whose resistance to the civil rights movement became synonymous with Southern racism, Rep. Charles Rangel said yesterday of the president: "George Bush is our Bull Connor." Mr. Rangel's metaphoric linkage of Mr. Bush to the late Theophilus "Bull" Connor—who in 1963 turned fire hoses and attack dogs on blacks, including Martin Luther King Jr., demonstrating in favor of equal rights—met with wild applause and cheering at a Congressional Black Caucus town hall meeting, part of the organization's 35th Annual Legislative Conference.[9]

Comparing President Bush to the infamous police commissioner is reprehensible and not the type of words one would expect an influential leader within the House of Representatives might use to describe the sitting president of the United States—for whatever reason. Moreover, it is the precise double standard utilized by certain black politicians, which has helped build the toxic cloud of racial acrimony that presents itself in current American society and is taking us blackwards: this is not to excuse whites or members of other ethnic groups using racially offensive language or overtly discriminating against blacks based on the color of their skin. Rather, in the America in which one is to be judged based on their individual skills, merits, and/or qualifications, it appears incongruent for blacks to advocate for special, rather than equal, rights while accusing those who disagree with their goals and aims of being racist.

Once again, black politicians apparently believe they are entitled to special, rather than equal, rights that permit them to hurl such scurrilous allegations against whites with little or no political ramifications. One can only imagine if a white politician had made a similar charge against a person of color—the outcome would have been entirely different, to say the least.

The other remarkable aspect of Rangel's attempt to link President George W. Bush to Bull Connor is both the forum in which he uttered the remarks, as well as those who stood beside him when he did so. Rangel was not bellowing from a street corner atop a soapbox in Harlem, New York; the congressman was addressing the Congressional Black Caucus's thirty-fifth Annual Legislative Conference before a town hall setting in Washington, D.C. Did the Congressional Black Caucus condone Rangel's remarks? There is nothing in the press that indicates they condemned them. In the absence of such criticism for employing such divisive language to politically wound the president of the United States, one is sadly left to assume that Rangel's views were not outside of the mainstream of the CBC itself—lest they would have criticized him or forced Rangel to apologize for uttering remarks not reflective of the organization as a whole. As noted above, two fellow CBC members were present with Rangel—along with New York junior senator Hillary Rodham Clinton (D-NY)—when he made his inflammatory comments. Apparently Rangel's congressional colleagues did not take exception to his remarks, nor did the apparently wildly cheering crowd before them. We will discuss the partiality of the CBC—or lack thereof—momentarily, but I wanted to first illustrate that Congressman Rangel felt as comfortable speaking before a CBC-sanctioned meeting in 2005 to use racially divisive language as he did in enlisting their support to defend him against House Ethics charges when he further played the race card for his perceived advantage in 2010.

Congressman Rangel would cruise to reelection in 2010. In the lame duck session of Congress that followed, outgoing Speaker Nancy Pelosi (D-CA), a close friend and ally of the embattled congressman, could no longer delay the sanctions phase the House of Representatives would mete out to Rangel. While the House elected not to expel Rangel from Congress, the members were resigned either to censure the Harlem Democrat or offer a formal reprimand. A censure is the more severe of the two sanctions and the offending member is forced to stand in the well of the House of Representatives while the Speaker of the House formally reads a statement of the charges against the member before their assembled 433 other colleagues. A reprimand, on the other hand, is a less serious sanction in which a majority of the House of Representatives votes to chide a member for their offending conduct.

While the Congressional Black Caucus did not "officially" engineer Rangel's campaign to receive a reprimand rather than censure, there are a number of interesting events that took place in the days leading up to judgment day in which the House would select the congressman's form of punishment. James Clyburn, the majority whip and second in line to the Speaker of the House, was the most senior black member serving in the House of Representatives at the time. The whip's responsibility is to gauge the temperature of the House majority by "whipping" a vote—deploying regional lieutenants to assess their colleagues' likelihood of voting for or against a close bill or resolution. Although Clyburn's office would claim they weren't whipping the Rangel censure vs. reprimand vote, members of the CBC could be seen with official whip cards as they deployed about the Capitol to mitigate the punishment their colleague would receive.[10]

Ultimately, Congressman Charlie Rangel would stand before his colleagues in the House of Representatives on December 3, 2010, and become the twenty-third member officially sanctioned by the body. Surrounded by his colleagues from the Congressional Black Caucus in the moment leading up to the 333–79 vote to censure him, Rangel stood alone as House Speaker Nancy Pelosi read the following statement:

> By its adoption of House Resolution 1737, the House has resolved that Rep. Charles B. Rangel be censured, that Rep. Charles B. Rangel forwith present himself in the well of the House for the pronouncement of censure, that Rep. Charles B. Rangel be censured by the public reading of this resolution by the speaker, and that Rep. Rangel pay restitution to the appropriate taxing authorities for any unpaid taxes . . . on income received from his property in the Dominican Republic and provide proof of payment to the [House ethics] committee.[11]

In a mere forty-five seconds Rangel's punishment had been administered but his forty-year career in the House of Representatives had been forever tarnished as a result. Why had the Congressional Black Caucus been unwavering in its support of Representative Rangel even though he had been found to have committed more ethical violations (eleven) than any member of Congress in history? Had the CBC been stalwart in their support due to the fact that Rangel had been a stellar representative in his congressional district? Overall the poverty rate at the time of his censure was 14 percent in the United States and 24.3 percent in the Harlem congressional district he served. The child poverty rate was a staggering 30.1 percent.[12]

Perhaps his leadership in Congress had not manifested itself to address serious problems of poverty and unemployment on behalf of his constituents. While one member of Congress cannot single-handedly combat these harrowing statistics, I do believe Rangel could have forged bipartisan coalitions with his colleagues to address and reverse the helplessness and poverty faced by many of his constituents through effective collaborations between state, federal, and local leaders.

Yet Rangel was reelected to serve the Fifteenth Congressional District of New York having received more than 80 percent of the vote of the ballots cast by his fellow constituents. Could the truth of the matter be as simple as the fact that no matter how egregious their conduct, the Congressional Black Caucus would stand up for ethically challenged fellow members? Did skin color matter more than the facts of alleged misconduct only in the instance where a black lawmaker was accused of ethical misconduct? Could the CBC uphold the cult of ethnicity mind-set that forsakes individuality for the preservation of unity based on race and/or ethnicity? Sadly, I believe the answer to be in the affirmative. While I have admired Representative Rangel over the years and found him to be an affable, likable man, ethics should be color-blind when an individual is given the trust and high honor of representing their constituents in public office.

Regardless of their skin color, I would have called for a member of the House to resign their office if they were found to have violated eleven specific rules of conduct. I was attacked in the media and in the blogosphere when I made such a call in an op-ed in *The Huffington Post* on November 10, 2010, entitled "Sorry, Charlie," in which I called for Rangel to step down.[13] I was further castigated for not protecting Rangel given his long service to the nation as well as the fact that he was one of the most senior black members in the Congress.

As is typically the case when I discuss issues on national television or in the print media, I was attacked along racial lines for offering my opinion in a racially neutral manner: ethics. One such enlightened individual had this to say when I noted that Rangel had created a climate of mistrust by his continued presence in the House of Representatives: "Ron [C]hristie you're a republican. Well you go to the events even if they do make you come in through the service entrance."[14] This is something I've grown accustomed to over the years, but which has particular salience as we discuss the entire notion of America retreating on the remarkable progress of racial parity since the civil rights era. Namely, those blacks who fail to go along with what purports to be mainstream thinking in the African American community are lashed out against by blacks and whites alike for daring to express a differing viewpoint. Because I tried to objectively look at Mr. Rangel's conduct through a non-biased lens to assess his conduct, many criticized me for speaking ill of a black elected official—the solidarity we ostensibly shared through skin color was stronger than the desire to push for blacks to be treated equally and without special treatment in American society today.

To this end, for citizens to have any faith in their elected representatives, they must be held to a higher standard of ethical conduct. How could I defend Rangel's longevity and unquestioned service to his country in the past when my present displeasure centered around the eleven ethical rules of the House of Representatives he was found to have broken?

Despite vigorous protests from the CBC that Rangel was not found to have enriched himself through his office, his conduct, if undertaken identically by one of his constituents, would have found that person in federal court and likely federal prison for tax evasion, among other possible crimes. But to decry a lawful investigation by the House Ethics Committee into his alleged conduct, compare the process to a lynching, and have other members of the Congressional Black Caucus support him based on his race is reprehensible. Do Rangel and his fellow colleagues of the Congressional Black Caucus not understand the ramifications of playing the race card well into the twenty-first century? I daresay Dr. Martin Luther King and other pioneers of the civil rights era would be appalled by those who would besmirch their efforts to achieve full racial equality in an America where all of her citizens would be judged by the content of their character rather than the color of their skin.

Our third inquiry revolves around the Congressional Black Caucus and its inability to function as anything other than a racist ethnocentric organization with the election of President Barack Obama as America's first black president. During his time in the Congress, Senator Obama had largely avoided being closely identified with the CBC and instead sought to represent his constituents in Illinois as a whole rather than focusing on their racial identity.

Regardless, the Congressional Black Caucus, once the euphoria of the 2008 election had subsided, were not quite certain what to do with America's first black president. The fact that the president was the son of a black father and a white mother had been irrelevant to the CBC members upon his election: he was black just like they were and ostensibly represented the hopes and dreams of the black race. During the first eight months of the Obama administration, the CBC had been largely muted in any concerns or criticism they might have with the first black president but tensions were lingering just beneath the smiling veneer they maintained publicly. Yet in 2009, just before the CBC Annual Legislative Conference held each September, the tensions that had been lingering under the surface emerged in regard to both their evolving view of President Obama as well as the political landscape, which had changed dramatically in the eight months since his inauguration.

For one, majority whip Clyburn would touch upon a theme we will explore at great length in chapter 7: namely, that the opposition to the president's legislative agenda was not based upon legitimate policy disputes, but on racism displayed toward America's first black president. In an interview published in *Politico* on September 23, 2009, as the Congressional Black Caucus Annual Legislative Conference got underway, Clyburn asserted:

> "It is a great year for the CBC to be celebrating. Many of us have spent a lifetime getting where we are now," Clyburn said in an interview with *Politico*. "But people who think the election of Barack Obama puts us in a postracial world are being a bit naïve at best."
>
> Clyburn said the U.S. economic downturn has made it easier for those who seek to exploit racial tension for their own political goals, and he suggested that some of the opposition to Obama's health care reform proposal is racism "hiding behind something else."
>
> "I would say that those of us who study the history of this country, we know that it was economic conditions in the South that gave cover to Nathan Bedford Forrest after the Civil War,"

Clyburn said, referring to the former Confederate general who helped found the Ku Klux Klan. "Without the economic conditions of the South, he would never have been successful in organizing the Ku Klux Klan, who terrorized so much of that region of the country."[15]

It is beyond ironic that Representative Clyburn would begin his remarks by noting that in 2009 the Congressional Black Caucus had much to celebrate but then immediately pivot to label rising uncertainty about America's fragile economy to those possessed with a racism akin to that of the Ku Klux Klan. Clyburn, of course, was making reference to the so-called Tea Party protests that had sprung up across the United States on April 15, 2009, and continued to grow in strength and intensity throughout the year.

Perhaps if Mr. Clyburn had not been so intent on labeling legitimate political unease with Democrats in Congress and the White House in complete control of the federal government as racist the congressman would have noticed that prior to his caustic comments a black member of the Tea Party had been beaten by a white union representative in an event that was captured on videotape for the world to see.

Just a month previous to Clyburn's remarks, Representative Russ Carnahan (D-MO) held a town hall meeting in his St. Louis area congressional district to discuss pending health care reform legislation in the Congress. Seeking to fill the hall with friendly supporters, Carnahan's staff allowed members of the Service Employees International Union (SEIU) to enter through a side entrance while Tea Party members waited patiently in line outside to gain entrance to the auditorium. At the same time, Kenneth Gladney, a black Tea Party supporter, was handing out "Don't Tread on Me" flags when he was assaulted by two SEIU members who subsequently threw him to the ground, punched him repeatedly in the face, where he was called "nigger." One of the alleged assailants was white and the other black.[16]

While it would ultimately take two years for the criminal complaint against the two alleged defendants to reach a jury for a verdict, the men were ultimately found not guilty and the charges were dismissed in July 2011. Shortly after the adjudication of the criminal proceedings, Gladney ultimately would file charges in a different court venue, this time alleging his civil rights had been violated. As of this writing, Gladney's civil rights lawsuit had yet to be adjudicated.

The important aspect of the Gladney case is that regardless of the guilt or innocence of the two defendants involved in the altercation, the manner in which the mainstream media sought to cover, or more accurately, failed to cover the incident is quite telling. Could the rationale behind the minimal coverage be that the events that unfolded did not fit the narrative the media sought to portray? The first incident of violence and racism that occurred at a Tea Party function, in which a white SEIU member allegedly punched an innocent black Tea Party member in the face and called him a "nigger" while a black SEIU member allegedly participated in the assault as well did not fit the narrative often related in the media, that it was the Tea Party members who were motivated by by racism, toward President Obama.

Sadly, the case would take an even more sinister turn in 2010, one that was also ignored by the mainstream media and officials of the Congressional Black Caucus in their bid to find equality and justice for all Americans before the law as articulated by their original mission statement from 1971.

On May 5, 2010, the Missouri NAACP held a press conference and rally on behalf of the two alleged assailants of Kenneth Gladney, the black Tea Party member just discussed above. The NAACP demanded that the county prosecutor *drop* assault charges against suspects Perry Molens and Elston McCowan. Let me allow Zaki Baruti, the organizer of the NAACP rally and press conference, to speak in his own words regarding why Gladney deserved to be beaten and that the charges against the assailants should be dropped:

> Back in the day, we used to call someone like that, and I want to remind you, uh, when this incident occurred, I was really struck by a front page picture of this guy, which we called, a Negro, I mean that we call him a Negro in the fact that he works for not for our people but against our people. In the old

days, we call him an Uncle Tom. I just gotta say that. Here it is, the day after a young brother, a young man, I didn't mean to call him a brother, but on the front page of the *Post-Dispatch*, ironically, he's sitting in a wheelchair, being kissed on the forehead, by a European. Now just imagine that as a poster child picture, not working for our people.[17]

The words expressed here are nothing short of stunning but hardly surprising. The new narrative we have seen unfold across America in the last few decades is that there is a group of blacks advocating for special, rather than equal, rights and protections under the law. If one adheres to the meme that blacks are victims, in need of government assistance, and held together cohesively as a group due to their racial/ethnic characteristics, almost any poor actions or deeds can be explained or excused away. Should one dare to express a differing viewpoint than the conventional "black mainstream" thinking—in this case, Gladney being a self-identified member of the Tea Party—an official of the NAACP is given a pass for calling Mr. Gladney an Uncle Tom, deserving of poor treatment. Why? Because with increasing frequency, those advocating for special, rather than equal, rights for blacks have also become quite comfortable fostering a culture of revenge in which self-appointed black leaders are not seeking equality and inclusiveness but are instead lashing out at those they deem to be supplicant to "white society."

Having watched the event on YouTube several times, Baruti's words alone do not give sufficient justice to the hatred portrayed on the screen. People are heard laughing and seen smiling when the NAACP official calls Kenneth Gladney a Negro and an Uncle Tom. In fact, if one didn't realize this was a political rally in support of the local prosecutor dropping assault charges against a white and black assailant for punching a black victim in the face, the impression left is that one is viewing a celebratory event. One can only imagine what the reaction had been if the victim in this case were a black SEIU member being assaulted by white Tea Party protestors. The results would have been entirely different, to say the least.

This is why I believe leaders such as Representative James Clyburn and organizations such as the Congressional Black Caucus breed cynicism and mistrust and are taking America blackwards, if you will; ostensibly they represent the best interests of people of color but, sadly, they have devolved into racist organizations that support a particular ideological and/or race based agenda. The Congressional Black Caucus has been clear in its disdain for groups, such as the Tea Party, that find legislative and political fault with the agenda advanced both by the congressional Democrats as well as President Obama. Rather than the CBC seeking to engage constituents to ascertain how their differing views could be bridged together to find compromise and balance, the Tea Party was often branded as racist or harboring views that would be analogous to the Ku Klux Klan.

Then, in the face of an apparently racist event where a black man is seemingly beaten and berated due to his political beliefs that run counter to those of many African Americans, Clyburn and other supporters of the president cowered, rather than led. They failed to denounce a vicious assault on a black man at a health care rally; assaulted both because of his affiliation with the Tea Party and called a nigger because he was black. For all its calls for equality, equal rights, and justice for all under the law, the Congressional Black Caucus failed to stand up for someone who was black because the gentleman in question was from a differing political and ideological perspective than their own.

In order to understand more clearly how the Congressional Black Caucus viewed both their role in the United States Congress as well as the communities they ostensibly represent, I visited their Web site on March 16, 2011, to ascertain their mission. In a welcoming letter by CBC chairman Emanuel Cleaver (D-MO) I read the following:

Dear Friend:
. . . Throughout our forty-year history, the Congressional Black Caucus has worked tirelessly to ensure that all Americans, regardless of race, color, or creed have the chance to pursue and achieve the American dream.

> Leading our communities and country with passion and commitment, the Congressional Black Caucus continuously strives to be a voice for the voiceless, earning the moniker "the conscience of the Congress."[18]

This is where I believe the true hypocritical nature of the Congressional Black Caucus is exposed. On the basis of its philosophical foundation in 1971, the CBC sought to be the conscience of the Congress and the voice for those whose voices couldn't be heard. Over time, this mind-set devolved into supporting each other as members of Congress based on their exterior racial and ethnic identification as being black, first and foremost. As for activities and incidents beyond the halls of Congress, the CBC would choose to support those causes that met their political and/or ideological needs. As such, I can draw no other conclusion than that the Congressional Black Caucus has worked tirelessly to ensure that Americans, *strictly* on the basis of race, color, or creed receive CBC's support so long as they adhere to the same ideological and political goals of the group.

The CBC could have served as a voice for Kenneth Gladney, beaten by thugs both white and black because he happened to be a conservative black man attending a health care reform meeting hosted by a Democratic congressman as a member of the Tea Party. The CBC didn't lend a voice to Gladney nor did they raise their voices when the Missouri NAACP sought to have the assault charges dropped against the two assailants or condemn the group for referring to the victim of a serious crime as a Negro and an Uncle Tom.

This is not an isolated incident: consider for a moment the condemnation of then judge Clarence Thomas by certain members of the Congressional Black Caucus when he was nominated an associate justice of the United States Supreme Court. His transgression? Thomas did not sufficiently support the "black community," a community in which one can infer that the prescribed ideological perspective is of a world in which blacks should be afforded special rights based on their racial and ethnic identity rather than as American citizens entitled to equal rights and freedom as enshrined in our Constitution.

The treatment of Judge Thomas offers a disturbing example of a phenomenon I have identified as our society heads blackwards—those blacks daring to express a differing ideological opinion than that of a self-identified black elite are subject to attack, criticism, and ostracism—lashed out against for refusing to embrace an acceptable "black" orthodoxy and instead accepting a more "white" perspective. Again, this is the notion that one's authenticity as a black person living in America is tied more to their ethnicity and racial identification rather than their unique status as an American citizen deserving equal, rather than special, rights before the law and society at large.

We shall explore this line of inquiry more closely in the pages that follow, but it is important to note at this juncture that Kenneth Gladney, a black self-identified member of the Tea Party movement, did not warrant the support of the Congressional Black Caucus or other leading "civil rights" groups because his political and ideological mind-set did not support the notion that blacks are entitled to special, rather than equal, rights due solely to the color of skin and one's ethnicity.

Viewed in this context, it is therefore not surprising that the Congressional Black Caucus stood up for Representative William Jefferson (D-LA) and Representative Charles Rangel (D-NY), one man a convicted felon and the other found to have committed more ethical transgressions than any other member of Congress in history. They stood up for these two men and stared down people like Kenneth Gladney because ideological purity and adhering to the mentality of the cult of ethnicity where race and identification of a distinct group of people were more important than standing up for the constitutional protections and responsibilities of being an American citizen.

If nothing else, the incident involving Kenneth Gladney proved to me beyond a shadow of a doubt that groups like the Congressional Black Caucus are racist and should be disbanded. They refused to stand up for the rights of an American citizen who had been beaten because of his race and political affiliation that didn't bear faith and fidelity to their ideological perspective.

Moreover, I find it repugnant that the Congressional Black Caucus refuses to admit members who are not themselves black. If that isn't the embodiment of the cult of ethnicity, I'm at a loss for words. Back in 2006, Stephen I. Cohen made an interesting pledge as he ran for Congress in Tennessee in a district that had a 60 percent black population: if he won, he told his potential constituents, he promised that he would seek to become the first white member of the Congressional Black Caucus. Cohen didn't seek membership to the CBC as a publicity stunt to join as the first white member of the caucus, but instead, he wanted to forge a working relationship with fellow members of Congress who represented majority African American districts. Cohen ultimately prevailed in his election to succeed the popular retiring Representative Harold Ford Jr. and he dutifully sought to join the CBC when he arrived in Washington, D.C., in January 2007. Immediately upon his request, Cohen was not only told he couldn't join the CBC, he was told he couldn't join because he was white. In a rather revealing report entitled: "Black Caucus: Whites Not Allowed," *Politico* delved deeper into the rationale behind the decision to deny Cohen's bid to join the CBC:

> Cohen said he became convinced that joining the caucus would be "a social faux pas" after seeing news reports that former Rep. William Lacy Clay Sr., D-Mo., a co-founder of the caucus, had circulated a memo telling members it was "critical" that the group remain "exclusively African-American."
>
> Other members, including the new chairwoman, Rep. Carolyn Cheeks Kilpatrick, D-Mich., and Clay's son, Rep. William Lacy Clay, D-Mo., agreed. "Mr. Cohen asked for admission, and he got his answer. . . . It's time to move on," the younger Clay said. "It's an unwritten rule. It's understood. It's clear."[19]

According to Representative Clay (D-MO), "it" is an unwritten rule that blacks are able to discriminate by race in the United States Congress and that should whites attempt to do so, that would constitute racism. "It" is understood and clear under these circumstances that blacks are entitled to special, rather than equal, rights not just in the

United States Congress but also in society in general *because* they are black and entitled to such treatment.

Finally, "it" is clear that any serious investigation regarding the conduct of CBC members in their personal or legislative capacity is off limits to the media as well as internal deliberation in the Congress itself because the CBC is entitled to special, rather than equal, rights afforded all American citizens. The so-called conscience of the Congress merely acted to protect itself and its special interests, making a mockery of its claim to give a voice to the voiceless. I was stunned to discover that eight out of approximately forty members of the Congressional Black Caucus were under investigation during the 111th Session of Congress. Beyond the charges of ethical lapses lodged against Representative Charlie Rangel previously discussed, Congresswoman Maxine Waters (D-CA) had also been under investigation for using her position as a senior member of the House Financial Services Committee to obtain a meeting with then Secretary of the Treasury Henry "Hank" Paulson to press for TARP (Toxic Asset Recovery Program) money to be steered toward a local community bank within her congressional district. The impropriety alleged in this instance is that Representative Waters failed to disclose that her husband had been a member of the board of directors of the same bank and that he stood to gain financially from the federal infusion of capital.

This is not to suggest, of course, that only members of the Congressional Black Caucus stood accused of unethical conduct during the 111th Session of Congress. Quite to the contrary. The overarching point here is that of a group of approximately forty members, the fact that eight, or nearly a quarter of its members, were under investigation by the House Ethics Committee. Moreover, certain members of the Congressional Black Caucus felt comfortable, if not entitled, to deflect criticism of alleged ethical misconduct and/or poor behavior as racist, rather than accepting the color-blind judgment of their congressional colleagues serving on the House Ethics Committee.[20]

Dare anyone accuse me of bias in drawing the conclusion that black members of the House believe they should be afforded special, rather than equal, treatment due to the color of their skin, I only offer

Representative William Lacy Clay's full statement on the admission of whites to the CBC and allow you the opportunity to draw your own conclusion:

> "Quite simply, Rep. Cohen will have to accept what the rest of the country will have to accept—there has been an unofficial Congressional White Caucus for over two hundred years, and now it's our turn to say who can join the 'the club,'" read an official statement released by Representative William Lacy Clay Jr. (D-MO) on the matter. "He does not, and cannot, meet the membership criteria, unless he can change his skin color. Primarily, we are concerned with the needs and concerns of the black population, and we will not allow white America to infringe on those objectives."[21]

The racially tinted prism through which the CBC viewed the world would once again rear its ugly head as the Obama presidency reached the end of its first year in office. With a bleak economy and high unemployment across the United States, the CBC and other like-minded "leaders" would begin to murmur that President Obama hadn't pursued a sufficiently "black" agenda. What is it precisely that would differentiate a black agenda from an American agenda? If blacks are somehow entitled to have a black agenda, shouldn't whites, Latinos, and other individuals press for such an agenda based on their racial and/or ethnic origin? Moreover, under this logic, shouldn't Asian Americans, Native Americans, and other ethnic members of our society be positioned and entitled to press for a social agenda based on skin color? The answer, of course, is absolutely not. Why not? Because in order for Americans to thrive as a people, we must recognize that our strength is derived from the independent contributions of individual citizens regardless of their skin color and not because of it. Self-segregation based on racial and/or ethnic characteristics will only lead to a balkanization of our society at the expense of national cohesion and pride.

Yet, in early March 2010, Congressional Black Caucus members took their private grievances with President Obama public, with former House Judiciary Committee chairman John Conyers saying that White House officials were "not listening" to black lawmakers while Florida representative Alcee Hastings would say that "there's not enough attention to poor people."[22]

Sometimes facts have a way of getting in the way of a good narrative. Let me take a moment to explain why. During his eight years in office, President George W. Bush expanded the federal budget for economically distressed areas by $700 billion through 2008; President Obama's budget in 2009 called for an additional $1 trillion. While President Bush increased federal education spending 58 percent faster than inflation, President Obama proposed to double that figure in 2009. And finally, when President Bush became the first American president to spend more than 3 percent of GDP on anti-poverty programs, President Obama had already increased spending in this area by 20 percent in March of 2009![23] This, of course, says nothing of the $812 billion stimulus bill President Obama would ram through the Congress or the $26 billion bailout sent to states and localities. In view of the better part of $1 trillion in new federal spending during President Obama's first year in office, I was astonished to see how he was criticized by the CBC for not devoting enough resources to the poor and those in need, given the dramatic spending increases sought by the Congress and sent to President Obama for his signature into law.

Continuing on the notion that President Obama did not spend enough on or pay particular attention to America's most at risk is an assessment I disagree with in two key areas. One, President Obama and his administration allocated nearly $1 trillion in expanded government spending for economically distressed communities across the United States, as noted above, in his first year in office. That level of spending can hardly be considered spendthrift. Most important, however, the complaints of the CBC fall into the all too familiar narrative of black people as victims and part of an overall African American community. Are all blacks poor? Of course not. But this narrative conveniently continues the victimology that all African Americans need a hand up and a handout by the government, rather than looking at people as unique individuals regardless of their race. Of course, I believe the CBC had an ulterior motive in mind in their publicly disclosed "disputes" with President Obama: access and power within the White House itself.

Politico published an interesting article entitled "Tension Between CBC, Obama" in which unnamed CBC sources cited changes that could place the White House and the CBC on solid ground:

> . . . There are relatively easy things the Obama Administration could be doing to curry favor with the CBC including adding more staffers with CBC experience and making sure to include CBC members in high-profile meetings. For example, they said CBC member Donna Christensen (D-U.S. Virgin Islands)—a physician and the CBC's leader on health care— should have been included in the White House health care summit.[24]

Rather than opine off the record to the reporters covering this story, senior members of the CBC went one step further to articulate their disagreements with the president. Former House Judiciary Committee chairman John Conyers offered that President Obama and the White House staff were "not listening" to the concerns of black lawmakers and fellow CBC member Alcee Hastings fumed that "there's not enough attention to poor people."

At its core, the Congressional Black Caucus was more interested in having its former staff inside the gates of 1600 Pennsylvania Avenue and attend high-profile White House events for the enrichment of their members, rather than the enrichment of the Americans they were elected to represent. While diversity of thought and opinion is critical for any president to make informed policy decisions, can one safely assume that the Congressional Black Caucus solely wanted the president to curry favor with them precisely because they were black, rather than offering specific subject matter expertise on an area the president and the country could depend upon?

Sadly, the Congressional Black Caucus was not the only group of so-called black leaders seeking to curry favor and attention from the president of the United States. That same month, March 2010, journalist and television talk show host Tavis Smiley abandoned the Covenant with Black America, where he had previously called on self-reliance, affordable health care, and the strengthening of the black community, as the path forward in favor of a more confrontational and controversial agenda.

Bringing together a panel of black "experts" at Chicago State University including the Reverend Louis Farrakhan, Reverend Jesse Jackson, Professor Cornel West, and Professor Michael Eric Dyson, among others, Smiley opined that President Obama had failed to pursue a legislative agenda to help blacks in particular, and called on the president to undertake such an agenda. To this end, Smiley noted:

> The bottom line is that the president needs to take the issues of Black America more seriously because black folks are catching hell, number one. Number two: this theory that a lifting tide lifting all boats—that theory was soundly dismissed. Thirdly, because black people are suffering disproportionately, it requires a disproportionate response.[25]

As I reflected upon Mr. Smiley's words, I thought about the efficacy of what he had said and that in many respects blacks were, in fact, suffering in disproportionate levels as compared to other Americans during the present economic stagnation. But rather than bring together a series of black journalists, thought leaders, and controversial individuals such as the Reverend Jesse Jackson and Louis Farrakhan, where were the wealth managers, educators, and housing experts who could shed light on real solutions to the problems that affected people with distressed income levels regardless of their race?

Or in regards to education, many students across the country are faced with failing and/or underperforming schools that exist to shuffle students from grade to grade rather than provide a solid educational foundation that will prepare children to compete in a technologically savvy global economy. Since blacks have disproportionately lower test scores in reading and math compared to their white and Asian classmates, shouldn't parents be given the opportunity to send their children to charter, magnet, or parochial schools if their public school is not adequately preparing them for success?

Perhaps Smiley and the other participants at his Black Agenda conference could have taken President Obama and congressional leaders to task for effectively eliminating the District of Columbia Opportunity Scholarship Program, which helped 1,700 low income students receive a scholarship up to $7,500 per year to attend a private school of their choice rather than remain in a failing public school. At the time Congress considered reauthorizing the program in 2009, approximately 38 percent of members of Congress were sending their children to private school and 20 percent had attended private school in their youth themselves.[26] For their part, Barack and Michelle Obama were fortunate enough to send their children to an elite private school in the District of Columbia, but the president and his administration had effectively blocked the door for inner city children to do the same. Why? As *The Washington Post* would write in a scathing editorial on the issue:

> Where is the humanity of not wanting to hurt children who won't be able to continue in their current schools if the scholarship program is eliminated? No one has been able to offer any evidence of the drawbacks of this small, local program while evidence of its benefits has been mounting. It has been disappointing that many of those one would expect to speak up for the educational rights of poor minority children . . . have been almost mute or has been the case with D.C. Delegate Eleanor Holmes Norton (D), downright hostile."[27]

Smiley and others could have assailed the president, Congress, and the local District of Columbia government for their decision to bow to pressure from the National Education Association (NEA), the powerful teachers union lobby, that opposes school choice. The District of

Columbia program is just one of countless such opportunities for parents to save their children from failing schools: a recent federal evaluation of the program showed that 91 percent of scholarship participants graduated from high school—a rate 21 percent higher than those children offered scholarships who didn't use them and thirty points higher than students who remained trapped in D.C. public schools.[28] How could the leadership of a White House and Congress exclusively controlled by the Democratic Party allow such a valuable lifeline to be extended to those with means but be denied to those living in poor neighborhoods in our nation's capital? What happened to the Congressional Black Caucus giving a voice to the voiceless here?

Oddly, at the same time the Obama administration was working to put the brakes on the D.C. Opportunity Scholarship Program, they took time to praise the efforts of Harlem innovator Geoffrey Canada's Harlem Children's Zone—a unique nonprofit that targets children beginning before they are born and ending with a college diploma for most of the participant students living in a ninety-seven-block area in Harlem, New York.

The program begins with Baby College, a nine-week prenatal and early childhood parenting preparation course.[29] Next, three-year-olds are enrolled in the Children's Zone preschool, where they will ultimately join the centerpiece of Canada's operation, the Promise Academy. Promise Academy students are taught grammar and writing skills in English but are also taught Spanish and French. Never too early to plant the seed of academic success, classrooms at the Promise Academy boast names such as Columbia and Harvard.[30] Students arrive at school as early as 7:30 A.M. for preschool activities (where they are served a healthy meal) and remain as late as 7 P.M. while participating in after-school enrichment activities.

Despite the Obama administration's frequent praise of the program and promise to set aside $10 million in the 2010 budget to replicate Canada's program in twenty cities, a remarkable lack of leadership in Washington, D.C., set back the progress of current and future students: with Democrats in control of both sides of Pennsylvania Avenue they failed to produce a budget for the federal government for the first time in modern history.[31] Perhaps rather than promoting a black agenda, more constructive engagement would occur if leaders inside and outside of Congress focused on problems facing individual Americans rather than submitting to the cult of ethnicity that dictates that government policies and priorities must be viewed through the prism of race, rather than looking at Americans as individual citizens in need of a hand up, not a handout.

Fortunately, a new generation of leaders such as Newark, New Jersey mayor Cory Booker, former Representatives Harold Ford Jr. and Artur Davis (D-AL), along with newly elected Republicans Tim Scott (R-SC) and Allen West (R-FL), have quietly but consistently shown that substance matters much more than style and that actions speak louder than words. These leaders will serve as trailblazers to move beyond the politics of racial divisiveness while capably demonstrating that blacks may seek and gain elected office beyond majority African American constituencies through hard work and proven competence.

Candidly, the relevance of a Congressional Black Caucus and calls for a black agenda has long since passed. Allowing and encouraging a group of advocates to press for special, rather than equal, treatment and rights under the law is abhorrent. The insistence of CBC members to remain exclusively black and refuse to admit non-black members only affirms this special sense of entitlement and preferred treatment because of their skin color and ethnicity rather than any other non-racial qualification.

It is further ironic to me that if a caucus of private citizens gathered to form an "Alliance for White People" that excluded blacks solely on the basis of their skin color, the "alliance" would be found to violate their civil rights protection. Sadly, the mere existence of a Congressional Black Caucus serves only to divide the country and isolate us from one another on lines of race and ethnicity rather than bring us together in solidarity as citizens of the United States of America. The CBC only seeks to divide the country on racial lines and risks creating antipathy against blacks perceived as seeking special, rather than equal, rights. In this vein, the need for black leaders would eventually evaporate, the void filled by responsible citizens called to serve their fellow Americans regardless of their race, color, or ethnicity, but motivated by the prospect of making the United States the strongest country in the world—comprised of those willing to lead who happen to be black rather than leading because of the color of their skin—a true embodiment of Dr. Martin Luther King's dream that is still sadly years away from fulfillment.

4. CANDIDATE OBAMA AND THE MANIPULATION OF RACE

||||||||||||||||||||||||||||||||||||||||||||||||||||

Setting the Stage for America Heading Blackwards

IF THERE IS ONE THING THAT POLITICAL SUPPORTERS AND OPPONENTS OF President Obama can agree on it is that the former junior senator from Illinois forever changed the American landscape when he was sworn in as the forty-fourth president of the United States on January 20, 2008. A barrier that I thought would be impenetrable during my lifetime had forever been shattered: the notion that a person of color in general and a black citizen in particular could never be elected president of the United States was now no longer a reality. Some 220 years after our founding and almost 150 years following the end of slavery the unthinkable had become the reality: America elected its first black president to become the most powerful leader in the world.

Rather than play the race card or seek to be the "genuine" voice of black America while running for higher office, as others had done before him, Obama inspired the nation and the world with his intellect, eloquence, and soaring rhetoric—making people young and old, black and white, rich and poor believe in his magical campaign slogan of hope and change. In fact, not only was the race of Candidate Obama not an issue in his initial quest for the Democratic nomination for president, many in the media and the punditry claimed that Mr. Obama had somehow *transcended* his race to become the first postracial candidate seeking the Oval Office.

Mr. Obama deftly gained support through the power and conviction of his ideas rather than by seeking as a racial prophet or icon. Despite the efforts of others to play the race card against him, Obama appeared to be above the fray and seemingly impervious to those who sought to define him by the color of his skin. Only when the hate-filled sermons of Mr. Obama's preacher, the Reverend Jeremiah Wright, came to light did Obama have to confront the issue of race relations in America. As Wright's angry and inflammatory words were broadcast across the country and around the world, Obama's campaign was quickly in serious jeopardy of being over before it had truly begun in earnest—all due to allegations that one of the senator's closest confidants and spiritual adviser was a racist.

The candidacy of hope and change was forced to respond to Wright's incendiary remarks, which had found an endless echo chamber in conservative talk radio and television outlets; silence by the candidate would have lent truth to claims that Obama had somehow subscribed to such comments attributed to his one-time pastor and spiritual adviser such as:

> In the twenty-first century, white America got a wake-up call after 9/11/01. White America and the western world came to realize that people of color had not gone away, faded into the woodwork or just "disappeared" as the Great White West kept on its merry way of ignoring black concerns.

Or:

> Racism is how this country was founded and how this country is still run! . . . We [in the U.S.] believe in white supremacy and black inferiority and believe it more than we believe in God.[1]

Suddenly the question of race had cast a very uncomfortable shadow over a candidacy that adroitly had avoided up to that point the subject. To extinguish the flames that had suddenly enveloped his campaign, Mr. Obama chose to address the nation from Philadelphia,

Pennsylvania, on March 18, 2008, to place distance between himself and Reverend Wright while trying to turn the page by seeking to inspire the nation on a topic that has challenged America from our founding.

Obama's meteoric political arc was at significant risk as he arrived in Philadelphia. He had gone from being a little known state senator to the United States Senate to now running for president of the United States in just four short years. For a candidate widely hailed for his oratory skills, Obama's words were immediately illuminating. As he began his remarks he noted:

> I chose to run for the presidency at this moment in history because I believe deeply that we cannot solve the challenges of our time unless we solve them together—unless we perfect our union by understanding that we may have different stories, but we hold common hopes; that we may not look the same and we may not have come from the same place, but we all want to move in the same direction—toward a better future for our children and our grandchildren.
>
> This belief comes from my unyielding faith in the decency and generosity of the American people. But it also comes from my own American story.[2]

Obama wisely initiated his discussion by describing all of the aspects that bound us together as Americans rather than immediately focus in on our differences. A better future would unfold if we could move in the same direction as a nation by stressing our common hope, Mr. Obama told us. Given our discussion regarding the dangers of multiculturalism in chapter 1, Senator Obama's opening words in his speech on race could well have been written to dispel that practice, while instead focusing on the unique aspect of what it means to be an American: our unique set of laws, culture, and citizenry. Obama went on to trace his ancestry and story now known to millions across the United States and around the world: born to a Kenyan father and white American mother, Mr. Obama would eventually be raised with the help of his white grandfather, who had served in General George Patton's Third Army in World War II, while his white grandmother had worked on a bomber assembly line in Fort Leavenworth in her husband's absence.

After describing his own life story as embodying the American dream, Obama immediately delved into the thrust of his argument:

> It's a story that hasn't made me the most conventional candidate. But it is a story that has seared into my genetic makeup the idea that this nation is more than the sum of its parts—that out of many, we are truly one.
>
> Throughout the first year of this campaign, against all predictions to the contrary, we saw how hungry the American people were for this message of unity. Despite the temptation to view my candidacy through a purely racial lens, we won commanding victories in states with some of the whitest populations in the country. In South Carolina, where the Confederate flag still flies, we built a powerful coalition of African Americans and white Americans.[3]

Cleverly invoking the motto on the Great Seal of the United States, *E Pluribus Unum,* "Out of Many, One," Obama gave the distinct impression that he was above the racial finger-pointing and divisiveness that precipitated his speech in the first place. Instead, Obama soothingly purported to offer what the American people had hungered for: his message of unity and common purpose for the citizens of the United States.

If only the rhetoric of unity and common purpose had remained the theme throughout the remainder of the senator's remarks as he discussed race relations in America in the twenty-first century. Unfortunately, several passages later Mr. Obama seemingly reversed course on his previous themes of racial harmony and reconciliation to engage in a stern bout of finger wagging at both blacks and whites alike when he offered his prescriptions to navigate the treacherous racial undercurrents that could well have sunk his presidential aspirations.

Of Reverend Wright, Senator Obama said that his former pastor, for all of his faults, was like family to him. And yet, in a refrain that is still discussed to the present day, Obama offered:

> [Reverend Wright] contains within him the contradictions—the good and the bad—of the community that he has served diligently for so many years.
>
> I can no more disown him than I can disown the black community. I can no more disown him than I can my white grandmother—a woman who helped raise me, a woman who sacrificed again and again for me, a woman who loves me as much as she loves anything in this world, but a woman who once confessed her fear of black men who passed by her on the street, and who on more than one occasion has uttered racial or ethnic stereotypes that made me cringe.
>
> These people are a part of me. And they are a part of America, this country that I love.[4]

Let me take a moment to discuss the inherent contradictions contained within Mr. Obama's statement. Without question, I believe Obama's repeated "do as I say, not as I do" approach to public policy is but one piece of the puzzle as to why the future president and subsequent actions taken by his administration may well have led to a backlash that persists to the present day.

First, Obama reversed his previous assertion in which he said the country must move forward together in the same direction by recognizing that we are of different races but moving toward a common goal with his commentary regarding Reverend Wright, above. His statement that Reverend Wright contained the contradictions—good and bad—of the community he served, and that Obama could no more disown his former pastor than he could the black community, is a remarkably startling view into the future president's true insights and impressions regarding the country he hoped to serve from the Oval Office. Most important in this particular instance: how could disowning one incendiary cleric, who is black, somehow equal disavowing the entire black culture and community in the United States?

As I have stressed repeatedly, the strength of our American society is based on the notion that we are comprised of strong individuals united by a common thread and purpose—our very citizenship of fifty states united. We have shown that the fabric of our society begins to unravel when people begin to think of themselves as members of distinct racial/ethnic groups rather than as individual actors. Here, Mr. Obama claimed that he could no more disown Reverend Wright than he could the black community. Who or what precisely *is* the black community? He did not identify a particular neighborhood or other geographical marker for his definition of what constituted a community.

Instead, Mr. Obama sought to use race and ethnicity to define his neighborhood—one solely predicated on the race of its inhabitants rather than a blend of society members as a whole. I worry about the manner in which then Senator Obama embraced this notion of apologetic multiculturalism as it related to the remarks regarding his former pastor. As we shall discuss shortly, more than three years into his presidency Mr. Obama took several steps to bolster such special treatment of racial and ethnic minorities in favor of their group, rather than national identity, in ways that I think have undermined the racial cohesiveness in society that he professed to strive for in his speech on race relations back in 2008.

For weeks prior to his speech in Philadelphia, the junior senator from Illinois was silent when Wright's racist views and sermons were revealed. I contend this was done for political expediency rather than dexterity; only when Wright's shadow threatened to tarnish Mr. Obama's image was he thrust into action to publicly distance himself from Wright. I believe the American print and broadcast media had largely given Mr. Obama a pass, given their fear in our present politically correct environment in America, by not immediately denouncing Wright's comments and urging Mr. Obama to do the same. One can only imagine what the newspaper headlines and commentary on the evening television news broadcasts would have been if Senator

John McCain (R-AZ), Obama's eventual rival for the presidency, had a white pastor and/or spiritual minister with similar views. Let me make clear, however, that I fully recognize that whites remain a majority of the population in the United States and that blacks comprise approximately 14 percent of our overall population. Given the history of slavery and racism in America, we must take seriously and eradicate the threat posed by white supremacist groups who seek to divide and discriminate based on skin color.

At the same time, I found the silence surrounding Reverend Wright's rants by the mainstream media when the story first broke deafening; I daresay Senator McCain would have encountered an immediate and entirely different response had he been in the identical position as his colleague from the U.S. Senate.

Quite to the contrary, then, I contend that then Senator Obama could have disowned his former pastor precisely because Reverend Wright, acting as an *individual,* uttered several incendiary remarks that offended the body politic of the *American community:* we are not comprised of white America or black America, but we are the United States of America. Wright's comments that the country believes in white superiority and black inferiority and that the horrific September 11 attacks upon our shores was a reminder that people of color had not gone away and instead the "Great White West" kept ignoring black concerns, were deplorable. They represented a narrow, bigoted viewpoint that Obama and the mainstream media would have done well to criticize. I believe not having done so was an implicit approval of Wright's behavior; hence, Obama's commentary regarding the circumstances Wright and other blacks of his generation had faced as well as their anger. Past discrimination does not excuse present racist proselytizing.

Similarly, the senator's next statement that he could no more disown Reverend Wright than he could his white grandmother is equally offensive in the manner in which Obama sought for his audience to interpret it. The notion that his white grandmother, a member of his family, is analogous to Reverend Wright, now representative of the black community, is cleverly offensive. Clever in that Obama wanted us to forgive Reverend Wright for his present sins—a man he could not disown—just as Obama himself was unable to disown his own grandmother for her racially laced remarks from long ago. One act or set of actions had nothing to do with the other, but Obama links the two together as if to say that if Candidate Obama could get over his grandmother's racial comments, the nation could move past his more-than-twenty-year association with Reverend Wright and elect him president of the United States, as Wright's comments had nothing to do with Mr. Obama personally. Additionally, one is given the free choice to choose their pastor or house of worship at will—one cannot choose their own family prior to one's own birth!

To continue with Mr. Obama's logic here, if Wright's comments were inextricably linked to the black community, they should be set aside or forgiven since they represent the views of that community—both good and bad. The offensive implication, of course, is that given the composition of the black community, warts and all, Reverend Wright was merely reflective of that community itself—he must not be held to account *individually* for all of the bad aspects of that community or his direct involvement in it. Once again, the double-edged sword of multiculturalism and the cult of ethnicity is revealed: reject individual obligation and responsibility for one's actions while instead escaping culpability by being affiliated with a group due to one's race and/or ethnicity—all the while assailing unnamed past oppressors rather than focusing on present and future individual actions.

Many Americans had taken great offense at Reverend Wright's rants and had questioned Mr. Obama's more-than-twenty-year association with the pastor as well as whether the remarks of the former could be said to capture and reflect the true beliefs of the latter. I believe that rather than bringing the nation together to discuss how to move past vexing questions of race, the true intent of the speech was more utilitarian: to encourage the nation to move past those vexing questions of race that had now imperiled Mr. Obama's candidacy.

From that day in March 2008 to the present day, I believe Mr. Obama has never been truly candid regarding his more-than-twenty-year association with Reverend Wright. His elusiveness in seeking to explain away his former spiritual minister in offhand and dismissive tones left people suspicious of the president's veracity. It strains belief that the Obamas attended Wright's church each Sunday for more than twenty years but neither he nor his wife ever heard anything similar to the "U.S. of KKK" or other offensive remarks that came to light. Like so much of the coverage of Candidate Obama in those days, the media chose to ignore murky areas in which a bright light ought to have shone; to conduct objective reporting rather than active cheerleading for Mr. Obama's continued success.

Accordingly, the disowning of Wright and his grandmother passage received scant coverage and Obama's speech on race was hailed as both visionary and remarkable. Before discussing said coverage, let us return to the remainder of Senator Obama's speech to finish our review.

Following the Wright/white-grandmother dichotomy, Obama took a moment to hector and wag his finger at both his black and white audiences on how *they* could move forward on a more constructive path on matters of race. First, Mr. Obama chided his black audience:

> For the African-American community, that path means embracing the burdens of our past without becoming victims of our past. It means continuing to insist on a full measure of justice in every aspect of American life. But it also means binding our particular grievances—for better health care, and better schools, and better jobs—to the larger aspirations of all Americans.[5]

Once again, blacks are reduced to being members of a particular racial and/or ethnic group with collective responsibilities rather than being individual Americans with their own personal aspirations and responsibilities. Why did no one question Mr. Obama's view articulated during his speech on race that blacks could best move forward on a path by only by "embracing the burdens of our past without becoming victims of our past"? While the legacy of slavery is a dark stain upon the history of the United States, what burdens would Mr. Obama like black folks to embrace, nearly 150 years after the practice of slavery had ended?

Quite to the contrary, the multicultural push for society to atone for past burdens has empowered new generations of black victims, victims that remain aggrieved by the past but unable to account for individual culpability in the present or future. I cannot imagine a more paternalistic or, frankly, condescending manner with which to treat a group of people collectively, due to the color of their skin, rather than praising or admonishing individuals for their singular behavior.

To this end, I believe that many of the problems that have imperiled the advancement of blacks in the United States for generation after generation are shockingly self-inflicted and have nothing to do with settling past wrongs and/or addressing previous discrimination. High numbers of out of wedlock births, disproportionately high percentages of blacks incarcerated in state and federal prisons, and distressingly low high school graduation rates for blacks are not to be set at the feet of American society as a whole but instead at the doorsteps of the individual actors who have made bad choices for their lives.

On the surface, Mr. Obama's call to all Americans not to get caught in past grievances appeared noble—except when viewed in the contextual light of the history of blacks in the United States since 1954. While the path to full integration in our schools, neighborhoods, and places of work has been painful and drawn out over decades, a widely disseminated report by a then–little known assistant secretary of labor by the name of Daniel Patrick Moynihan published in 1965 spoke to the ills of the black family, ills which have only worsened in the ensuing forty-seven years.

The title of the report, "The Negro Family: The Case for National Action" (aka "The Moynihan Report"), touched on the real issue of despair in the black community (such as it is): the breakdown of the two-parent family unit. In the relevant section of his report, Mr. Moynihan noted:

At the heart of the deterioration of the fabric of Negro society is the deterioration of the Negro family. It is the fundamental source of the weakness of the Negro community at the present time.

There is probably no single facet of Negro American life so little understood by whites. The Negro situation is commonly perceived by whites in terms of the visible manifestations of discrimination and poverty, in part because Negro protest is directed against such obstacles, and in part, no doubt, because these are facts which involve the actions and attitudes of the white community as well.[6]

If Senator Obama's true intent in his remarks on race in 2008 was the amelioration of relations between people from differing racial and/or ethnic groups in the United States rather than a blatant attempt at political salvation, I believe Mr. Obama missed a landmark opportunity to focus the attention and the blame for the deterioration of many black families in honest context. Namely, Senator Obama could have discussed the impact of the breakdown of the black family unit functioning as a married mother and father with children. While there is no universal explanation as to why many blacks lag behind their fellow citizens in regards to wealth, education, and opportunity, it is without question that the very issue that plagued many blacks in 1965 was still prevalent some forty-five years later when Mr. Obama delivered his remarks in Philadelphia: the breakdown of the black family.

Rather than confront this unfortunate self-perpetuating cycle— lack of strong parent figures leads to children having children and continuing the cycle—Obama instead chose to urge blacks to resist the temptation to blame others rather than taking personal responsibility to honestly assess their situation by placing ultimate responsibility in the hands of individuals themselves. To put the dismal statistics of children having children into vivid perspective, consider the following.

Every February, we as a country take a moment to honor and reflect on the accomplishments of black Americans, during Black History Month. According to the State University of New York, when

Black History Month first began in 1950, 77.7 percent of blacks were living in a two-parent household. Shockingly, the U.S. Census Bureau reported in 2010 that the number of blacks living in a two-parent household had dropped to *38 percent* just sixty years later—a nearly 50 percent decline.[7] To put these sad and stark statistics in glaring context, a majority of black children born today are brought into the world by single, unmarried women.

That is, if they were even born at all. A report issued in 2011 revealed very disturbing and uncomfortable data regarding the abortion rate of black children in New York City. According to figures released in the City of New York's vital statistics report based on data from 2008, two out of every five pregnancies in New York City end in an abortion, giving the city an overall abortion rate of 41 percent.[8] But when one looks at the abortion rate among black women in the city, the abortion rate is reportedly 59.8 percent.[9] If these statistics represent the abortion rate in New York City for black women, can other urban cities not be far behind?

Ironically, there are few cities in the United States where the self-perpetuating cycle of children having children and failing to break out of poverty and underperforming schools, is worse than in our nation's capital—the District of Columbia. A cursory review of the statistics reveals that when broken down by ward, the areas in Washington, D.C., with the highest rates of youth violence also have the highest rates of out of wedlock birth. As *Washington Post* columnist Colbert King noted in a 2011 essay entitled "Celebrating Black History as the Black Family Disintegrates":

> Boys get guns, girls get babies. To buttress that point, I referred to the Web site of the D.C. Campaign to Prevent Teen Pregnancy, which posted maps from 2005 and 2006 identifying the location of juvenile arrests and births to 15- to 19-year-olds in the District. Neighborhoods plagued by youth violence, the maps showed, were the same neighborhoods where birth rates among teenagers were highest.[10]

While these most recent statistics were taken from 2010, I'm willing to wager that the figures have not changed dramatically since Mr. Obama delivered his speech on race in 2008.

Again, rather than address the true cause of hopelessness among many who are relegated to urban quagmires from which there are few avenues of escape, the aspiring presidential candidate elected not to confront the truly difficult, uncomfortable statistics in his remarks when he could have shown brave and true leadership to have shined a revealing light on a distressing trend while offering meaningful solutions to address the issue. Instead, he focused on the themes that he thought would get him elected, rather than addressing the stark realities facing many black urban children and their single-mother parents today.

Returning to our analysis of Senator Obama's speech on race, I was equally disappointed in Mr. Obama's admonition to white Americans on matters of race relations regarding what the candidate actually said versus the topics he chose to discuss; a dichotomy between what was in the best interest of the country to improve the delicate issue of race relations in America versus what was in the best interest for his personal and political future. To the white listeners before him in Philadelphia and across the United States Mr. Obama opined:

> In the white community, the path to a more perfect union means acknowledging that what ails the African-American community does not just exist in the minds of black people; that the legacy of discrimination—and current incidents of discrimination, while less overt than in the past—are real and must be addressed. Not just with words, but with deeds—by investing in our schools and our communities; by enforcing our civil rights laws and ensuring fairness in our criminal justice system; by providing this generation with ladders of opportunity that were unavailable for previous generations. It requires all Americans to realize that your dreams do not have to come at the expense of my dreams; that investing in the health, welfare, and educa-

tion of black and brown and white children will ultimately help all of America prosper.[11]

Widely praised in the media for his comments regarding white and black reconciliation, I find Mr. Obama's charge to white Americans equally quixotic, as was his charge to blacks. First, what is one to make of the statement that "what ails the African-American community does not just exist in the minds of black people?" Is there such a thing as the African American community to which then Senator Obama can make a particular identifiable reference to, other than people of a particular racial group or ethnicity? Along these lines, is there such a thing as the "white American" community, since he denotes one specifically for blacks? Once again, I contend we have returned to Arthur Schlesinger's cult of ethnicity where Americans are grouped together along racial and ethnic lines rather than being judged separately as individuals.

While I recognize this was the senator's speech on race, I remain curious as to why he and others can readily point to the "African-American community" as if this is an idiomatic expression that garners immediate universal recognition and understanding. If whites hail from different geographic regions, economic strata, and educational backgrounds in the United States, are they said to hail from the same community since apparently all blacks are part of the African American community?

To this end, I found it rather insulting that Senator Obama would chide whites that what ails the black community doesn't merely exist in blacks' minds. Again, just as it can be said that all white Americans do not hail from similar economic, social, and educational circumstances, why is it that Mr. Obama can make such a sweeping statement about the "African-American community"? In other words, whether intentional or not, Obama was encouraging whites to look at blacks as being identical—ethnic victims suffering from the legacy of slavery and discrimination, rather than judging people as individuals. More than anything else, I am struck at how condescending this statement is when put in context; it is as if Obama sought to characterize all blacks as being poor victims who need a little benevolence from paternalistic white folks to move beyond their past grievances caused by slavery and racism. As a product of Columbia University and Harvard Law School, Obama should have known better than to portray all blacks as victims of discrimination when he himself is a vivid illustration of how hard work and the power gained through a solid education, would emancipate those in difficult financial circumstances rather than nice words about race relations.

Unfortunately his is the narrative that is prevalent in current academic, media, and sociological discussions of blacks in America today: victims of the legacy of slavery and Jim Crow, who are unable to overcome their present circumstances due to wrongs against their ancestors from long ago. This maintains and perpetuates the popular stereotype of blacks as being readily grouped together in identical socioeconomic, academic, and cultural surroundings. While this is nothing further from the truth and the present reality in America well into the twenty-first century, this chronicle of the "state of African Americans today" neatly fits an imagined normalcy for blacks as members of an aggrieved group rather than assessing people of color on their individual strengths and merits. That this stereotype has helped lead America blackwards in our contemporary society is apparent: blacks need special, rather than equal, rights. If affirmative action and other set-aside programs are not provided to address past discrimination, then the dissenter must be racist. Similarly, to suggest that all blacks are not victims of past and present discrimination—a common sentiment in the minds of all African Americans—one must be racist as well. Under this tortured and preposterous notion, this author—as an opponent of affirmative action programs and other programs designed to provide special, rather than equal, rights—must also be racist.

Consider carefully the words Senator Obama chose in his "landmark" speech on race to insinuate that civil rights laws were not being enforced in 2008. Here, Obama noted that America could come together as a nation "by enforcing our civil rights laws and ensuring fairness in our criminal justice system."[12] Tellingly, Senator Obama did not cite one specific example of how such laws were not being enforced, nor did he offer any specific reason as to why such laws needed to be strengthened. As we discussed in the previous chapter, when he became president of the United States, Obama did make good on his promise to dramatically increase domestic discretionary spending. What President Obama did not do, which in large measure led to a recoil against him and his administration, was the inability to adjudicate fairly under the color of law with prejudice toward none, instead of several instances in which the Obama administration sought to favor members of one racial/ethnic group at the expense of another—all while characterizing some of the president's political detractors as being racist. These are topics we shall pursue in the chapters to follow.

Ergo, setting aside Mr. Obama's multicultural identification of blacks as being part of a distinct group while failing to do so for whites, the senator's call to action for whites to curb racial discrimination rang hollow to me as well. Here, he called upon increased spending on our schools and communities, as well as enforcement of civil rights laws and fairness in the criminal justice system, while providing ladders of opportunity that were not present in previous generations. Does the reference to "our schools" and "our communities" make reference to predominantly black communities or does Mr. Obama mean all schools and communities regardless of the racial and/or ethnic group to which the students belong?

If we accept the premise that the senator is referring specifically to communities of color, then I pose one scenario that lays bare the folly of his assertion in regards to education funding: namely, the financial resources that have been and continue to be spent to educate children in the District of Columbia. Our nation's capital is a majority black city, with most of its black citizens residing in the Seventh and Eighth wards. The District of Columbia spent $1.29 billion on public education in 2009.[13] This compares to the entire GDP of the Central American country Belize, which was $1.38 billion in 2008.[14] Put another way, the District of Columbia spent $28,170 *per student* in the 2009 school year.[15] This figure is just beneath the $32,550 tuition costs for Harvard University in 2009.[16] If the District of Columbia spends more per pupil than any other state in the union at a figure on pace with educating students at Harvard University while ranking near the bottom in student ability as assessed by test scores, can an increase in spending really be said to provide a solution for racial discrimination in America?

Late in 2011, Harvard professors Roland Fryer and Will Dobbie produced a fascinating piece of scholarship entitled "Getting Beneath the Veil of Effective Schools: Evidence from New York City," in which they collected significant data from thirty-five charter schools in New York City to ascertain how best to improve the efficacy and delivery of public education in America. Of particular interest to our discussion at this juncture, the authors revealed that the "traditionally collected input measures—class size, per pupil expenditure, the fraction of teachers with no certification and the fraction of the teachers with an advanced degree—are not correlated with school effectiveness."[17] Instead, the authors discovered that with over forty years of qualitative research, "frequent teacher feedback, the use of data to guide instruction, high dosage tutoring, increased instructional time and high expectations" explain the contrast in school effectiveness between charter schools and traditional public education facilities.[18] These statistics provide an important counterargument to the one offered by then Senator Obama that "our schools" and "our communities" need additional resources to be competitive. To the contrary, for blacks to receive equal rather than special treatment in our classrooms today, teachers must be held accountable by parents concerned not with the size of the school's budget, but by the amount of tutoring and high-level instruction, and setting high expectations for students to define and achieve success.

I will leave Senator Obama's call for enforcement of civil rights laws and the adjudication of justice for a later discussion. Suffice it to say, early actions by President Obama and members of his administration led many to criticize that despite his promise to ensure equal access and protection under the law regardless of skin color, the president and his political allies either specifically chose to act or declined to do so based entirely on the race and/or ethnic identity of the entity pressing the administration to act or react in a certain manner.

Finally, how much longer did Senator Obama wish for the "ladders of opportunity" to be in place for black Americans to ensure they had a better shot at the American dream than their ancestors? My brother and I were fortunate to receive our college degrees prior to our parents and I know many blacks from all socioeconomic income levels who can point to the same occurrence within their own family. This is not to discount that racism and discrimination exist in the United States today. Of course it does. But the then junior senator from Illinois took the easy route out by tasking whites to be mindful that discrimination does not just exist in the minds of blacks but that if only whites made investments in areas of interest to Mr. Obama, then the country would be on the glide path to racial Shangri-la.

A more balanced and mature call to action that Senator Obama missed in his speech on race was an honest assessment of the difficult yet steady progress that had been made in the United States since the 1960s. At the same time, Mr. Obama could have encouraged his fellow citizens to live up to the inspiring legacy left behind by Dr. Martin Luther King, Representative John Lewis (D-GA), and others while recognizing that America continues to move beyond the painful legacy of slavery and overt discrimination from the Jim Crow era. By urging his fellow citizens to pull together as Americans rather than calling upon blacks and whites to act as members of racial and ethnic groups, the senator missed a real opportunity to further the dialogue and constructively move the country forward while leaving behind racial recriminations and resentments.

However, this was not the narrative the mainstream media wished for Americans to hear in their ostensibly evenhanded and unbiased coverage of Senator Obama's speech. Instead, the American broadcast media, smitten with Mr. Obama from the opening days of his candidacy, failed to critically and constructively analyze his speech on race other than to say that Obama had put the Reverend Wright distraction behind him. My friend Chris Matthews went even several steps further in his praise, calling Obama's remarks a speech "worthy of

Lincoln" and the most important speech on race in American history—
surpassing Dr. Martin Luther King's "I have a dream" speech on
the steps of the Lincoln Memorial. Consider Matthews's following
statement:

> Did Barack Obama distance himself enough from Reverend
> Wright? Did he calm the fears of the white voter? How did the
> speech play? We'll have much more on this momentous day
> and what I personally view as the best speech ever given on race
> in this country. One that went beyond "I have a dream," to "I
> have lived the dream but have also lived in this country."
>
> . . . I think this is the kind of speech I think first graders
> should see, people in the last year of college should see before
> they go out in the world. This should be, to me, an American
> tract. Something that you just check in with, now and then, like
> reading *Great Gatsby* and *Huckleberry Finn*. Read this speech,
> once in a while, ladies and gentlemen. This is us. It's us with the
> scab ripped off. It's white people talking the way they do when
> they're alone with other white people, some people. It's black
> people talking the way they are when there's not white people
> around. It's an honest statement from a guy who comes from
> both backgrounds. We have never heard anything like this.[19]

Now in fairness, Chris Matthews is well known for his effusiveness
and a frequent tendency toward the melodramatic when excited and
on the air. I take no particular pride in chiding my friend in this regard. At the same time, I believe the very manner in which the media
took pains to build Mr. Obama up as being somehow postracial or
transcendent of race would come back to haunt him and help create a
degree of resentment among many once he assumed the presidency—
particularly since Mr. Obama and his supporters did little to discour-
age the impression that political disagreements and opponents of
President Obama were either racist or motivated by race.

For the present discussion, however, I wish to return to Matthews's
remarks regarding Obama's speech on race. For one, I believe Dr.

Martin Luther King's "I have a dream" speech is one of the most important oratorical discourses in American history if not the world. Conversely, Obama's speech on race was more of a salve seeking to heal a political wound than it was historically important or worthy of being placed in the pantheon of outstanding rhetoric. Given the importance of Dr. Martin Luther King's speech in American history, compared to Senator Obama's attempt to recover from largely self-inflicted wounds, we will not take the effort or opportunity to examine whether Chris Matthews's belief that Obama's remarks had transcended King's is an accurate statement. I believe the record stands for itself.

Similarly, an objective observer might easily conclude that Obama's speech certainly was not on par with the mastery of the written word of such American luminaries as Mark Twain and F. Scott Fitzgerald. That discussion is also not warranted or necessary at this juncture as the comparison by Matthews appears to be more of a subjective personal opinion rather than an established truth by historians or political observers.

But Chris Matthews's enthusiastic reaction to Senator Obama's remarks represented just the tip of the iceberg when it came to mainstream media reaction to his widely heralded speech on race. In an editorial entitled "Mr. Obama's Profile in Courage," *The New York Times* couldn't resist gushing praise for the senator's remarks—even choosing the title of former Senator John F. Kennedy's 1955 Pulitzer Prize–winning study of eight individuals whose bravery and integrity deserved special recognition. The gauzy attempt to equate the trajectory of Obama and Kennedy is unmistakable as was the overt desire to confer stature and gravitas on a man who had not yet been elected president of the United States let alone capture his party's nomination for the office. These early attempts in print and broadcast media to gloss over the senator's real record (such as had been amassed in a very short career both in Springfield and Chicago) to vault him to immediate senior statesman status would come back to haunt Mr. Obama, particularly by those who were able to assess the president's actions with his deeds and draw their own conclusion regarding his competence in office.

In the cited example, *The New York Times* would editorialize regarding the "transformative" speech on race:

> Inaugural addresses by Abraham Lincoln and Franklin D. Roosevelt come to mind, as does John F. Kennedy's 1960 speech on religion, with its enduring vision of the separation between church and state. Senator Barack Obama, who has not faced such tests of character this year, faced one on Tuesday. It is hard to imagine how he could have handled it better . . .
>
> We can't know how effective Mr. Obama's words will be with those who will not draw the distinctions between faith and politics that he drew, or who will reject his frank talk about race. What is evident, though, is that he not only cleared the air over a particular controversy—he raised the discussion to a higher plane.[20]

I hesitate in my criticism and analysis at this juncture because I recognize there will be many to accuse me of seeking to score political points at the president's expense. Having worked on Capitol Hill for nearly a decade before joining the White House staff of George W. Bush, it will be easy for my detractors to conclude my motivation for critically assessing Mr. Obama's remarks has more to do with politics than honest disagreement with the content of his remarks.

And yet, nothing could be further from the truth. Instead, *The New York Times* editorial above exemplifies all of my frustration with the coverage of then Candidate Obama as he sought the presidency and the real disservice that was done to the country by the failure to fully vet the person who would eventually become the most powerful leader on the planet.

Put less delicately, had Mr. Obama been a black Republican seeking his party's nomination and had he delivered identical remarks in Philadelphia, Pennsylvania, during the spring of 2008, I do not believe that candidate would have received such glowing coverage from outlets such as *The New York Times*. Candidly, conservative black

Republicans are rarely favorably portrayed in today's media outlets, for they fit neither the stereotype nor the image in which blacks are generally depicted: blacks as victims; blacks in need of government assistance; blacks seeking special, rather than equal, rights.

In media coverage of his race speech, Senator Obama was cast as the victim of the outrageous and fiery rhetoric cast forth by his pastor, Reverend Wright. No matter that Obama had chosen to attend Wright's church for more than twenty years, be married by Wright, or have the pastor baptize his children. While *The New York Times* and commentators like Chris Matthews lavished praise on the aspiring president's speech on race, I instead found the remarks tailored to fit the convenient story line that only serves to underscore black inferiority in American society today. Focusing on skin color, rather than our shared differences as American citizens, only fosters the notion that inequality occurs in America today due to racial differences and that blacks are entitled to special, rather than equal, treatment in our society.

In other words, the media overlooked the fact that Senator Obama's decision to address the nation on matters of race relations had little to do with his proffered desire to strengthen the union of the United States but rather, to strengthen his own political standing among an electorate that had begun to question Obama's long association with a pastor whose racist and offensive language had offended many. Surprisingly, this naked attempt at political resuscitation not only stemmed the negative accounts that had been written about Obama and Wright's association, but Obama was seemingly given statesmanlike status for his bravery of tackling the issue of race. Consider, for example, the manner in which many in the media began to compare the junior senator from Illinois with the former congressman and sixteenth president of the United States.

And while Senator Obama's remarks were certainly unusual—detailed speeches discussing matters of race in our society today are decidedly rare—*The New York Times* and other glowing commentary in the media equating Obama's remarks with famous speeches given by previous presidents such as Lincoln, FDR, and Kennedy seemed to be a stretch, at best. Instead, such efforts left me with the impression that Senator Obama was being given special, rather than evenhanded, treatment in the media because of his race.

While the passage of time has dulled the nearly incessant Obama-Lincoln comparisons as the young senator from Illinois sought to follow in the footsteps of the former congressman from his adopted home state, one snippet from an Associated Press article describing Obama's quest for the presidency is revealing as it perpetuated a narrative of Obama as a "national uniter"—a theme *The New York Times* and other media outlets would dutifully promote both in the days prior to as well as following Mr. Obama's speech on race. Consider the following:

> AP— Barack Obama announced his bid for president Saturday, a black man evoking Abraham Lincoln's ability to unite a nation and a Democrat portraying himself as a fresh face capable of leading a new generation . . .
>
> "Let us transform this nation," he told thousands shivering in the cold at the campaign's kickoff . . . He tied his announcement to the legacy of Lincoln, announcing from the building where the future sixteenth president served in the state Legislature.
>
> "We can build a more hopeful America. And that is why, in the shadow of the Old State Capitol, where Lincoln once called on a house divided to stand together, where common hopes and common dreams still live, I stand before you today to announce my candidacy for President of the United States of America," Obama said.[21]

Again, there can be no question that President Abraham Lincoln stands as one of America's strongest leaders for his ability to bring a divided nation together that had been torn apart both by slavery and a Civil War that threatened to destroy the United States of America just seventy years after its founding. At the same time, to equate then Senator Obama as one whose words, hope, and promise as a leader as he sought to put a largely personal crisis behind him based largely on race in any way measured up to the task before Lincoln as he delivered his presidential inaugural address to offer his wisdom and calm a nation wracked by divisions caused by slavery and race following his election is laughable by way of comparison.

President Abraham Lincoln arrived for his inaugural address on March 4, 1861, at a time of great uncertainty in the United States about its present course and seemingly uncertain future. Just two weeks prior, Jefferson Davis had been inaugurated as the new president of the Confederate States of America; Lincoln's arrival to Washington had been shrouded in secrecy due to concerns about his safety. Ignoring the advice of his security detail, President-elect Lincoln boldly rode with President James Buchanan for his inaugural remarks in an open carriage to address the nation upon his being sworn into office by Chief Justice Roger Taney.[22] There is much to be admired about President Lincoln's inaugural address for his desire to keep the country intact as the threat of secession loomed large. In his remarks, Lincoln pleaded with his national audience to seek reconciliation and constructive engagement rather than destroy the fabric of American society through the secession of Southern states. Here he wrote movingly:

> Before entering upon so grave a matter as the destruction of our national fabric, with all its benefits, its memories, and its hopes, would it not be wise to ascertain precisely why we do it? Will you hazard so desperate a step while there is any possibility that any portion of the ills you fly from have no real existence? Will you, while the certain ills you fly to are greater than all the real ones you fly from, will you risk the commission of so fearful a mistake?[23]

Lincoln was hailed for his persistent ingenuity to keep America intact from the threats and perils of a war that could destroy the young constitutional republic in his first term in office. And yet, did the junior senator hailing from the same state as our sixteenth president deserve such glowing coverage in the media for a speech set more to salvage Mr. Obama's political future rather than the national fabric of present American society?

Beyond the specious comparisons of Obama's speech on race to echo the inaugural addresses of Lincoln and Roosevelt, the *Times* also hailed that Senator Obama had ostensibly risen above traditional divides on race. To the contrary, I believe we have seen how Obama spoke in terms specifically designed to separate Americans based exclusively on the color of their skin and ethnicity rather than bring the country together by assessing our fellow citizens as individuals rather than members of distinct groups.

Moreover, I believe *The New York Times* and other members of the mainstream media, whether they would ever publicly or privately admit it, had engaged in journalistic affirmative action toward Senator Obama rather than honestly assess his strengths and weaknesses as a viable candidate to become the next president of the United States. Had they engaged in a more evenhanded assessment of his experience, his stature, and his attempt to disassociate himself from a pastor in whose pews he sat for twenty years by delivering a speech on race in which his pastor's repugnant behavior was largely dismissed and apologized for by circumstance, Senator Obama's views would have been placed in context. This contextual foundation could have elicited more pointed questions from the media to solicit responses from the candidate himself as to what he genuinely believed, not only regarding Reverend Wright but about the delicate issue of race in America at that point in 2008. These questions were not only never asked, but the media appeared far more interested in bolstering Senator Obama's stature and eventual coronation than they were about making serious inquiries about his true beliefs on a variety of subjects that ultimately did the American people a great disservice for not fully vetting a candidate seeking the most powerful job in the world.

I believe Obama's speech on race was born of political necessity for his survival to remain in the race to receive the Democratic nomination for president than it was a desire for him to expand the intellectual debate or discourse on race in the United States. Unfortunately, the media took it upon themselves to elevate Obama's words as part of their narrative that Obama was a uniquely historical figure who had transcended his race.

Unfortunately, the analysis and assessment of the speech by Chris Matthews and others in the media trended along the multicultural/cult of ethnicity lines for assessing people as members of racial and ethnic groups than analyzing individual behavior and/or actions for responsibility and culpability. Had the media devoted any level of objective analysis to Obama's speech on race, they would have found certain inconsistencies in his call for unity and reconciliation. Shouldn't the man who desired to be the leader of all Americans have spoken with one clear voice rather than asking whites and blacks to listen to differing messages as to how best to put racial strife behind us?

For that matter, had the mainstream media been paying particular attention to the behavior of the Obamas themselves at this point of the campaign, rather than accusing the Republicans and conservative talk radio of using Reverend Wright as a racist diversion to derail Obama's candidacy, they could have asked very pointed questions of Senator Obama regarding divisive comments made by his wife Michelle just one week prior to his address in Philadelphia. As it turned out, *The New Yorker* had published a profile on would-be First Lady Michelle Obama that was meant to be flattering yet it revealed an interesting insight into the woman who would become the first black First Lady in American history. Consider the following as she offered her assessment of America as reported in the magazine:

> [Michelle] Obama begins with a broad assessment of life in America in 2008, and life is not good: we're a divided country, we're a country that is "just downright mean," we are "guided by fear," we're a nation of cynics, sloths, and complacents. "We have become a nation of struggling folks who are barely making it every day," she said, as heads bobbed in the pews. "Folks are just jammed up, and it's gotten worse over my lifetime. And, doggone it, I'm young. Forty-four!"[24]

A divided country. A country divided by fear. A country that is just downright mean. One would have expected such words from Reverend Wright but certainly not from the wife of the presidential contender whose campaign was predicated on the notion of "Hope and Change You Can Believe In." And yet, although the article chronicling Michelle Obama's candor in politics was published one week prior to her husband's "landmark" speech on race, it received scant attention in the media. Americans were not fully acquainted with the Obamas in March 2008; nor would they become more familiar with the future First Family until well into President Obama's term in office.

That the Obamas were somewhat of a blank slate before the 2008 elections is beyond question. Given the perspective of space and time, it is interesting to see how President Obama failed not only to live up to his own calls for unity and reconciliation during his speech on race in 2008 but once in office, Obama and his supporters would seek to muzzle political opponents with charges of racism—charges that have led not only to a backlash against the president's political fortunes, but increased the flames of racial tension in the United States, rather than quell them.

5. A NATION OF COWARDS

||||||||||||||||||||||||||||||||||||||||||||||||

How the Obama Administration Deepened Racial Divisions Rather Than Unify the Country

WITH THE REVEREND WRIGHT MATTER FIRMLY BEHIND HIM, SENATOR Obama's glide path for the Democratic Party nomination took on an air of inevitability as the primaries and caucus elections drew to a close. Fighting off a spirited challenge from Senator Hillary Rodham Clinton, Obama had achieved what no one had done before him: he had secured the nomination of a major political party as their standard-bearer to become the next president of the United States as a black man.

The mainstream media coverage of this accomplishment was incessant; regardless of my political affiliation as a strong conservative Republican, I was proud of my country for its ability in overcome the overt discrimination and racist legacies of the past to embrace a young black man to be his party's nominee for president. This was an accomplishment that I never thought I would see in my lifetime—particularly not from the Democratic side of the aisle that had stymied passage of the Civil Rights Act of 1964. For all the talk of the Democrats favoring the rights of minorities while the Republican Party sought to stymie black progress, one only needs to briefly revisit the manner in which the Civil Rights Act of 1964 was passed to understand this assessment is less than accurate. During Senate consideration of the landmark civil rights legislation, a group of eighteen Southern Democratic senators led a filibuster to torpedo passage of the bill. Senator

Strom Thurmond (D-SC) was one of the most outspoken opponents of the bill and he spoke for twenty-four hours straight in opposition— utilizing language similar to secession advocates in the Civil War by equating passage of the civil rights bill with infringing on the sovereign rights of Southerners by the federal government.

For me, I found the fact that the Democratic Party would nominate an African American to be their presidential standard-bearer just forty-four years following opposition in the party to passage of the Civil Rights Act of 1964 was nothing short of astounding. I therefore found it ironic that Senator Obama's historic speech upon his nomination by the Democratic Party to be their presidential nominee had the feeling more of a coronation or deification of a Greek god than a politician seeking the most powerful job in the world. That evening in late August 2008, Senator Obama strode upon an elaborately constructed stage with Greek columns that oddly evoked images of a Greek temple. With the various factions of the Democratic Party well behind him, Obama sought to unify the country behind his candidacy as he spoke to the nation from Denver, Colorado, at the culmination of the Democratic National Convention.

Well aware of the media's preoccupation of Senator Obama as the candidate who was "postracial" or somehow *transcended* his race, the candidate did not disappoint his audience when he accepted his party's nomination on August 28, 2008, by drawing upon his biracial heritage as an inspiration for the country—the very same day on which Dr. Martin Luther King had delivered his iconic "I have a dream" speech forty-five years prior:

> Four years ago, I stood before you and told you my story, of the brief union between a young man from Kenya and a young woman from Kansas who weren't well-off or well-known, but shared a belief that in America their son could achieve whatever he put his mind to.
>
> It is that promise that's always set this country apart, that through hard work and sacrifice each of us can pursue our individual dreams, but still come together as one American fam-

ily, to ensure that the next generation can pursue their dreams, as well. That's why I stand here tonight. Because for 232 years, at each moment when that promise was in jeopardy, ordinary men and women—students and soldiers, farmers and teachers, nurses and janitors—found the courage to keep it alive.[1]

After utilizing the promise of his own past as future inspiration, Senator Obama methodically drew distinctions between himself and his opponent in the general election, Senator John McCain (R-AZ). As he drew to the close of his speech, Obama once again sought to unify the country rather than focus on the issues of division and mistrust. As Obama spoke of his understanding of the American spirit he noted:

And it is that promise that, forty-five years ago today, brought Americans from every corner of this land to stand together on a Mall in Washington, before Lincoln's Memorial, and hear a young preacher from Georgia speak of his dream.

The men and women who gathered there could've heard many things. They could've heard words of anger and discord. They could've been told to succumb to the fear and frustrations of so many dreams deferred.

But what the people heard instead—people of every creed and color, from every walk of life—is that, in America, our destiny is inextricably linked, that together our dreams can be one.

"We cannot walk alone," the preacher cried. "And as we walk, we must make the pledge that we shall always march ahead. We cannot turn back."

America, we cannot turn back.[2]

Obama as healer. Obama as bridge builder. Obama as the living embodiment of Dr. Martin Luther King's dream; a postracial American renaissance man who would show the world that the race card that had been the currency of much of the debate regarding race relations in the United States over the previous fifty years had been cut up and thrown away in favor of a new breath of air in the form of hope and change that would forever change our political and cultural land-scape. If America was ready to embrace the change, Obama was ready, willing, and able to provide it.

It comes as little surprise that the mainstream media reaction to Obama's acceptance speech for the Democratic nomination and his steady march toward judgment day on November 4, 2008, was noth-ing short of breathless admiration. More comparisons to President Lincoln; more references to the birth of a new Camelot era. In short, Senator Obama was an obligingly blank sheet of canvas that the media all too eagerly took the opportunity to fill in with vivid color and tex-ture what an Obama presidency would mean for the United States as well as the rest of the world. Questions regarding the Reverend Wright controversy had been shelved. Michelle Obama's comments from ear-lier in the year about America being a country that was "just down-right mean," "guided by fear," and being comprised of a nation of cynics, sloths, and complacents were not only ignored, but there was the sense that the American press did not want to disrupt the perfect storm that they had largely created themselves: the perfect postracial, Kennedy/Camelot presidential candidate who would return glamour and elegance to the White House just by his very presence while re-pairing the image of the United States to the world at large that had been ostensibly "broken" during the presidency of George W. Bush.

A spell had been cast upon many in the American populace by the mainstream media outlets that supposedly reported the news in a non-partisan and dispassionate manner. Unfortunately for Senator Mc-Cain, a brave naval aviator who had served his country with distinction and honor, the battle waged with Obama was one he could not possibly have won, given the manner in which the deck had been stacked against him: an adoring media shining a bright spotlight on Obama's personal story leading to an entirely predictable outcome. And so it was, on the evening of November 4, 2008, when Senator Barack Obama became president-elect of the United States, that the true sensa-tion known as "Obama mania" had gripped many citizens across the country.

Strangers hugged in the streets, horns blared, and the almost cult-like devotion toward Obama that had gripped the country for the past several months had barely reached its crescendo. The impossible dream come true and narrative complete, Obama traveled to Hyde Park in Chicago to address the thousands—crowds that were later estimated to be 240,000—who had thronged to hear their inspirational leader declare victory for himself and the movement to change America that they had championed. Continuing with the themes that were the landmark of his campaign: Obama as healer and a uniter of America in the spirit of Abraham Lincoln, the president-elect declared:

> Let us resist the temptation to fall back on the same partisan-ship and pettiness and immaturity that has poisoned our poli-tics for so long. Let us remember that it was a man from this state who first carried the banner of the Republican Party to the White House—a party founded on the values of self-reliance, individual liberty, and national unity. Those are val-ues we all share, and while the Democratic Party has won a great victory tonight, we do so with a measure of humility and determination to heal the divides that have held back our prog-ress. As Lincoln said to a nation far more divided than ours, We are not enemies, but friends . . . though passion may have strained it must not break our bonds of affection. And to those Americans whose support I have yet to earn—I may not have won your vote, but I hear your voices, I need your help, and I will be your President too.[3]

In retrospect, these words are remarkably important given the manner in which the president-elect himself promised to govern once he had been sworn into office. Obama promised not to resort to the pettiness, the immaturity, and the partisan tone that had turned Washington, D.C., political discourse into spirited shouting matches rather than civil debate. He further promised that Americans should look upon their fellow citizens as friends rather than enemies and that he would help restore bonds of affection that had been strained by conflict.

As he drew to a close, the president-elect ended as he had begun his speech that evening—with a riveting call to action. Here, Obama thundered to the jubilant crowd:

> This is our time—to put our people back to work and open doors of opportunity for our kids; to restore prosperity and promote the cause of peace; to reclaim the American Dream and reaffirm that fundamental truth—that out of many, we are one; that while we breathe, we hope, and where we are met with cynicism, and doubt, and those who tell us that we can't, we will respond with that timeless creed that sums up the spirit of a people:
> Yes We Can.[4]

But could he? Could Obama possibly live up to the enormously high series of expectations that he and the mainstream media had set for his presidency? Could a politician whose career trajectory had soared without the corresponding high-level and microscopic examination of his temperament, politics, and personal management style transform the country in the manner in which he had promised? His fundamental pledge to restore the American dream to fulfill the promise that we would pull together as citizens of the United States under the motto of "Out of Many, One," promised the dawn of a new sense of civic hope, responsibility, and engagement. Newspaper columns and television broadcasts were filled with human-interest stories touting the triumph of the new prophet, who would singlehandedly transform America by his very presence.

CNN.com writer John Blake's assessment of the president-elect on November 5, 2008, was indicative of much of the narrative the media had unfolded for their reading and viewing audience to consume: a transformational leader transforming America and the world. Under the blazing headline "Obama Victory Caps Struggle of Previous Generations," Blake quoted civil rights era hero Reverend James Zwerg, who stood shoulder to shoulder with John Lewis on a Bloody Sunday so long ago in Selma, Alabama, described Obama in the following manner:

"Obama's message reflects much of the same idealism that [the Rev. Martin Luther King Jr.] spoke of when he talked about coming together to improve our country," Zwerg says. "He's really rekindled the same enthusiasm for change among young people, which is terrific."[5]

To be certain, Obama inspired many younger voters and blacks that had previously not been actively involved in presidential electoral politics. However, American University issued a report in the days following the election to note that while many had predicted that Obama would generate the largest number of voters going to the polls in American history, this simply did not occur. There was a significant increase in the black vote from 2004 to 2008—13 percent of the overall electorate and a 2 percent increase from the previous election.[6] But overall, 60 percent of the 208.3 million eligible voters cast votes in the 2008 election, statistically equal to the 60.6 percent of voters who went to the polls in 2004 for President Bush's reelection.[7]

This statistic is important because it is one of several indicators that what had been offered in the fawning media coverage regarding President Obama as truth when the reality turned out to be something entirely different than what had been portrayed—an important predicate for the ensuing acrimony that would engulf the Obama presidency. For the present inquiry, however, let us return to the euphoric atmosphere surrounding the incoming forty-fourth president of the United States and discuss how the unrealistically high expectations for his presidency, along with subsequent actions taken by the administration itself, have led to an America more divided and polarized on matters of race than ever before.

In the days leading up to President-elect Obama's inauguration, the images of Obama and his wife and daughters were ubiquitous. Seemingly every magazine cover, newspaper photograph, or special edition periodical carried glossy pictures of America's new First Family. *Time* magazine's coverage was emblematic of the "Obama-mania" that had swept through the mainstream media outlets. In a two-month span from October 27, 2008, to the December 29, 2008, issue in which Obama would be hailed as *Time*'s "Man of the Year," the president-elect's face would grace the cover of the magazine on five separate occasions. What was revealing about this coverage on the front cover of the magazine, however, was the manner in which Mr. Obama was depicted. On the October 27, 2008, issue, Obama's face appeared on the cover of the issue—along with those of Presidents Lincoln and Roosevelt and his opponent in the race, Senator John McCain (R-AZ).

Further revealing the hopes and aspirations of the media for the subject they had ostensibly covered through a neutral lens of objectivity, the November 24, 2008, issue of *Time* portrays an Obama likeness dressed similarly to FDR (complete with FDR's signature top hat) with the headline, "The New New Deal." The thinly disguised elevation and comparison of President-elect Obama to two significant presidencies in troubling times during U.S. history was not a hard story line to miss.

As inauguration day drew closer still, gift shops in airports and train stations across Washington, D.C., had been turned into virtual shrines for the Obamas with patrons seeking to buy the endless supply of T-shirts, cups, glasses, key chains, and any other paraphernalia that could bear the Obama visage.

Continuing the media and Obama-driven narrative that the young forty-fourth president-elect of the United States was the twenty-first century's reembodiment of America's sixteenth president, Obama retraced Lincoln's arrival from Springfield, Illinois, to Washington, D.C., for his inauguration. Capturing both the tone and texture of the event, *The New York Times* reported:

> As he did throughout his campaign, Mr. Obama evoked imagery of Abraham Lincoln, in word and deed, as he took an abridged version of Lincoln's journey by rail to the capital before his own inaugural festivities in 1861. The trip offered Mr. Obama one more opportunity to savor his victory before he inherits the challenges that await him . . .
>
> "What is required is a new declaration of independence, not

just in our nation, but in our own lives—from ideology and small thinking, prejudice and bigotry—an appeal not to our easy instincts but to our better angels."

The trip picked up momentum as it drew closer to Washington, with larger crowds gathering to wave, cheer, and merely catch a glimpse of Mr. Obama, who on Tuesday will be the first African-American sworn in as president.[8]

I daresay that a new declaration of independence free from the bigotry and prejudice that marred America's past evokes more than imagery of Mr. Obama standing in the shadows of Abraham Lincoln: this new narrative placed Obama as a new leader set to emancipate America in a way that would eclipse the bravery, hard work, and ability to heal the nation of the sixteenth president and his fellow man from Springfield, Illinois.

On the eve of Mr. Obama's inauguration, something took place that had never occurred before: all of the bridges connecting Washington, D.C., to the surrounding suburbs were closed as a security precaution for the festivities set to occur the following day. More than a million people would assemble on the National Mall to observe the transfer of power from the forty-third to the forty-fourth president of the United States and to become part of history themselves. While citizens from a previous generation could lay claim to where they were when President Kennedy had been assassinated in 1963 or when the space shuttle *Challenger* had tragically exploded in 1986, many wanted to tell subsequent generations they were there when Barack Obama became the first black president of the United States sworn into office.

With such daunting expectations of the new president and his administration also came great hope and optimism across the United States that Barack Obama would prove different from his predecessors. Eager to seize the moment and channel the energy of the million people gathered in the nation's capital as well as of countless tens of millions of others watching across the country and around the globe, President-elect Obama placed his hand on the Bible used by President

Lincoln during his first inaugural and recited the oath of office making him the forty-fourth president of the United States on the West Front of the U.S. Capitol. Nearly immediately after thanking his predecessor for his service to the American people, Obama outlined the purpose of his inaugural remarks, along with the theme of his nascent presidency. Here he noted:

> On this day, we gather because we have chosen hope over fear, unity of purpose over conflict and discord. On this day, we come to proclaim an end to the petty grievances and false promises, the recriminations and worn-out dogmas that for far too long have strangled our politics. We remain a young nation. But in the words of Scripture, the time has come to set aside childish things. The time has come to reaffirm our enduring spirit; to choose our better history; to carry forward that precious gift, that noble idea passed on from generation to generation: the God-given promise that all are equal, all are free, and all deserve a chance to pursue their full measure of happiness.[9]

Unlike all the speeches he had given before, Obama's inaugural address now had real meaning. He was no longer a legislator casting votes in the Illinois and subsequently, the United States Senate. He was no longer a candidate on the campaign trail, shaking hands, delivering speeches, and stumping for votes. Barack Obama was now the president of the United States and he would be judged both by the words he spoke and the actions he undertook in support of his promises made to advance the country.

Before analyzing the implications of Obama's inaugural address as the benchmark for a backlash against him and his administration, consider for a moment that Obama himself had been criticized by Senator Hillary Rodham Clinton during the campaign for being a candidate of all words and no substance. In his now infamous "Just Words" speech to rebut Senator Clinton's assertion, then Candidate Obama had declared:

Don't tell me that words don't matter. "I have a dream." Just words. "We hold these truths to be self-evident, that all men are created equal." Just words. "We have nothing to fear but fear itself." Just words. Just speeches. It's true that speeches don't solve all problems, but what is also true is that if we can't inspire the country to believe again, then it doesn't matter how many plans and policies we have.[10]

But now, President Obama's words *did* matter, as they would be the yardstick against which the American people could judge him. The old adage "actions speak louder than words" certainly applied to the young president, whose career path thus far had been marked by much promise and anticipation but little tangible accomplishments to demonstrate his prowess in elective office.

On that brisk January day in 2009, President Obama proclaimed that Americans had chosen hope over fear and unity of purpose over conflict and discord. He called for an end to the partisan bickering and petty grievances that had dominated the American political landscape. Perhaps most important, President Obama had called on his fellow citizens to reaffirm the enduring spirit that had made the United States the greatest country in the world: that we must carry forth the God-given promise that all Americans were equal, free, and deserved a chance to pursue their full measure of happiness without consequence. Were these just words spoken for history and posterity or did the president mean what he said and would accordingly lead by example to be the standard-bearer for a new generation of leadership in America?

As he returned to the White House for the first time as president of the United States, Barack Obama's first official act was to issue a proclamation declaring January 20, 2009, as the National Day of Renewal and Reconciliation. In seeking to set a new tone for the civil and political discourse on his first day in office, Obama pronounced:

On this Inauguration Day, we are reminded that we are heirs to over two centuries of American democracy, and that this legacy is not simply a birthright—it is a glorious burden. Now it falls to us to come together as a people to carry it forward once more.

So in the words of President Abraham Lincoln, let us remember that: "The mystic chords of memory, stretching from every battlefield and patriot grave to every living heart and hearthstone all over this broad land, will yet swell the chorus of the Union, when again touched, as surely they will be, by the better angels of our nature."[11]

Now the time for comparisons was over. No more associations with Presidents Lincoln or Roosevelt. No more allegorical assessments to Dr. Martin Luther King. The time had come for President Obama's own words and actions, successes and failures, to stand on their own strength and merit. Given the entire tenor of his campaign for the presidency, the words articulating his aspirations for a more compassionate America, where our strengths would be drawn from our diversity and our diversity would comprise our strengths, had now arrived. As he promised both his supporters and those who had not voted for him, Barack Obama had called for a better country where the glorious burden of two centuries of our unique democracy had been placed upon our shoulders and that we were compelled to follow his example to make the country more cohesive and inclusive by setting aside our past grievances and prejudices to fully embrace the ideal of the United States: *E Pluribus Unum*—"Out of Many, One." America was ready to embrace this call to action and a change in our social, political, and cultural fabric: the question remained whether Barack Obama was the right leader at the right time to lead such a charge.

As the euphoria surrounding Obama's inauguration slowly subsided and America grew accustomed to watching its first black president and his telegenic family move into the White House and their new surroundings, Americans regarded their new president with respect and curious interest to see whether the tremendous hope and change he had promised would soon be delivered to a country exhausted after eight years of a Republican administration, two wars, and a deteriorating economic and employment forecast. The question remained whether the new president and the officers in the Cabinet he had chosen to lead America forward were up to the challenge and the daunting promises they had endeavored to fulfill.

Wednesday, February 18, 2009

Not even a month into his term in office, President Barack Obama encountered an unexpected controversy regarding his promise of a new tone and a new style of civil and political discourse in America. After countless promises to regard our fellow citizens as individuals and to recognize both the legacy of slavery and our ability to treat our neighbors with respect without acrimony, while choosing hope over fear and unity of purpose over conflict and discord, seemingly the impossible had occurred: the fledgling administration had fallen into its first controversy surrounding race, in a way that was entirely unexpected at the time but seemed to set the tone for the true sincerity of whether the president and his team had meant what they had said on the campaign trail, or whether their soothing assurances were nothing more than an empty vessel.

On February 18, 2009, another milestone was about to occur—the first black attorney general of the United States was set to address his fellow workers at the Department of Justice to commemorate Black History Month in the first year of the first term with America's first black president. Attorney General Eric Holder Jr., a man known for his legal as well as political acumen, was unwittingly about to change the course of the Obama presidency with words he thought would be received favorably but would instead seep out as a stain on the new administration that would prove impossible to remove. As he spoke to fellow employees at the Justice Department, the attorney general noted:

> Every year, in February, we attempt to recognize and to appreciate black history. It is a worthwhile endeavor for the contributions of African Americans to this great nation are numerous and significant. Even as we fight a war against terrorism, deal

with the reality of electing an African American as our President for the first time and deal with the other significant issues of the day, the need to confront our racial past, and our racial present, and to understand the history of African people in this country, endures. One cannot truly understand America without understanding the historical experience of black people in this nation. Simply put, to get to the heart of this country one must examine its racial soul.

Though this nation has proudly thought of itself as an ethnic melting pot, in things racial we have always been and continue to be, in too many ways, essentially *a nation of cowards.* [emphasis added] Though race related issues continue to occupy a significant portion of our political discussion, and though there remain many unresolved racial issues in this nation, we, average Americans, simply do not talk enough with each other about race. It is an issue we have never been at ease with and given our nation's history this is in some ways understandable. And yet, if we are to make progress in this area we must feel comfortable enough with one another, and tolerant enough of each other, to have frank conversations about the racial matters that continue to divide us. But we must do more—and we in this room bear a special responsibility. Through its work and through its example this Department of Justice, as long as I am here, must—and will—lead the nation to the "new birth of freedom" so long ago promised by our greatest President. This is our duty and our solemn obligation.[12]

These words, however well intentioned, sent shock waves through the American social, political, and cultural establishment. Had the country's first black attorney general just accused his country of being a nation of *cowards* on matters of race less than a month after the first black president had been sworn into office? Didn't this run counter to the message of hope and change that President Obama had promised when he said America would put aside its petty grievances and false promises while ending the recriminations and worn-out dogmas that had strangled our politics?

In the days that followed Holder's remarks, President Obama was remarkably silent on the views expressed by the nation's top law enforcement officer. In a pattern reminiscent of the Reverend Wright flap from a year prior, Obama seemed to be weighing his political options rather than forcefully and decisively expressing his views one way or the other. His silence was remarkably odd given the repeated admonitions that he and his administration would change the tone in Washington and across the country. From his acceptance speech for the Democratic nomination to his election night victory speech to the inaugural address and subsequent Presidential Proclamation on Reconciliation and Renewal, the attorney general's remarks seemed incongruent with where the president had stood on matters of national unity and race relations. Or were they? Was this a break with administration policy, or did it represent the president and the attorney general's true feelings now that the election was behind them?

And just as a matter of optics, Holder's speech was an odd event: the country's first black attorney general in his first major speech to the nation castigating his fellow citizens for cowardice on matters of race. Hadn't Mr. Holder been assigned one of the most prestigious positions in the Cabinet due to his political and legal skills, with his race presumably not at issue in his selection? On a day when the attorney general was delivering remarks to *celebrate* the contributions blacks had made to their country, he also turned around and insulted that very country for its insensitivity on issues of race.

The mainstream news media, still in the afterglow of the Obama inauguration, seemed stunned by the attorney general's declaration, as did many Americans across the country. This wasn't the hope and change tone that was promised, and Mr. Holder seemed to wade into many of the petty grievances that had divided the country for decades on matters of race. Wasn't the attorney general playing the race card by accusing the country of being a nation of cowards on matters of race? It seems difficult to believe that people would want to engage in honest dialogue, as Mr. Holder suggested in his remarks, by first accusing America's historic notion of being an ethnic melting pot of being cowardly.

CNN was representative of much of the coverage in the immediate aftermath of Holder's remarks: not editorially critical, but shocked by such a militant and even angry tone adopted by a senior official of President Obama's leadership team when the country was still engaged in a honeymoon with their new president and First Family. In an article posted on CNN.com by reporter Terry Frieden, he noted that:

> Following his address, Holder declined to say whether his unexpectedly stern message would be translated into policy.
>
> "It's a question of being honest with ourselves and racial issues that divide us," Holder told reporters in a hastily arranged news conference. "It's not easy to talk about it. We have to have the guts to be honest with each other, accept criticism, accept new proposals."
>
> The nation's top law enforcement official vowed to "revitalize the Civil Rights Division" at the Justice Department but offered no specifics.[13]

As we shall see shortly, while the attorney general professed that he would revitalize the Civil Rights Division of the Department of Justice, he and his colleagues would do so in a manner never imagined by those who voted for an administration that promised to look at people as individuals rather than being part of specific racial groups and/or ethnic entities. For an administration that promised to treat all equally under the color of law, a disturbing phenomenon in just the opposite direction was set to occur.

At the time of these remarks I remember thinking that my original suspicions about President Obama and those closest to him had been proven correct: he and his aides would say whatever they needed to say on matters of race to avoid defeat, but their publicly espoused comments of a nation having put aside its racist past and acrimony were false. Once safely secure and in the White House, I thought that the president and the First Lady would reveal their true colors on race; after all, hadn't Michelle Obama said the first time she was proud of her country was when her husband decided to run for president?

And for all of the comparisons to Abraham Lincoln and Dr. Martin Luther King, President Obama's silence in regards to the words spoken on a day ostensibly to celebrate Black History Month was stunning to me. In the absence of presidential articulation or rejection of such divisive commentary, couldn't his silence be equated to acquiescence if not outright support?

For all of the words, all of the speeches, and all of the promises made by President Obama that he would be a different type of leader by setting a new tone and a new example in Washington, D.C., for the rest of the nation to follow, his administration's angry assessment of the United States following the election that sent the first black man to the Oval Office seemed to be in distinct contrast to what the country had just done by electing him. If Barack Obama, a biracial child born of an immigrant African and a white American, didn't embody the melting pot legacy of the country, I honestly didn't know who would. Perhaps for the first time, those Americans around the country who had bought into the notion of Obama being postracial or transcending his race were taken aback by the commentary given by the attorney general during his speech.

At the same time, many of the conservative commentators who had warned of Obama's true feelings on matters of race began to speak out in earnest in light of the Holder controversy. Distinguished professor of economics at George Mason University Walter Williams was representative of the concern and anger expressed by conservatives in regards to the thoughts proffered by the attorney general:

> The bottom line is that the civil rights struggle is over and it is won. At one time black Americans didn't share the constitutional guarantees shared by whites; today we do. That does not mean that there are not major problems that confront a large

segment of the black community, but they are not civil rights problems nor can they be solved through a "conversation on race." Black illegitimacy stands at 70 percent; nearly 50 percent of black students drop out of high school; and only 30 percent of black youngsters reside in two-parent families. In 2005, while 13 percent of the population, blacks committed over 52 percent of the nation's homicides and were 46 percent of the homicide victims. Ninety-four percent of black homicide victims had a black person as their murderer. Such pathology, I think much of it precipitated by family breakdown, is entirely new among blacks. In 1940, black illegitimacy was 19 percent; in 1950, only 18 percent of black households were female-headed compared with today's 70 percent. Both during slavery and as late as 1920, a teenage girl raising a child without a man present was rare among blacks.

If black people continue to accept the corrupt blame game agenda of liberal whites, black politicians, and assorted hustlers, as opposed to accepting personal responsibility, the future for many black Americans will remain bleak.[14]

As we have discussed previously, the civil rights era, which brought much equality and a true opportunity for blacks to achieve the American dream, was, in fact, over. When Senator Obama offered his much vaunted speech on race in America, I was in the significant minority when I thought that he had failed in a major opportunity to confront the true issue confronting many black families head-on: the breakdown of the two-parent household to provide a stable environment for their children. Daniel Patrick Moynihan had noted this decline nearly forty years prior but generation after generation of so-called black leaders sought to pin the blame on racism and the lack of equality in the United States. Williams was absolutely correct in his assessment that with the constitutional protections afforded to all in the United States, the notion that we must continue to push for civil rights and equality is absurd. Without discounting racism that still exists, blacks have been given the opportunity to compete as equals, regardless of the color of their skin. What was needed was not an additional conversation on race, but a conversation, as President Obama himself had assured us during his inaugural address, where he recognized the following:

> The time has come to reaffirm our enduring spirit; to choose our better history; to carry forward that precious gift, that noble idea passed on from generation to generation: the God-given promise that all are equal, all are free, and all deserve a chance to pursue their full measure of happiness.[15]

Again, were those just words, just speeches given by the president to mask his true feelings and intentions? There is one other aspect of Dr. Williams's assessment of the "Nation of Cowards" speech I would like to address before turning to President Obama himself on this matter. At the beginning of his column, Dr. Williams correctly noted:

> Attorney General Eric Holder said the United States is "a nation of cowards" when it comes to race relations. In one sense, he is absolutely right. Many whites, from university administrators and professors, schoolteachers to employers and public officials accept behavior from black people that they wouldn't begin to accept from whites. For example, some of the nation's most elite universities, such as Vanderbilt, Stanford University and the University of California, have yielded to black student demands for separate graduation ceremonies and separate "celebratory events." Universities such as Stanford, Cornell, MIT, and Cal Berkeley have, or have had, segregated dorms. If white students demanded whites-only graduation ceremonies or whites-only dorms, administrators would have labeled their demands as intolerable racism. When black students demand the same thing, these administrators cowardly capitulate. Calling these university administrators cowards is the most flattering characterization of their behavior. They might actually be stupid enough to believe nonsense taught by some of their sociology

and psychology professors that blacks can't be racists because they don't have power.[16]

We have previously touched on much of the material above in our brief discussion regarding how many in academia have capitulated to behavior by certain blacks in which exclusion based on the color of skin is fine if blacks elect to do so. At this juncture it is fair to say that if there were truly an honest dialogue to be had on race relations in the twenty-first century just three months following the election of America's first black president, the question might be better posed as to why blacks clung to such crutches as separate living facilities, graduation ceremonies, and other special, rather than equal, accommodations of blacks based solely on the color of their skin. I fully recognize that many African American students attending our colleges and universities today find a certain level of comfort and familiarity in living and/or associating with students with similar backgrounds to their own. At the same time, while such self-segregation might be beneficial to a particular group of students in the short term, I believe the long-term consequences can be far more destructive—one cannot self-segregate by race once in the workplace and in our society as a whole. Our students should be taught to be accepting and tolerant of other ethnic groups by accepting people as *individuals*. Unfortunately, the mind-set is such that the threat of being called racist is such a powerful weapon that certain blacks have wielded the term as a club to obtain special, rather than equal, rights at the expense of their fellow citizens based merely on skin color. Hence the proliferation of self-segregated facilities at our colleges and universities in the name of diversity today, which I believe causes more harm than good in helping foster a cohesive environment in which we celebrate the diversity of our collective experiences rather than focusing on skin color and ethnic characteristics.

A vivid illustration of this troubling entitlement mind-set occurred while I was a resident fellow at the John F. Kennedy School of Government Institute of Politics at Harvard University during the fall 2011 semester. One evening, I had ventured across campus to observe a lecture and book launch entitled "Harvard and Slavery: Seeking a Forgotten History," a fascinating look at how slavery has impacted the university from the nineteenth century to the present day. As lead author and professor Sven Beckert discussed the findings of his research along with his student research assistants, the audience was invited to participate in a question-and-answer session.

Midway through the give-and-take with the audience, a young black student raised his hand and wanted to know what Harvard University was going to do to eradicate not only the stain of slavery on the institution, but to address past wrongs done to African Americans in the United States through reparations. A celebration to highlight more than five years of research of slavery at Harvard had immediately been transformed into a difficult and uncomfortable discussion about how blacks were owed money and other forms of assistance from whites for a practice of slavery that has been outlawed in the United States with passage of the Thirteenth Amendment in December 1865.

Many in the audience were stunned by the sudden turn of events, but equally troubling, I noticed that most of the African Americans present in the audience were clapping and cheering the calls for reparations and additional compensation today for past wrongs committed by whites against blacks. This exchange was troubling to me on several levels. For one, the "Harvard and Slavery" discussion had been designed as a book launch and an opportunity for the lead professor and his student researchers on the project to discuss their findings and outline how they would continue their scholarly efforts in the weeks and months to follow. Immediately upon the one student's injecting reparations and the need for Harvard and the United States to address past wrongs stemming from slavery to economic inequality and discrimination in the present day, there was an uncomfortable tension that soon enveloped the room.

Many supporters who had arrived to learn more about the project began to stream toward the exits. While Professor Beckert valiantly sought to regain control of the room, the positive atmosphere had evaporated, and was replaced by many calling for "past wrongs to be made right by Harvard." How, precisely, was that to be done? A white colleague of mine with whom I sat that evening was as incredulous as I was as to what had just occurred. And yet, no one dared to confront the student to ask questions such as "When will enough be enough for society to move on to stop blaming whites who were born in the last several decades for wrongs committed by potential relatives of theirs born several hundred years ago?" Or, "Why does or why should society owe something to you based on the color of your skin rather than giving you an opportunity to achieve your dream in America based on equal treatment under the law?" The disturbing trend that is taking us blackwards lies with the culture and mind-set that has fostered in recent years: unless one subscribes to the ideological belief that blacks are entitled to special, rather than equal, treatment in American society due to their racial and/or ethnic identity, one is somehow racist for believing otherwise. Once again, it was the club of racism being used to promote a viewpoint shared by certain black political and media elite, which has crept into our academic settings that blacks should be treated and viewed differently due to the color of their skin. Having witnessed this event up close, I believe such offensive behavior did more to set back relations between students, faculty members, and the Cambridge community who were present based on race and ethnicity rather than bringing people together based on our common unity as American citizens.

In his controversial bestselling book *The Secret Knowledge: On the Dismantling of American Culture,* author David Mamet examines this identical issue with a particular emphasis on the effect such entitlement status based on race/ethnicity has had upon our contemporary American society. In particular, Mamet posits:

> If, for example, African Americans are to have a special judicial status because of a legacy of slavery, how might one determine, conclusively, that that legacy has dissipated and it is time to welcome the descendants of its victims back into the general population? (Could such a "legacy" exist for a thousand years? Even the most vehement supporters of the idea would probably

say no. Then, for how long? And how might one recognize its absence, and upon what authority announce it?)[17]

As we shall soon discover, this honest assessment of race and of treating one group of citizens differently based on race would be a hallmark of the Obama administration and its supporters, which would lead to a rising anger in the manner in which individuals were treated in American society based exclusively on the color of their skin and/or ethnic group identification.

For the present inquiry regarding Attorney General Holder and his assessment that America was a nation of cowards on matters of race, it would take President Obama more than *two weeks* to fully respond, in large measure because the White House press corps didn't urge the president or his spokesman, Robert Gibbs, to be more forthcoming on the subject. Consider the lone question asked of the White House press secretary *two days* following the Holder thoughts of America as a nation of cowards:

QUESTIONER: Okay. And also, does the President agree with a statement by Attorney General Holder the other day that on things racial, we are essentially a nation of cowards? MR. GIBBS: I have not talked to the President about that. I think what the Attorney General discussed was—or talked about—was that for many years in this country all races have struggled with discussions about race. I would point you to the President's speech on the topic during the campaign as his thoughts on that matter.[18]

Objectively speaking, the silence from the White House and the reporters assigned to cover the president and his activities was appalling. First, Attorney General Holder delivered his remarks on Wednesday February 18, 2009, at the Department of Justice. Later that afternoon, Press Secretary Robert Gibbs answered reporters' questions on Air Force One returning to Washington, D.C., and not a single reporter asked a question about the attorney general's remarks and whether they were reflective of the president. Gibbs again held a question-and-answer session with the White House press corps on February 19, 2009, and not a single question was asked regarding the event.

Finally, more than two days following Mr. Holder's speech, Gibbs was asked a grand total of *one* question regarding the controversial remarks and the transcript above is shocking in what the president's spokesman had revealed; Gibbs hadn't bothered to ask the president about whether the chief law enforcement officer of the United States declaring that the country he had elected to serve was a nation of cowards on matters of race was indicative of the president and/or his administration's position.

Amazingly enough, it would take the president nearly two-and-a-half weeks to answer the American people directly on this question and only during an interview with a friendly outlet in the form of *The New York Times*. "Attorney General Chided for Language on Race," we were told in the headline. If ever there was a question that the president wasn't upset by the attorney general's speech on race where he referred to his fellow countrymen as being a nation of cowards, both the length of time in which it took for Mr. Obama to respond as well as the content of his response when he finally elected to comment spoke volumes. According to *New York Times* reporter Helene Cooper, this is how the president tried to delicately walk past the comments made by his attorney general regarding America being a nation of cowards:

> "I think it's fair to say that if I had been advising my attorney general, we would have used different language," Mr. Obama said, in a mild rebuke from America's first black president to its first black attorney general.[19]

The president's response here is nothing short of incredible and led to more questions being asked of Mr. Obama on the subject than he had answered in his short interview with *The New York Times*. First, one would assume that the president of the United States would have taken time to advise his Cabinet—including his attorney general—on the tone and direction his fledgling administration would undertake during their opening days in office. But even taking his comment at face value, what different language would the president have used? He offered the following to *The New York Times* as if this follow-up response provided any specific clarity:

> "We're often times uncomfortable with talking about race until there's some sort of racial flare-up or conflict," he said, adding, "We could probably be more constructive in facing up to sort of the painful legacy of slavery and Jim Crow and discrimination."[20]

Again, the president's response here is not only quixotic, but brings about more questions than answers in regards to his thoughts on race in general, and the words articulated by his attorney general on the topic in particular. The fact that people could be uncomfortable talking about race until there is some sort of conflict or flare-up is immaterial to whether the president agreed with his attorney general that America was a nation of cowards on that very subject. How, precisely, could people be more constructive in facing up to the painful legacy of slavery and Jim Crow and discrimination at a time when the United States had just sworn in its first black president and attorney general? Obama's election and elevation of several people of color to lead his Cabinet would indicate that the United States had moved beyond conversations of race as it related to Jim Crow and discrimination, and had instead indicated a willingness to move *beyond* race by the very fact that he had been elected to the presidency.

Moreover, both political parties in 2009 were run by black men—with the president as the titular head of the Democratic Party and former Maryland lieutenant governor Michael Steele serving as the first black elected head of the Republican National Committee. Perhaps the time for talking about past wrongs had ended, given the desire of American citizens to elevate those they felt most qualified to prestigious positions regardless of the color of their skin.

Finally, as *The New York Times* interview with the president, ostensibly to address the brewing Holder controversy, drew to a close, Mr. Obama failed to address the issues that many of his fellow citizens had hoped he would address to put the controversy behind the country. Instead, President Obama concluded:

> "I'm not somebody who believes that constantly talking about race somehow solves racial tensions," Mr. Obama said. "I think what solves racial tensions is fixing the economy, putting people to work, making sure that people have health care, ensuring that every kid is learning out there. I think if we do that, then we'll probably have more fruitful conversations."[21]

Again, what amazes me about this exchange with *The New York Times* to quell the furor that had erupted regarding Attorney General Eric Holder's proclamation that America has been and continues to be a nation of cowards on matters of race is that President Obama simply never addressed what a senior member of his Cabinet had declared as fact. Notwithstanding the fact that it had taken the president a couple of weeks to address the issue in the first place, he simply punted when given the opportunity to firmly embrace or repudiate the statement by offering an oblique commentary about not having such discussions on race and instead focusing on jobs, the economy, and making sure students were learning in school.

Perhaps what struck me the most about President Obama's nonresponsiveness to the questions posed to him regarding Attorney General Holder's comments is that they were eerily reminiscent of the manner in which then Senator Obama addressed the furor that had erupted regarding Reverend Jeremiah Wright and his denunciations of America. First, Obama said nothing, and then he sent out surrogates seeking to quell the issue and only waded into the matter once the controversy threatened significant damage to him personally. The difference, of course, is that candidates make calculated political decisions that inoculate themselves from political harm. The president of the United States, however, doesn't have the luxury to vote "present" or decide to abstain on an important issue such as race in America when the head of the Department of Justice has announced that America had been and remained a nation of cowards on matters of race.

The president missed an early opportunity to exert leadership and demonstrate to the American people that he would not tolerate divisive comments on matters of race from percolating within his administration. Had President Obama forcibly rebuked Holder and denounced such divisive language as not representative of his administration, an administration that was focused on jobs, the economy, and the welfare of the nation's schoolchildren, I think the issue would have been placed swiftly and immediately behind him. By instead electing to duck the issue, and to parse and dissemble about constructive ways to discuss race in America, I believe the American people began to return from their initial honeymoon with the president and question why it had taken him two and a half weeks to gently "rebuke" the attorney general when stronger words and actions would have put an end to the matter once and for all.

Instead, the entire episode cast the White House and his administration in a rather unfavorable light. For one, the president found himself engulfed in a racial controversy once again: almost a year to the day that Americans had listened to Senator Obama deal with the Wright controversy, now he found himself dodging, rather than defending his attorney general's belief that America was a nation of cowards on issues of race.

Second and perhaps more important, the spotlight had been shifted from President Obama and his aura of being postracial and/or transcending race and being put in the position of having to defend very divisive issues on matters of race when Americans had most recently celebrated the fact that they had voted for a new American president who happened to be black, as opposed to electing a black president. While subtle, this distinction is crucial: being told by the nation's chief law enforcement officer—a man who happened to be black—that America still remained a nation of cowards on matters of race thrust this very divisive and uncomfortable issue on the forefront of the American political landscape when most of her citizens were concerned with finding or keeping their jobs and ensuring the ability to remain in their homes.

The net result of the manner in which President Obama handled this situation unfortunately shifted the public's attention from the celebratory and historic nature of his presidency to an area that he had adamantly avoided during the campaign trail: a stark discussion of race, this time with the spotlight of the American and international media thrust upon him. As we shall see in the following pages, the initial chink of President Obama's armor exposed an Achilles' heel of vulnerability in handling delicate issues of race and equality that would result in a swell of anger and recoil against the president and his administration, leading to large numbers of white voters fleeing Obama and putting his reelection for a second term in office very much in doubt in November 2012.

6. OF POLICE OFFICERS ACTING STUPIDLY AND BLACK PANTHERS AS "MY PEOPLE"

||||||||||||||||||||||||||||||||||||||||||||||||||||||||||

Cementing the Impression Blacks Were Entitled to Special, Rather Than Equal, Rights in the Obama Era

*Get past "Obama the personality" and see "Obama the president"...
Otherwise all you're being is a political-celebrity groupie instead of a
citizen... It all starts with acknowledging he's my president, and not
my homie.* —Jeff Johnson, Black Entertainment Television (BET)

WHILE PRESIDENT OBAMA AND HIS ATTORNEY GENERAL HAD HOPED THEY
had put racially divisive issues behind them early in their term of office,
events would unfold later in 2009 that would force even the most ardent admirer of the president to question whether he and those surrounding him favored special rights for blacks rather than equal rights
shared by other Americans. The first incident involved a matter that
took place on the day Obama was elected president of the United
States and involved members of the New Black Panther Party, a racist
and anti-Semitic group, who had gathered in front of a polling station
in Philadelphia, Pennsylvania, and allegedly intimidated voters as
they made their way to the polls to select the country's next president.

In video footage captured by an observer that would soon capti-
vate viewers around the world, two Black Panthers, Minister King
Samir Shabazz and Jerry Jackson, are seen standing in front of the

polling station, wearing military inspired clothing—black berets, black tunics with a variety of Black Panther insignias, and black combat boots.[1] One of the individuals carries a black nightstick or billy club approximately two feet long. Both members of the Black Panthers are positioned in such a way that any voter attempting to enter or exit the polling station would necessarily have to come within close proximity of the two men.

The Philadelphia Police Department was alerted to a report of voter intimidation at the polling station and soon dispatched two officers to investigate in further detail. When the police told the two men that "You cannot be out here intimidating voters," one of the Panthers responded that their removal from the polling station was "another white man trying to bring the black man down."[2]

The question remains, of course, what the two men had done in the first place to warrant the attention and subsequent action of the Philadelphia Police Department. As it turns out, one of the poll watchers dispatched by the Philadelphia Republican Party, who was credentialed to observe voting in the polling place was labeled as a "race traitor" by the Black Panthers; the gentleman in question happened to be black. The man and his wife, also a poll observer, felt intimidated and threatened by the Black Panthers and refused to leave the polling station for fear of their personal safety. They sought additional members from the Philadelphia Republican Party to come to their assistance.

After more poll observers were sent to investigate by the Philadelphia Republican Party for potential voter intimidation, consider the following narrative from the Department of Justice memorandum recommending the actions of the New Black Panthers warranted pursuing legal action for violating the safeguard provisions of the Voting Rights Act—ironically the very statute that was enacted to eliminate whites from intimidating blacks in Southern polling stations in the 1960s:

> After [additional Republican Party observers] Mauro, Myers, and Hill arrived, they approached the entrance to the polling place. Samir Shabazz, when engaging and speaking with Mauro

and his fellow poll watchers, tapped the baton in the palm of his other hand. Hill told us that the leather thong on the end of the baton was wrapped around Shabazz's hand while he did this. Mauro heard the Black Panthers call him and his poll watching colleagues "white supremacists." Mauro said that Samir Shabazz also yelled at the poll watchers "fuck you, cracker" as he alighted. When Hill sought to enter the polling location, he said Jackson and Shabazz formed ranks, meaning stood side by side to create a larger obstacle to Hill's entry into the polls. The weapon was in plain view as Hill approached. Hill reported that as he departed the polling place, Samir Shabazz yelled "how you [sic] white motherfuckers gonna like being ruled by a black man?" Meyers told us that the Black Panthers called him a "cracker" and opined that Meyers would "soon know what it was like to be ruled by the black man." Meyers "found the guy to be intimidating." Morse, the videographer, also said that he was "scared to death" of the Black Panthers. Hill, Meyers, Mauro . . . are witnesses with knowledge concerning intimidation and threats by the [New Black Panther Party] members.[3]

Following the election in which the senator became president-elect, the Department of Justice initiated an investigation to see whether or not the New Black Panthers had engaged in voter intimidation by their presence, brandishing of a nightstick, and/or offensive language hurled at certain voters and poll observers as they entered and exited the voting station in question in Philadelphia.

When the facts and events described above were presented to career, nonpolitical attorneys at the Department of Justice Civil Rights Division, they were tasked to determine whether, in fact, a potential violation of the Voting Rights Act had occurred. The relevant statute they reviewed was Section 11(b) of the Voting Rights Act, which states:

No person, whether acting under color of law or otherwise, shall intimidate, threaten, or coerce, or attempt to intimidate, threaten, or coerce any person for voting or attempting to vote, or intimidate, threaten, or coerce, or attempt to intimidate, threaten, or coerce any person for urging or aiding any person to vote or attempt to vote, or intimidate, threaten, or coerce any person for exercising any powers or duties under section 1973a(a), 1973d, 1973f, 1973g, 1973h, or 1973j(e) of this title.[4]

Department of Justice officials methodically interviewed eyewitnesses at the polling station, observed the footage captured by the videographer in which the New Black Panthers were observed brandishing the nightstick while standing in front of the entrance to the building as well as hurling some of the racial epithets noted above. Don't take my word for such menacing behavior—consider the actual video recording of the incident, which is posted on YouTube.[5] Following its review, the Department of Justice applied the statutory language of the Voting Rights Act to the Black Panthers' behavior on Election Day 2008 and recommended that a suit be brought against them for violating the intimidation provisions of the Voting Rights Act.

The chronology now becomes important, as the Department of Justice filed its suit on January 7, 2009—in the waning days of the outgoing Bush administration—in the U.S. District Court for the Eastern District of Pennsylvania, just prior to the inauguration of President Obama. After the suit was filed and the New Black Panthers failed to appear in court on April 17, 2009, to answer the charges against them, the Department of Justice was told by the court they would be given until May 1, 2009, to file for default judgment—the result of which the New Black Panthers would be deemed to have been in violation of the Voting Rights Act for their failure to appear in court. On April 28, 2009, the New Black Panthers were notified by the Justice Department of its intent to file for a default judgment with the court for the Panthers' failure to respond to the charges of violating the Voting Rights Act—a move that would have handed the Justice Department an uncontested victory against them.

Before proceeding with the chronology of the case and the growing backlash against the Obama administration for its apparent willingness to dispense justice favoring blacks and discriminating against whites in civil rights disputes, it is important to recognize that the New Black Panther Party was no stranger to the Department of Justice as to its extreme racist and anti-Semitic views. According to a Department of Justice memorandum discussing the actions and activities of the group:

> The violent and racist views of the New Black Panther Party for Self-Defense are well-documented. The Southern Poverty Law Center has described the party as an active black separatist group, [e]schewing the health clinics and free breakfast programs of the original [Black] Panthers . . . to focus almost exclusively on hate rhetoric about Jews and whites.[6]

It was at this juncture that the actions of the Holder Justice Department and the Obama White House have been called into question for the partiality in how the New Black Panther case was ultimately adjudicated by the Department of Justice. As noted above, the failure of the New Black Panthers to appear in court or otherwise respond to the allegations that two of their members had sought to intimidate voters at a polling station in Philadelphia should have resulted in a default judgment for the Department of Justice against the Panthers. The Federal District Court had given the Justice Department until May 1, 2009, to file their default judgment motion. On May 1, Justice instead asked the court for a two-week extension to May 15, 2009.

On May 15, 2009, despite the fact that the New Black Panther Party members were observed in real-time video photography wielding a nightstick and otherwise seeking to stand in such a way as to impede passage into the polling station, and despite the recommendation of the Justice Department's career prosecutors that they be held accountable for potential crimes committed, the DOJ abruptly dropped its case against the Black Panthers with no further explanation.

What was perhaps more troubling was the original relief sought by the Justice Department when it filed suit against the Black Panthers in 2009, while the Bush administration was still in office, versus the relief the Obama Justice Department ultimately sought with the Federal District Court on May 15, 2009. While I recognize most of my reading audience is not comprised of lawyers, I want to visibly demonstrate and then comment briefly on the wide variance in what was originally submitted by the Justice Department prior to President Obama's arrival versus what was submitted and ultimately accepted, afterward.

In its complaint, *United States of America v. New Black Panther Party for Self Defense et al.*, filed on January 8, 2009, the Justice Department sought the following relief:

> Permanently enjoins Defendants, their agents and successors in office, and all persons acting in concert with them, from deploying athwart the entrance to polling locations with either weapons or in the uniform of the Defendant New Black Panther Party, or both, and from otherwise engaging in coercing, threatening, or intimidating, behavior at polling places during elections.[7]

In plain language, this order would have prohibited members of the New Black Panther Party, present or future, from deploying to polling stations *anywhere* with either weapons or insignia indicating their affiliation with the New Black Panthers, and prohibiting them from coercive, threatening behavior at polling places during elections. Now contrast the original relief sought by the Department of Justice following Eric Holder's confirmation and subsequent assumption of office as attorney general of the United States:

> Defendant Minister King Shabazz is enjoined from displaying a weapon within 100 feet of any open polling location on any election in Philadelphia, Pennsylvania, or from otherwise engaged in coercing, threatening behavior in violation of Section 11(b) of the Voting Rights Act.

> And that the Court only "maintain jurisdiction over this matter until November 15, 2012."[8]

The practical impact in what the department originally sought and what it ultimately obtained against the New Black Panther Party before and after President Obama assumed office is remarkably significant. Less than five months into the leadership of President Obama and Attorney General Holder, not only were the charges dropped against the members of the New Black Panther Party who had been present at the polling station but the charge against the organization itself was also dismissed.

Perhaps more important, the Department of Justice only sought in the present filing with the court to prohibit King Samir Shabazz and *only* Mr. Shabazz from being within one hundred feet of polling stations in Philadelphia where he might be in a position to intimidate, coerce, or otherwise threaten voters. No other members were so restricted and, in fact, the narrow tailoring of the relief order would indicate that Shabazz would have been free to hop on a commuter train either to Wilmington, Delaware, or Trenton, New Jersey, both less than an hour from Philadelphia, and engage in identical behavior.

Equally as troubling, the Holder Justice Department only sought for the court to have jurisdiction over this matter until November 15, 2012—just one week following the U.S. presidential election to be held on November 6, 2012. Did the Justice Department not believe that Mr. Shabazz would not engage in identical behavior at the identical polling station in Philadelphia after only one presidential election cycle? Perhaps this is an innocuous question with a straightforward explanation, but the DOJ offered no further rationale as to its decision-making process in this matter. For its part, the Department of Justice refused to comment on its abrupt decision to file a case against the New Black Panther Party in January 2009, only to dismiss its own complaint five months later, other than the following press account in the conservative-leaning *Washington Times:*

A Justice Department spokesman on Thursday confirmed that the agency had dropped the case, dismissing two of the men from the lawsuit with no penalty and winning an order against the third man that simply prohibits him from bringing a weapon to a polling place in future elections.

The department was "successful in obtaining an injunction that prohibits the defendant who brandished a weapon outside a Philadelphia polling place from doing so again," spokesman Alejandro Miyar said. "Claims were dismissed against the other defendants based on a careful assessment of the facts and the law."

Mr. Miyar declined to elaborate about any internal dispute between career and political officials, saying only that the department is "committed to the vigorous prosecution of those who intimidate, threaten or coerce anyone exercising his or her sacred right to vote."[9]

What is perhaps most remarkable about the statement issued by the DOJ spokesman above is the comment that claims were dismissed against two defendants following a careful assessment of the facts and the law. Yet, it was the identical criteria that led the same Justice Department to file suit in the first place after carefully examining the law and the facts and electing to file a motion with the Federal District Court. There are only two unquestioned variables in this matter that bear mention at this juncture: first, career civil service attorneys investigated and filed their suit against the New Black Panther Party for voter intimidation prior to the swearing in of the Obama administration team, and second, officials appointed by the president of the United States and the attorney general subsequently overruled the counsel of their nonpartisan lawyers to pursue the case further as well as decreasing the ultimate remedy sought by the Department of Justice.

While the facts and ultimate outcome of this dispute were downplayed right after the announcement that the Department of Justice would entirely drop charges against two defendants and downgrade charges and the ultimate remedy against the third defendant, conservative columnists and news outlets condemned the decision for having a racial double standard. An editorial by the conservative-leaning

Washington Examiner summed up much of the skepticism if not out-right sense of entitlement for blacks and supporters of the Obama administration at the expense of others, when they wrote of the Justice Department's move to overrule the career attorneys' decision to prosecute the Black Panthers:

> Even though career attorneys at Justice had won a default judgment against the hate group for voter intimidation, the department dismissed the case against two of the men and merely sought a restraining order against the third, rather than seeking appropriate penalties, including jail time, for all three. That decision was approved by an Obama appointee, Associate Attorney General Thomas J. Perrelli. No satisfactory explanation for the decision has been tendered by anyone in the administration.
>
> The lesson is clear enough though: if you intimidate voters in the services of Obama's election, your offense can be overlooked.[10]

As I previously discussed in my book *Acting White,* the behavior of President Obama and Attorney General Holder is difficult to square when you consider that then Senator Obama had introduced legislation in the Senate to eliminate the very form of voter intimidation that was on display in Philadelphia. The bill, entitled the Deceptive Practices and Voter Intimidation Prevention Act (S. 453), was introduced by Senator Obama (D-IL) on January 31, 2007. At the time, when he spoke in favor of his bill to crack down on voter intimidation at the polls before the House Judiciary Committee that spring, Senator Obama noted:

> There is no place for politics in this debate . . . Both parties at different periods in our history have been guilty in different regions of preventing people from voting for a tactical advantage. We should be beyond that.[11]

By not aggressively pursuing legal action against the New Black Panthers and three of its members who were responsible for overt intimidation of voters in a Philadelphia polling station, an impression was left to many that the Obama administration believed that blacks were entitled to special, rather than equal, rights and that whites would be held to a different standard under the color of law. To use Senator Obama's words above, it would appear to many that the dismissal of the New Black Panther voter intimidation case was precisely and entirely about politics, and that seeking and pursuing justice was not the motivation of the Obama administration in cases where blacks were the alleged perpetrators of crimes and the victims of malfeasance were white. The United States Commission on Civil Rights would initiate an investigation in the fall of 2009 to determine whether the Department of Justice had been applying the law in a racially neutral manner or whether they treated certain racial and/or ethnic minorities differently than whites—the question presented was whether blacks were being given special, rather than equal, treatment at the DOJ due to the color of their skin rather than the color-blind application of the law to a particular set of facts at hand. We shall shortly revisit the New Black Panthers investigation and the manner in which it would hang like an albatross around the neck of the Obama administration well into 2011 and beyond.

At this juncture, however, I would like to turn our focus to yet another racially motivated tempest that would dominate the headlines during the summer of 2009 and fuel rather than quell the impression that President Obama favored blacks at the expense of whites and propelled America blackwards against an administration increasingly viewed as providing special, rather than equal, rights to ethnic minorities. While the Obama administration sought to distance itself from two relatively high-profile incidents involving race and the Department of Justice during the first six months in office, the president himself would wade directly into the treacherous waters of racial politics and further cement the notion that he and his administration sought to favor blacks and ethnic minorities at the expense of others.

The notion that special dispensation and treatment should be afforded to blacks and not whites from the Obama White House arrived in the form of President Obama opining about the treatment and arrest of his friend, Harvard professor Henry Louis Gates Jr., by the Cambridge Police Department that summer. The facts of this particular incident are well known—Gates had arrived home without his keys, he and his driver sought to wedge open a door to gain entry, and a neighbor called police to alert them of a possible break-in. When confronted by police, Gates told them "you don't know who you're messing with," and refused to calm down when asked repeatedly to do so. Subsequently, Gates was arrested for disorderly conduct and racial harassment, the latter charge having arisen when Gates allegedly said: "Why are you doing this? Is it because I'm a black man and you're a white officer?"[12] July 22, 2009, would prove to be a pivotal day for the Obama administration, particularly following the less-than-adroit handling of two high-profile cases in which race had been handled—some would say mishandled—by the Department of Justice.

On this day, President Obama conducted an evening news conference to rally support for the flagging popularity of his and congressional Democrats' efforts to overhaul and revitalize the nation's health care delivery system. He had made it to the final question fifty-five minutes after he began his give-and-take session with the White House press corps when he was asked by Lynn Sweet from the *Chicago Sun-Times* to comment on the arrest of Professor Gates. Here is the president's response—a portion of which would reverberate around the world for the manner in which President Obama would opine on a matter in which he admitted he knew little of the actual facts involved:

SWEET: Thank you, Mr. President. Recently, Professor Henry Louis Gates Jr. was arrested at his home in Cambridge. What does that incident say to you and what does it say about race relations in America?
THE PRESIDENT: Well, I should say at the outset that "Skip" Gates is a friend, so I may be a little biased here. I don't know all the facts. What's been reported, though, is that the guy forgot

his keys, jimmied his way to get into the house, there was a report called into the police station that there might be a burglary taking place—so far, so good, right? I mean, if I was trying to jigger into—well, I guess this is my house now so (laughter)—it probably wouldn't happen. But let's say my old house in Chicago—(laughter)—here I'd get shot.

But so far, so good. They're reporting—the police are doing what they should. There's a call, they go investigate what happens. My understanding is at that point Professor Gates is already in his house. The police officer comes in, I'm sure there's some exchange of words, but my understanding is, is that Professor Gates then shows his ID to show that this is his house. And at that point, he gets arrested for disorderly conduct—charges which are later dropped.

Now, I don't know, not having been there and not seeing all the facts, what role race played in that, but I think it's fair to say, number one, any of us would be pretty angry; number two, *that the Cambridge Police acted stupidly* [emphasis added] in arresting somebody when there was already proof that they were in their own home; and number three, what I think we know separate and apart from this incident is that there is a long history in this country of African Americans and Latinos being stopped by law enforcement disproportionately. That's just a fact.

As you know, Lynn, when I was in the state legislature in Illinois, we worked on a racial profiling bill because there was indisputable evidence that blacks and Hispanics were being stopped disproportionately. And that is a sign, an example of how, you know, race remains a factor in this society. That doesn't lessen the incredible progress that has been made. I am standing here as testimony to the progress that's been made.

And yet the fact of the matter is, is that this still haunts us. And even when there are honest misunderstandings, the fact that blacks and Hispanics are picked up more frequently and oftentimes for no cause casts suspicion even when there is good cause. And that's why I think the more that we're working with

local law enforcement to improve policing techniques so that
we're eliminating potential bias, the safer everybody is going
to be.[13]

When I discussed President Obama's comments regarding the Cambridge Police Department "acting stupidly" in *Acting White,* the prism
from which I viewed that exchange revolved around the fact that I
believed Obama had destroyed any credibility to the notion that his
presidency would be "postracial." On that question, then as now, there
is no question the president's first seven months proved that comments
and actions taken by his administration had demonstrated the fallacy
to that proposition.

President Obama and his coverage in the mainstream American
media portrayed him to be a different type of leader: a healer, a uniter,
someone in the mold of President Abraham Lincoln, who could bring
the country together and emerge stronger from difficult challenges.
The reality, however, was that despite the hype, the buildup, and the
excitement behind Obama's candidacy for the presidency, there was
little examination of either his record as a state and ultimately United
States senator for clues as to what type of leader he would be. Obama
had proven that he was a prodigious fund-raiser, possessed remarkable
oratory skills, and had admirably overcome adversity from a difficult
childhood.

As the first senator elected directly to the presidency since President Kennedy in 1960, many Americans had little notion of how
Obama would govern if elected president. Every president over the past
forty-eight years (with the notable exception of Gerald Ford) prior to
Obama's election had held elective office and amassed a record of leadership as either vice president of the United States or a governor of a
state; Obama had neither.

While not dispositive of the acumen of Obama's leadership skills
one way or the other, the failure of the mainstream media to fully vet
the candidate other than to discuss the historic arc of his candidacy
ultimately did a great disservice to the country. While many Americans believed in the campaign theme of hope and change as indicative

of how Obama would govern, it was apparent midway through his first year in office that Obama had proven an irresistible blank screen upon which the media and his admirers could project the qualities of the leader they had *hoped* he possessed.

The unfortunate reality many Obama supporters had come to discover in July 2009 is that the candidate of hope and change had begun to polarize the nation along racial grounds, and to cause many to wonder if America's first president who happened to be black had, in fact, become America's first black president: willing to tip the scales of justice and power in favor of people of color at the expense of others, rather than leading the country forward in an evenhanded and neutral way under the color of law.

Perhaps more vividly than Attorney General Holder's "nation of cowards" remark or the manner in which his Justice Department had adjudicated the New Black Panther case, President Obama's flippant remark that he believed a white police officer had "acted stupidly" for arresting a black Harvard University professor was far more revealing to his constituents than he could have imagined. Was this just a flip comment made in support of a friend of the president of the United States at the conclusion of a news conference where he revealed his bias, or were other, darker issues at play here?

For one, it showed the chief law enforcement officer of the United States peeking over the blinder that had been placed across his eyes to administer justice without regard to personal preference or belief. It was as if the scales of justice had been tipped and a verdict rendered because the black law professor's word was to be taken at a higher value than that of a white Cambridge police officer. President Obama himself had admitted during his press conference that he did not know all of the facts involved in the case; to weigh in on a local dispute in the manner in which he did led many to believe that Mr. Obama was more interested in justice for his friend than he was for the facts to speak for themselves. Obama openly called Gates his friend and admitted that his opinion on the matter was biased—what could he possibly have thought could have been gained by weighing in on a local matter in which he did not have all of the facts and evidence at hand?

One of the most important and difficult responsibilities a president undertakes when he or she assume the oath of office is to unify the country and to lead regardless of the race, color, or political affiliation of his or her constituents. Obama had made that promise repeatedly, from his acceptance speech on election night 2008 to his inaugural address in January 2009. Yet instead of leaving behind the petty grievances that had marked the American political landscape, President Obama made himself look petty and diminished the office he was elected to protect by appearing more interested in favoring his friends and political supporters than adjudicating the law in a color-blind manner.

In what the president and his White House advisers had hoped was a flip, off-the-cuff remark regarding racial profiling and Obama's record to end the practice instead turned into a worldwide discussion about why he would accuse the Cambridge police of "acting stupidly" and make such a statement without knowing all of the facts while admitting his bias toward Professor Gates. The situation spiraled further out of the president's control when Dennis O'Connor, the head of the Cambridge Police Superior Officers Association, held a news conference and had the following to say regarding Obama's comments: "His remarks were obviously misdirected but made it worse yet by suggesting somehow this case should remind us of a history of racial abuse by law enforcement."[14]

While the White House had hoped that the interest in the president's comments regarding the conduct of the Cambridge Police Department would fade with time, the exact opposite had occurred. Outraged by the sense that the president had waded into a local issue and had subsequently brought bad publicity to the Cambridge Police Department, the local police unions stood in solidarity with the arresting officer by demanding that the White House issue an apology for Mr. Obama's comments.

Mr. O'Connor offered very pointed remarks to the president of the

United States regarding the conduct of his department in handling the arrest of Mr. Gates when he declared:

> Whatever may be the history, we deeply resent the implications and reject any suggestion that in this case or any other case that they've [Cambridge Police officers have] allowed a person's race to direct their activities. However we hope they [the White House] will reflect upon their past comments and apologize to the men and women of the Cambridge Police Department.[15]

As a consequence of the brewing controversy sparked by the president's remarks, mainstream media outlets, conservative talk radio, and newspaper headlines were captivated with the president's clumsy injection of himself into a local police matter and his apparent maligning of the Cambridge Police Department by accusing them of having "acted stupidly" for arresting his black friend. When his press secretary was unable to tamp down the story, President Obama himself stood before the White House press corps less than forty-eight hours after his ill-messaged press conference to resolve the international furor he had created and hoped his misstep had created a "teachable moment" on race relations in America:

> My hope is, is that as a consequence of this event this ends up being what's called a "teachable moment," where all of us instead of pumping up the volume spend a little more time listening to each other and try to focus on how we can generally improve relations between police officers and minority communities, and that instead of flinging accusations we can all be a little more reflective in terms of what we can do to contribute to more unity.
>
> . . . I just wanted to emphasize that—one last point I guess I would make. There are some who say that as President I shouldn't have stepped into this at all because it's a local issue. I have to tell you that that part of it I disagree with. The fact that

this has become such a big issue I think is indicative of the fact that race is still a troubling aspect of our society. Whether I were black or white, I think that me commenting on this and hopefully contributing to constructive—as opposed to negative—understandings about the issue, is part of my portfolio.[16]

Perhaps the true teachable moment regarding President Obama and his handling of the Gates affair was its illuminating insight into his thought and leadership process. If nothing else, the American people gained a valuable lesson regarding the president's leadership skills in a moment of crisis: in the two days after making his caustic remarks, the president remained silent, instead electing to send out his staff to chastise the media for making such a fuss over the furor the president had himself created. Rather than immediately apologize for his poor choice of words, the White House added additional fuel to the fire by suggesting that the media had been partially to blame for engaging in frenzy by reporting on the story instead of discussing the president's continuing efforts to work with Congress to pass health care–reform legislation. When his staff's explanations failed to stem the tide of a growing scandal, the president decided to stand before the American people and seemingly chastise *them* for comments *he* had made.

Moreover, Mr. Obama hoped that people (never mind that he was the one who instigated the inflammatory conversation in the first place) would spend a little more time listening to one another and try to improve relations between police officers and minority communities. To listen to the president's phraseology, it was as if some ignorant busybody had taken a microphone and spoken to the American people and recklessly fanned the flames of racial tension: "instead of flinging accusations we can all be a little more reflective in terms of what we can do to contribute to more unity." The very person who had flung accusations of Cambridge police officers "acting stupidly"—perhaps in a knee-jerk response to a reporter's question—was now asking the

American people to be a bit more reflective and to contribute more to unity in the country? The very individual who had chided his constituents to mend rather than burn bridges to constructively come together in unity was the one operating the flamethrower.

Finally, the president took the opportunity to defend himself while criticizing those who would question why he would inject himself in a local law enforcement matter best left in the Commonwealth of Massachusetts rather than 1600 Pennsylvania Avenue. Listening and reflecting upon the president's choice of words here is very instructive: "The fact that this has become such a big issue I think is indicative of the fact that race is still a troubling aspect of our society." With all due respect to the president of the United States, *he* was the one who instigated the "big issue" by disclosing his thoughts about the Cambridge Police Department. Professor Gates had insisted that his arrest had everything to do with the fact that he was black. President Obama immediately sided with Gates and talked repeatedly about repairing relations with the police department and minority communities. The principal law enforcement officer of the United States had listened to a narrative that he thought fit the pattern of how he saw the United States and her citizens: a black man being confronted by white police officer equals police racism and police acting stupidly.

While the president thought he had played a constructive role by inserting himself into the Gates affair and adding meaningfully to the debate, he instead angered many people who believed in him, believed in his promise to change the tone in Washington, D.C., and who believed that Obama would put petty grievances behind him for the betterment of the country. For all of the president's hectoring about teachable moments, constructive dialogue, and coming together in unity, he never uttered two words that would have helped restore the trust he had broken with the American people: "I'm sorry."

While not a firm believer in the reliability of daily tracking polls, I was interested to read a poll released by Scott Rasmussen on the perception by citizens across the country regarding President Obama's handling of the Professor Gates affair. In a survey conducted on July

28–29, 2009, Rasmussen asked participants to rate the president's handling of the Gates matter in his press conference and subsequent attempts to quell the swirling cauldron he had created:

How do you rate the way the president has handled the situation over the past week?

13% Excellent
17% Good
18% Fair
44% Poor
8% Not sure[17]

What I found most remarkable about the poll question above is the number of people who rated the president's handling of the Gates situation as being fair or poor—a remarkable 62 percent versus 30 percent surveyed who felt he had handled the matter in an either excellent or good manner. The president who likened himself to Abraham Lincoln and the sixteenth president's ability to bring the country together during tumultuous times had instead created a scandal regarding race, which 62 percent of the country felt he had handled either fairly or poorly. Suddenly the great uniter had turned into the great divider.

In a blatant attempt at political triage, his staff arranged for President Obama to host Professor Gates and his arresting officer, Sergeant James Crowley, at the White House for a "beer summit," where all parties involved could put the matter behind them—the two men from Cambridge could then return to their regular routines and the occupant of 1600 Pennsylvania Avenue could return to governing the country. Ironically, this attempt to calm the roiling waters only ensured that the media would preoccupy itself with the story for another week. Perhaps more than anything, the Gates incident had shown the American people a side of their president that was entirely unexpected.

There is an important distinction to be made when looking at the actions of the Justice Department in failing to prosecute the New Black

Panther Party for violating the Voting Rights Act and the conduct of the president of the United States in the Gates case. More directly, a question persists whether there was and remains a concerted effort in the Obama administration to either act or fail to act, and to confer special, rather than equal, rights for certain citizens due to their racial and/or ethnic identity rather than to treat all Americans equal under the laws of our society.

As it pertains to actions undertaken by the Obama Justice Department, the Federal District Court for the Eastern District of Pennsylvania entered a default judgment against the New Black Panther Party for their failure to answer the charges brought against them by the Department of Justice in regards to violating the rights of white voters to enter the polling booth in Philadelphia, on Election Day 2008—a case that was brought in the waning days of the presidency of George W. Bush. When Obama assumed the presidency and Eric Holder was confirmed as attorney general of the United States, the political appointees of the Obama administration elected *not* to prosecute the case further—over the strong opposition of the career attorneys who had investigated the case and brought suit on behalf of the government— even though the Panthers had lost the case by default.

While the Black Panther matter could be said to be a matter of opinion that was handled at the Department of Justice, President Obama had, without provocation, injected himself into a matter of race, something that he had spent his entire political career seeking to avoid. The net result of which was the carefully calibrated image of being postracial and a great reconciler had been exposed as being more of a political mirage than a reality.

Moreover, at its core, President Obama had articulated a belief that many found offensive when dealing with matters of race that we have discussed thus far: assuming a black individual was the victim and a white individual was in the wrong. I have always found it remarkable that the Cambridge Police Department had been called out to Professor Gates's house in the mistaken belief that someone was trying to break into his home and steal his personal property. Rather than calmly explain himself and the circumstance of trying to wedge the door open on account of having left his keys behind, Professor Gates had become angry and confrontational with police. A simple "I'm sorry for the confusion, officer" would have sent both men on their respective ways that afternoon. Instead, Professor Gates accusing the police officer of racism set off a disastrous chain of events that would lead to an arrest and a difficult conversation on race held by the president of the United States that alienated rather than drew people closer together. The evidence of this? A Pew Research Center poll on President Obama's handling of the matter had broken down on racial lines. In a survey conducted July 22–26, 2009, just prior to the infamous "beer summit," Pew found 41 percent of respondents had disapproved of Obama's handling of the matter with just 29 percent in favor.[18] Did the erosion of the president's support derive from the impression that Mr. Obama and his government could be biased in their treatment of America's citizens based not on the facts of a particular matter, but on the skin color of the alleged actor? Were blacks receiving special dispensation from the government to either act or fail to do so to promote the notion they were privileged to receive special, rather than equal, rights at the expense of their fellow citizens merely due to their race?

Rather than subsiding, troubling questions would persist about the sincerity of the president and his administration to treat all Americans equally under the color of law as 2009 gave way to 2010. We shall discuss the disturbing pattern of President Obama and his supporters ultimately accusing his political opponents as being racist and the resulting anger it has caused in the American societal fabric today in the chapter that follows.

Presently, I would like to return to the aftermath of the Department of Justice decision to curtail its prosecution against the New Black Panther Party earlier in 2009. The United States Commission on Civil Rights had been very concerned about allegations the Department of Justice applied the law in a manner that treated Americans differently under the color of law based on the color of their skin. Of particular apprehension were allegations that the Justice Department had elected to ignore or mitigate the severity of charges against black defendants in cases where whites were the victims while correspondingly pursuing litigation in which whites were alleged to have committed crimes against black victims.

Congress established the United States Commission on Civil Rights in 1957 to serve as an independent and bipartisan agency to investigate complaints and allegations that citizens were being deprived of their right to vote by reason of their race, religion, sex, age, or national origin. Within this vein, the commission initiated an investigation into the handling of the New Black Panther Party in the spring of 2009 to ascertain the answers to two key questions: first, had the Department of Justice acted properly in its handling of and subsequent decision to drop the undisputed charges against the Black Panthers? Second, did the department apply the law in a racially neutral manner?

Initially, the commission had sent the Justice Department letters in June 2009 asking it to shed light on the legal and factual basis behind its dismissal of the case against the New Black Panther Party. When the department elected to either ignore the requests of the commission and/or exert a number of legal privileges to shield its internal deliberations, the commission moved to subpoena two of the lead civil service (nonpolitical appointee) lawyers to offer their insights behind encouraging the Department of Justice to sue the New Black Panther Party on November 18, 2009. These two individuals, Christopher Coates, chief of the Voting Section of the Civil Rights Division, and J. Christian Adams, a senior trial attorney, were ordered by the Justice Department not to comply with the subpoena or the Civil Rights Commission's investigation.

While we are constrained in our ability to conduct an exhaustive discussion regarding information sought by the U.S. Civil Rights Commission regarding the Black Panther Party litigation and the Department of Justice's apparent unwillingness to comply with such requests, there are a few important factors that bear consideration. First, there was a strong belief among certain career civil service attorneys involved in the Black Panther investigation that the Department of Justice had fostered a hostile climate toward enforcing the law in cases that involved black defendants versus the vehement denials of such conduct by political appointees of the president of the United States and the attorney general.

Next, the Department of Justice sought to avoid participation in the commission's investigation to the greatest extent possible by ordering attorneys not to testify, relocating another to South Carolina to be beyond the statutory subpoena reach of the commission's headquarters in Washington, D.C., and otherwise being only grudgingly cooperative.

Within this backdrop, I found it to be incongruent at best that the heralded arrival of America's ostensibly first postracial president would impede an investigation of the U.S. Civil Rights Commission (a) given the important and historic mission of the commission since its founding in 1957 and that (b) then Senator Obama had authored a bill that would strengthen the sanctions involved with voter intimidation. If anything, one would have imagined that President Obama would have asked, if not ordered, his attorney general and the Department of Justice to comply fully with any and all information requests presented them by the commission. Instead, the Justice Department employed a number of maneuvers to circumvent the commission's work, which soon proved ineffective once one of the trial attorneys previously ordered not to cooperate resigned from the DOJ and elected to participate in an open hearing to offer electrifying testimony as to what he had seen and heard during his employment.

On May 14, 2010, Thomas Perez, assistant attorney general for the Civil Rights Division, testified before the Civil Rights Commission regarding his department's involvement in the New Black Panther litigation and claimed that the Justice Department had dismissed the charges based on a thorough review of the law and the facts. The same day, J. Christian Adams, a civil service (i.e., not a political appointee of the Obama administration) trial attorney assigned to the New Black Panther case, resigned in protest over what he characterized as inaccurate testimony by the head of the Civil Rights Division. Adams's abrupt resignation from the Department of Justice would usher in one of the most dramatic instances of political theater I've viewed personally in more than twenty years in Washington, D.C.: Adams's decision to voluntarily testify before the Civil Rights Commission on July 6, 2010, to offer his view of the inner workings of the Obama/Holder Justice Department.

In a preview of his explosive testimony, Adams authored an op-ed in the *Washington Times* on June 25, 2010, which recounted his decision to terminate his employment at the Department of Justice as well as his view on the dismissal of the New Black Panther litigation. Most important, Adams spoke of a Justice Department that was more interested in settling racial scores than impartially applying the rule of law to matters before the department. In the relevant sections, Adams opined:

> The New Black Panther case was the simplest and most obvious violation of federal law I saw in my Justice Department career. Because of the corrupt nature of the dismissal, statements falsely characterizing the case and, most of all, indefensible orders for the career attorneys not to comply with lawful subpoenas investigating the dismissal, this month I resigned my position as a Department of Justice attorney . . .
>
> Most disturbing, the dismissal is part of a creeping lawlessness infusing our government institutions. Citizens would be shocked to learn about the open and pervasive hostility within the Justice Department to bringing civil rights cases against nonwhite defendants on behalf of white victims. Equal enforcement of justice is not a priority of this administration. Open contempt is voiced for these types of cases.[19]

As I read Adams's chilling account I was reminded once more of Arthur Schlesinger's warning from chapter 1 regarding the acceptance and acquiescence of a "cult of ethnicity" that had taken hold in the 1970s and the 1980s, in which the vision of America as a melting pot of opportunity where people put aside their racial and/or ethnic allegiance to honor their special status of being an American citizen was abandoned. Schlesinger's fear was that if pushed too far, the consequences of adopting an acquiescence of the cult of ethnicity mentality would have a devastating impact upon our American society; America would become not a nation of individuals but a nation of groups whose race and ethnicity would be their defining identity and whose ethnic ties to their specific communities would be paramount.

If Adams's allegations were true, had America taken a dangerous step down the path of racial exclusion and exclusivity rather than celebrate the unique aspect of being an American is our citizenship rather than the color of our skin? Further still, it would have seemed inconceivable during Obama's campaign for the presidency that once elected, he would allow the Department of Justice to favor blacks at the expense of whites, administering justice based on race rather than a fair application of the law to right past wrongs, and engage in "payback time." Wouldn't the net result of such activities retard, rather than improve, racial cohesiveness?

Moreover, given the tenor of President Obama's first term in office, bracketed on one end by his attorney general's admonition that America had been a nation of cowards on matters of race and Mr. Obama's "teachable moment" on race relations following the Gates affair on the other, one could have further presumed the administration could have grasped the opportunity to demonstrate its racial neutrality under the color of law. Indeed, given President Obama's eagerness to wade into a local law enforcement matter between the Cambridge Police Department and one of the town's most storied professors, I found the unwillingness of the president to order an exhaustive and full review to determine whether his Justice Department was not operating in a racially neutral manner to be particularly shocking.

On July 6, 2009, despite the personal risk involved in defying a department order barring his testimony even following his voluntary termination, J. Christian Adams raised his right hand before the U.S. Civil Rights Commission and proffered truthful testimony on what he had experienced in pursuing justice against the New Black Panther Party for voter intimidation before and after the Obama administration had come to power. Seated less than ten feet away from Adams during the proceedings, I was stunned on several levels of what I had heard firsthand that morning.

For one, the hearing room of the U.S. Civil Rights Commission looked no bigger to me than a seminar room at a medium-sized college or university. The number of print journalists was minimal and the only camera crew whose presence I could identify was from the Fox News Channel. The absence of a large media presence was surprising to me; I could only imagine how difficult it would have been to gain entrance if the Bush administration had been alleged to have dismissed charges of voter intimidation by white supremacists of black voters in rural South Carolina—particularly if such an occurrence had taken place within the first year of the Bush administration, with John Ashcroft, a Pentecostal minister's son, at the helm of the Justice Department.

Next, I was struck at how physically uncomfortable Adams looked while delivering his opening statement and answering the questions posed to him by the commissioners. Later press accounts would allege that Adams was motivated to speak out by his affiliation as a Republican and/or his dislike of the Obama administration. From my seat in the hearing room I found Adams to be credible given his obvious discomfiture being present as an almost reluctant witness driven by his desire for the truth to come to light rather than seeking to gain notoriety or fame from his appearance. There were many questions posed of Adams that he was either advised by counsel not to answer or that he replied would force him to reveal confidential and/or privileged information that he did not feel comfortable in doing so. Having observed his testimony from start to finish, it was apparent to me that Adams was not out to settle a score or conduct a scorched earth campaign against the administration; he clearly felt compelled to offer a different explanation than what the commission had previously heard from the assistant attorney general in charge of the Civil Rights Division, and a political appointee of the president, an explanation from the perspective of a former civil service employee who served regardless of the party affiliation of the occupant of 1600 Pennsylvania Avenue.

Of all that I had heard during Adams's riveting testimony that morning in July 2010, I was most surprised to learn of his firsthand description of the discrimination encountered by blacks working in the Department of Justice Civil Rights Division who elected to pursue enforcement actions against blacks accused of suppressing the rights of whites and others to vote. As I was shocked to observe, Adams had painted a picture in which the Department of Justice consciously created a climate in which black employees who either volunteered or were otherwise assigned to work on cases in which there were white victims at the hands of alleged black transgressors were harassed for doing so.

As such, Mr. Adams described two cases matching this description: the New Black Panther litigation referenced above as well as the Ike Brown case. Briefly, Mr. Brown, who is black, was alleged to have systematically violated the rights of whites living in Noxubee County, Mississippi. At the time of the lawsuit, blacks outnumbered whites 3 to 1 in the county; the George W. Bush administration ordered the Department of Justice to launch an investigation to ascertain if Brown had sought to disenfranchise whites by meddling with absentee ballots, manipulating the voter rolls, and paying off notaries public. In 2005, the Civil Rights Division initiated legal proceedings that ultimately brought about a successful prosecution against Mr. Brown, which was further upheld on appeal from the defendant.

What struck me that morning was the comment by Mr. Adams that prior to the Brown case filed in 2005 and the present New Black Panther case he was there to discuss, the Civil Rights Division had *never* filed litigation under the Voting Rights Act in a case in which the victims were white and the alleged perpetrators were black. Mr. Adams (and at a future hearing his supervisor, Christopher Coates) would testify to the open hostility for pursuing litigation against blacks in this manner.

I was stunned when Adams said the following about how one person in the department felt about pursuing such litigation: "At least one attorney stated, 'I'm not going to work on the case because I didn't join the voting section to sue black people.'"[20] As the Civil Rights Commission would note of Voting Rights chief Christopher Coates in its interim report issued in November 2010: "Robert Kengle, deputy in the Voting Section, allegedly stated to Mr. Coates during a trip to investigate the Ike Brown case, 'Can you believe we are being sent down to Mississippi to help a bunch of white people?'"[21] While that comment was allegedly made during the Bush administration, I found it a telling barometer of the atmosphere that was permitted to exist in the Department of Justice Civil Rights Division then and now.

From Coates's sworn testimony before the United States Civil Rights Commission, there were more than several incidents, when taken in their totality, indicated that the Department of Justice was (a) not interested in applying the law equally toward blacks and whites in the Voting Rights Division, and (b) this was an impression well understood by many who worked in the Department. For one, he relayed a story in which the deputy assistant attorney general told employees that she had no interest in enforcing a particular provision of the National Voter Registration Act because the section (Section 8) had nothing to do with increasing voter turnout; conversely, the particular section in question set forth uniform standards for states to fairly administer the registration of voters for federal office and imposed requirements on when valid voter registration applications would be accepted as well as rules for removing names from voter registration rolls. Consider the following:

> Specifically, Mr. Adams testified that, during a meeting on November 30, 2009, Deputy Assistant Attorney General Julie Fernandes, when asked about Section 8 [of the National Voter Registration Act] said, "We have no interest in enforcing this provision of the law. It has nothing to do with increasing turnout, and we are just not going to do it." Everybody in the Voting Section heard her say it.[22]

Part of the rationale behind passage of the National Voter Registration Act in 1993 was that it would facilitate an easier opportunity for people to vote as well as encourage minorities and lower socioeconomic groups to participate in the electoral process. One can infer from Adams's testimony above that a senior political official (appointed by the Obama White House) at the Department of Justice had no interest in protecting the integrity of the voter registration rolls for fear that doing so might invalidate or disqualify voters. The implication here, of course, is that the Department would not want to risk doing so for removing blacks and/or other minorities from being eligible to vote—ostensibly for Democratic candidates, if not President Obama, himself.

As chief of the Voting Section at the Department of Justice, Mr. Adams (a civil service employee retained regardless of the political party in power at the time) repeatedly sought authority from his political supervisors to investigate eight particular states that appeared to have significant noncompliance issues with the dictates in the National Voter Registration Act for maintaining a voter registration system that purges ineligible citizens from being able to vote. Here, Adams noted:

> During the time that I was Chief, no approval was given to this project. And it is my understanding that approval has never been given for that Section 8 list maintenance project to date. That means that we have entered the 2010 election cycle with eight states appearing to be in major noncompliance with list maintenance requirements of Section 8 of the NVRA. And, yet, the Voting Section, which has the responsibility to enforce that law, has yet to take any action.[23]

Without commenting directly on the testimony or the allegations asserted by Mr. Adams above, the assistant attorney general in charge of the Civil Rights Division asserted in a letter to U.S. Civil Rights Commission chairman Gerald Reynolds that the division was committed to applying the laws fairly and in a race-neutral manner. Yet, given the sworn testimony of a civil service employee from the Justice Department who resigned, in part, because he believed that the Obama administration was more interested in pursuing cases in circumstances in which the alleged perpetrator was white and the presumed victim was black, rather than in cases in which the rights of white citizens had allegedly been violated, deserves more than a blanket denial by the administration.

Finally, this impression of separate and unequal treatment for blacks rather than whites under the color of law in the Obama administration is vividly illustrated in the following quotation from an unnamed DOJ official in *The Washington Post* during the investigation of the handling of the New Black Panther Party litigation:

> Civil rights officials from the Bush administration have said that enforcement should be race-neutral. But some officials from the Obama administration, which took office vowing to reinvigorate civil rights enforcement, thought the agency should focus on cases filed on behalf of minorities.
>
> "The Voting Rights Act was passed because people like Bull Connor were hitting people like John Lewis, not the other way around," said one Justice Department official not authorized to speak publicly, referring to the white Alabama police commissioner who cracked down on civil rights protesters such as Lewis, now a Democratic congressman from Georgia.[24]

Ironically, as will be explored in greater detail in chapter 7, administration officials were quick to allege racism and play the race card when states across the United States imposed stricter requirements to ensure voters were legally registered—a move called a new poll tax to disenfranchise blacks from the ability to vote. Yet, the same administration officials were content to focus the efforts of the Civil Rights Division to pursue cases that were filed on behalf of minorities, while overlooking or failing to investigate cases in which whites were the victims of discrimination at the hands of alleged black perpetrators.

Once again, a seemingly clear case in which officials within the Obama administration and across the country sought to promote separate but inherently unequal playing fields based on the color of one's skin—a scenario in which blacks were to be granted special, rather than equal, rights. Of this interesting social dichotomy, play-wright and social commentator David Mamet would note:

> The Fifteenth Amendment makes it illegal to discriminate against anyone on the basis of race, color, or previous condition of servitude. If this is illegal in consideration of the first, most basic right of the citizen, surely it is illegal (as it is ridiculous) to discriminate *in favor* of an individual on such a basis.[25]

Finally, beyond the charges that the Department of Justice failed to adopt an ethic in which the law would be applied in a racially neutral manner, there was also the allegation that a tone was set within the department in which whites were made to feel uncomfortable at the expense of others—based solely on skin color. In his testimony be-fore the U.S. Civil Rights Commission, former Voting Rights chief J. Christian Adams described an uncomfortable climate at the De-partment of Justice in which race was very much a factor in the minds of many of those in the Civil Rights Division. In particular, he related a disturbing story about Attorney General Holder's visit to the Voting Rights Section in March 2009 and the manner in which political appointee Acting Assistant Attorney General Loretta King introduced the just confirmed attorney general. While the following is a quotation from a blog released the same day as Adams's testimony before the commission, the content is in line with the notes I took while listening to his testimony:

> I am reminded of a visit to the Voting Section by newly con-firmed Attorney General Eric Holder in March 2009. General Holder came to the conference room to meet the assembled Voting Section. He was introduced by then political appointee Acting Assistant Attorney General Loretta King.
> Loretta King had the honor of introducing General Holder. She would subsequently participate in the dismissal of the New Black Panther voter intimidation case.[26]

Adams then described how Ms. King excitedly told the assembled gathering of staff how happy she was to look every morning and see the photographs of Attorney General Holder and President Obama— a point at which she said that she was excited to have two black men running the country. At this comment, many, but not all of those present, apparently cheered in approval.

I was present during Mr. Adams's testimony on this point and as I listened, I could hardly believe what I had just heard. People actually cheered? It would have been one thing if this were a reunion gathering of campaign staff from President Obama's successful bid for the Oval Office gathered outside of a government building to celebrate their historic victory. I was shocked that the acting assistant attorney general had felt comfortable making such a statement and even more surprised that the attorney general himself hadn't immediately made clear to King and the assembled staff the impropriety of such a racially tinged introduction.

I can only imagine if one of Attorney General John Ashcroft's political appointees had made the same comment, except this time taking pleasure that two white men were running the United States of America. One can guarantee that there would have been swift calls for the resignation of the acting assistant attorney general for making the comments as well as the resignation of the attorney general for failing to repudiate such repugnant language. Was there a double standard involved if such language were to have been used by a Republican administration versus the historic election of President Obama and the introduction of America's first attorney general that happened to be black? Let me be the first to recognize that the excitement displayed over the first black president being elected and subsequently selecting the first black attorney general are cause for celebration on a number of levels. Obama's election and Holder's confirmation as attorney general were two events many blacks thought they would never see in their lifetimes. The important point here is that while the introduction of the first black attorney general was meant to be celebratory in nature, the door had been opened to make those present who were not black uncomfortable due to the tone of the introduction, itself.

Finally, Loretta King's inappropriate introduction of Attorney General Holder had come just weeks following his "nation of cowards" comment. One would have thought that he would have been more sensitive to such racially inflammatory language, but perhaps he found no fault with her introduction any more than he had in expressing his own views just weeks prior.

Frankly, the totality of Adams's testimony had saddened me greatly. I had arrived hoping to gain more insight into why the New Black Panther litigation had been dropped by the Department of Justice, and I left feeling almost numb. It was as if all of the politically correct talk of hope and change had not only been a farce, but that there were lawyers in senior political (as opposed to civil service) positions at the department who had no interest in pursuing justice in instances where whites were alleged to be the victims at the hands of black perpetrators of a serious crime. If Adams's testimony is to be believed—and from my front row chair I found his participation in the hearing to be riveting, if not depressing, yet believable—there were further problems within the Department of Justice that warranted attention by President Obama and Attorney General Holder. Did they really allow such a hostile atmosphere for racially neutral enforcement of the law to exist? Or worse, did they encourage such behavior, either directly or indirectly?

Sadly, the U.S. Civil Rights Commission would issue its interim report to the Congress and the American people in November 2009 with predictable press coverage; outside of the Fox News Channel and conservative talk radio and commentary, the story was couched as being a politically motivated attack against the Obama administration and the attorney general by Christian Adams and others with a partisan agenda. This despite the fact that the United States Commission on Civil Rights is an independent and bipartisan agency that was established in 1957 with the specific mission to "investigate complaints alleging that citizens are being deprived of their right to vote by reason of their race, color, religion, sex, age, disability, or national origin, or by reason of fraudulent practices."[27]

Lost in such dismissive commentary is the fact that the very agency charged to be independent of political control had failed to account why it had dismissed a lawsuit against the New Black Panther Party in which the Department of Justice had prevailed. Moreover, the allegations lodged during open commission hearings in which witnesses testified under oath (under penalty of perjury) regarding a systemic atmosphere within the Civil Rights Division in which blacks were free to perpetrate crimes against white defendants without fear of prosecution were never addressed in their entirety. If anything, the commission's report left far more questions posed than answers presented.

Apparently Congress, the White House, and the mainstream media merely yawned and diverted their attention elsewhere—seemingly the interim report from the U.S. Commission on Civil Rights entitled, "Race Neutral Enforcement of the Law? DOJ and the New Black Panther Party Litigation," held little interest for them. At the same time, the White House, Department of Justice, and the national news media would take particular interest and attention to the actions of several states that moved in 2011 to tighten the integrity of their ballot boxes by requiring citizens to show photo identification prior to casting a vote in a state and/or federal election. This move was decried as a poll tax—a move designed to keep blacks from voting in the 1950s and 1960s—and proof of a new wave of racism sweeping across the United States. Suddenly, Mr. Holder and the Civil Rights Division at the Department of Justice were rapt at the prospect of prosecuting racism against blacks, but remained seemingly indifferent to pursuing black perpetrators of crime against white defendants.

The New York Times found the perfect individual to vocalize this allegedly new racist attack against blacks in the form of Representative John Lewis (D-GA). Lewis is a hero from the civil rights era and was famously beaten on what became known as Bloody Sunday in Selma, Alabama, on March 7, 1965.

Writing in an op-ed published on August 26, 2011, and entitled "A Poll Tax by Another Name," Lewis would assert:

Despite decades of progress, this year's Republican-backed wave of voting restrictions has demonstrated that the fundamental right to vote is still subject to partisan manipulation. The most common new requirement, that citizens obtain and display unexpired government-issued photo identification before entering the voting booth, was advanced in thirty-five states and passed by Republican legislatures in Alabama, Minnesota, Missouri, and nine other states — despite the fact that as many as 25 percent of African-Americans lack acceptable identification.

To be certain, I do not condone any form of racism in our society, particularly not as it relates to the privilege of American citizens being denied the opportunity to cast their ballot to choose their leaders. This is of paramount concern to ensure the ugliness of Jim Crow is never seen again across our great country.

At the same time, the main thrust of Lewis's argument above is at best paternalistic and at worst belittling to blacks across America. Today, regardless of the color of one's skin, one is required to display proof of identification before they are allowed to purchase a drink, buy over-the-counter allergy medication, drive a car, fly on an airplane, or serve in the United States military. To suggest that requiring the display of valid identification is a blatant attempt to suppress the votes of blacks is a serious charge of racism itself without any proof.

Moreover, Representative Lewis notes than approximately 25 percent of the black population has no valid form of identification. If true, this is an important inequity that must be fixed, as I believe all Americans should have a valid form of identification in our society today. But the suggestion that blacks are too feeble to obtain proper ID makes blacks look inferior to their fellow citizens.

On June 5, 2011, Congresswoman Debbie Wasserman Schultz, the newly minted chair of the Democratic National Committee (DNC), opened up a new line of attack against efforts to require the use of photo identification cards during elections in certain states. Speaking to journalist Roland Martin on his TV One television program, Wasserman Schultz asserted that:

[N]ow you have the Republicans, who want to literally drag us all the way back to Jim Crow laws and literally—and very transparently—block access to the polls to voters who are more likely to vote for Democratic candidates than Republican candidates. And it's nothing short of that blatant.[28]

Once again, blacks apparently need special, rather than equal, treatment in our society, according to the view of Wasserman Schultz and other opponents of the measures designed to enhance the integrity of the ballot box. Given that the laws treat all voting citizens *equally*, without regard to skin color, why should blacks today deserve special treatment without proof of demonstrable harm? Even *PolitiFact.com* looked into the congresswoman's statement that Republicans wanted to drag the country back to Jim Crow laws and found that it was demonstrably false.[29] Assessing her claims of Republican efforts to revert to Jim Crow–era tactics to disenfranchise blacks, the *Tampa Bay Times* offered this blistering assessment:

Wasserman Schultz's comparison reduces an overwhelming apartheid system to one of its facets, voting laws. And Jim Crow was pure racism, whereas the intent behind today's proposals is, at most, partisan gain—albeit at the expense of some would-be voters, many of whom are likely to be minorities. Reasonable people can disagree about the wisdom of the new laws, but they would not return the United States to Jim Crow. Saying so offers more heat than light. On balance, we rate her comment False.[30]

For his part, Attorney General Eric Holder waded into the issue on December 12, 2011, when he delivered remarks at the Lyndon Baines Johnson Presidential Library, declaring:

Over the years, we've seen all sorts of attempts to gain partisan advantage by keeping people away from the polls—from literacy tests and poll taxes, to misinformation campaigns telling people that Election Day has been moved, or that only one adult per household can cast a ballot.[31]

Holder is absolutely correct to assert that over the years people have been kept away from the polls due to literacy tests and poll taxes. But to continue with the sentiment that America is still mired in the 1960s and President Lyndon Johnson hadn't signed the Voting Rights Act into law and the Department of Justice hadn't created an entire *division* to ensure discrimination by race at the ballot box was eliminated is absurd. And yet, while the Department of Justice was content to allow the New Black Panther lawsuit to drop in the face of demonstrable evidence that Voting Rights Act safeguards had been violated against whites, the attorney general announced that his Justice Department would work to ensure that racially neutral laws designed to protect the integrity of the voting process would not violate the civil rights of minorities, the elderly, and the poor. The apparent unwillingness of the attorney general to apply the force and color of law equally to all of America's citizens was a task too difficult for him and his department: only by perpetuating the myth that blacks were too ignorant of society around them would the attorney general act in such a manner that demonstrated that blacks needed special, rather than equal, rights and treatment under the law.

Consider yet another example of Mr. Holder's view that blacks require different treatment under law and in our society as a whole. Change of control of the House of Representatives would compel the attorney general to appear before Congress in March 2011 to testify about his department's activities—testimony in which I believe Congress should have demanded his resignation, for failing to manage the Department of Justice in a manner in which all citizens were treated equally under the color of law rather than receive special and inherently unequal treatment based on the color of their skin.

On March 1, 2011, Attorney General Holder appeared before the

House Appropriations Subcommittee on the Judiciary to answer questions regarding a steep increase in the president's budget for the Civil Rights Division for 2011 and 2012. Ultimately, the attorney general was asked to explain the dismissal of the New Black Panther Party litigation by his Justice Department. While first noting, "This Department of Justice does not enforce the law in a race-conscious way," Attorney General Holder offered an entirely different perspective when pressed to offer a concrete rationale behind the decision to dismiss charges against the Black Panthers after the Department of Justice had already prevailed in the litigation.[32] John Culberson, a Republican representative from Texas, started the fireworks when he read the statement by Bartle Bull, once publisher of the *Village Voice,* former campaign manager of Attorney General Robert F. Kennedy's bid for the White House in 1968, and civil rights activist from the Lawyers' Committee for Civil Rights Under Law in Mississippi. Bull declared that he had never seen such a blatant form of voter intimidation in all of the political campaigns he had worked, including his civil rights work in Mississippi during the 1960s.[33] According to *The Wall Street Journal* and similar accounts published the following day, a visibly angry Attorney General Holder responded to the congressman by saying:

> Think about that. When you compare what people endured in the South in the sixties to try to get the right to vote for African Americans, and to compare what people were subjected to there to what happened in Philadelphia—which was inappropriate, certainly that . . . to describe it in those terms I think does a great disservice to people who put their lives on the line, who risked all, *for my people.* [emphasis added][34]

My people? Who were Attorney General Holder's people? Certainly as the chief law enforcement officer of the United States other than the president, the attorney general was making reference to the citizens of the United States of America, correct? Straight to the point: did "my people" signify that he was discussing only black people, rather than the American citizens he had taken an oath to protect, support, and defend under the Constitution?

And yet, the attorney general of the United States, just barely one year removed from referring to America as a "nation of cowards" in regard to race, had the audacity to testify before the House of Representatives and to profess anger that what people had risked during the civil rights era for "his people" had no basis in comparison to what the Black Panthers had done in Philadelphia during the 2008 presidential election cycle.

For those who have watched and listened to the attorney general over the years, this form of racial identification—cult of ethnicity branding of politics—is nothing new. What I find most disturbing about this incident was the reaction of the president and his White House staff. The exchange between Attorney General Holder and Congressman Culberson (R-TX) occurred on March 1, 2011. I was somewhat surprised that the reaction of the White House and the press corps that covers the president was precisely . . . nothing. No questions were posed to the White House press secretary, Jay Carney, in the week following the "my people" comment, nor was President Obama asked to offer his thoughts on the matter or whether he agreed or disagreed with his attorney general. Never shy before the cameras, not a single reporter thought to ask the president about such an inflammatory remark.

The president of the United States and the attorney general owe their allegiance to all of the citizens of America, not just those of a particular racial or ethnic affiliation. Holder's explicit identification with "my people" and the failure of the president to condemn such language as not representative of all Americans shows a lack of understanding of the Constitution both men swore to defend. Over the course of two years, the Obama Justice Department displayed a remarkable callousness to racial sensitivity, inflaming the nation by calling her citizens cowards on matters of race, fostering a climate where alleged black victims of crimes were favored at the expense of white victims, and the attorney general saw blacks rather than all Americans as his people. And the president's strategists wondered why they were steadily losing the support of white voters from the time of his historic election. I think we have a few insights as to why that occurred. As we shall see in chapter 7, it is hardly surprising that the president and his supporters have unleashed a backlash that only they can stop, before the voters do it for them in the November 2012 presidential election.

7. PLAYING THE RACE CARD HAS TAKEN AMERICA BLACKWARDS IN THE OBAMA ERA

||||||||||||||||||||||||||||||||||||||||||||||||||||||||||||

The Civil War happened because the Southern states, particularly the slaveholding states, didn't want to see a president who was opposed to slavery. In this case a lot of people in this country, I believe, don't want to be governed by an African American, particularly one who is inclusive, who is liberal, who wants to spend money on everyone and who wants to reach out to include everyone in our society. That's a basic philosophical clash.[1]

—Representative James P. Moran (D-VA), January 25, 2011

As THE EUPHORIA SURROUNDING PRESIDENT OBAMA'S ELECTION BEGAN to subside in the spring of 2009, Americans settled back and became better acquainted with their new leader. Perhaps Attorney General Holder's comment regarding America as being a nation of cowards had not yet resonated; President Obama's approval rating on April 7, 2009, stood at a respectable 62 percent, down slightly from 67 percent when he assumed office in late January.[2] Obama's numbers were approximately in line with those of President George W. Bush after being in office just over two months—President Obama remained popular and in the midst of a honeymoon period with his constituents.

As such, I was interested to read an article in *The Washington Post* a day earlier entitled "Blacks at Odds over Scrutiny of President." Odd. Why would blacks be at odds with those who sought to analyze or criticize the agenda of America's new president? President Obama had outlined an aggressive if not exhaustive agenda during his first quarter in office—a desire to enact sweeping health care reform, pass a jobs/ stimulus bill, and tighten regulations in the financial services industry. A very ambitious agenda, I thought, for a very ambitious young president in his opening months in office.

Nonetheless, the *Washington Post* article went on to discuss how there was a division deepening between two groups of the African American community: those who wished to continue to celebrate the Obama presidency for its historic nature and those who sought to examine Mr. Obama more objectively now that the election was over.[3] I confess I was always interested when I read phrases like "the African American community" because I never knew what that meant. Was I a member of a specific community based strictly on skin color, or were there other characteristics I shared with other African Americans that I was unaware of? I say this not to be contentious or contrary—I just have always found it odd that others assume a certain degree of solidarity or shared experience based exclusively on skin color—in this instance, being black as opposed to other deeply significant (and potentially divisive) factors such as income or religious beliefs, for example.

Nonetheless, I was surprised at the racially divisive nature of the piece even though I am certain that was not reporter Krissah Thompson's intended effect. After noting Obama's 91 percent favorable view in the African American community, the piece discussed hostility encountered by journalist Tavis Smiley when he criticized Obama's policies and encountered a phenomenon once the sole province of black conservatives: He was called a sellout, an Uncle Tom, and an Obama hater for his views.[4] I have often found this form of black-on-black racism akin to a bucket of crabs where one crab never reaches the top because others try to bring it down before it is allowed to escape.

Let me take a moment to explain this most unorthodox of terms. Civil rights activist and singer Harry Belafonte is emblematic of the type of individual who fights racism yet never hesitates to bring down other blacks who fail to share his view and the view of a self-anointed black cultural elite about what blacks should and should not think. The overwhelming majority who share Belafonte's mind-set would be content to see black conservatives fail in their endeavors rather than be successful in expressing and following a different ideological and philosophical path to achieve the American dream.

As Republicans sought to coalesce around a nominee to take on President Obama in the 2012 election cycle, a little-known businessman named Herman Cain rapidly rose through the Republican field and briefly into the lead for the nomination based on his dynamic charisma, his innovative tax plan (9-9-9), and his being outside the DC Beltway mentality. Rather than applaud Mr. Cain for captivating the attention of conservative Republicans and Tea Party activists as he traveled the country to support his candidacy, Belafonte and other so-called black thought leaders sought to tear Cain down *because* he was black and dared to offer a different political and cultural viewpoint than was considered "mainstream" in the "black community."

In a particularly revealing interview with *CNN Headline News* anchor Joy Behar, Mr. Belafonte offered the following:

> The Republican Party, the Tea Party, all those forces to the extreme right have consistently tried to come up with representations for what they call black, what they call the real Negroes [this in reference to former secretaries of state Colin Powell and Condoleezza Rice]. They're heroes for some people. But for a lot of us, they're not. Herman Cain is just the latest incarnation of what is totally false for the needs of our community and the needs of our nation. I think he's a bad apple. And people should look at his whole card. He's not what he says he is.[5]

There are many statements to unpack in Mr. Belafonte's commentary above. First, it is interesting that he sought to accuse the Republican Party and Tea Party activists of trying to come up with representatives of what were either "real blacks" or "Negroes." Had a black conservative made the same identical commentary about a black Democrat, the condemnation in the media would have been swift and furious. In this particular case, Mr. Belafonte, making such comments about black conservatives, hardly raised an eyebrow in the collective conscience of the mainstream media.

Next, it is Mr. Belafonte's view that Herman Cain, a successful CEO, businessman, and former director of a Federal Reserve Bank, was totally false and not in tune with the needs of the black community and the needs of the nation as a whole. How would Cain have been perceived as being "authentic" and real for the needs of the country in general and the "black community" in particular? I believe the mind-set of Mr. Belafonte and others would rather hold Mr. Cain and fellow black conservatives back and "inside the bucket," rather than escape the monolithic mind-set that postulates that blacks are entitled to special, rather than equal, rights—and that anyone who dared to think or articulate views to the contrary should be scorned and held back in failure rather than succeed and prosper by expressing differing views than the self-appointed black cultural and political leaders.

Sadly, the hateful comments directed toward Mr. Cain are not in isolation; I cannot think of a black conservative in public life who has not received such malevolent commentary. I should know; I have hundreds of e-mails offering similar assessments regarding television and radio commentary in which I offer conservative and independent analysis regarding the political issues of the day. A brief sample of what arrives in my e-mail on a nearly daily basis is below:

> Ron. can you stop by and pick the cotton on my plantation? You uppity Uncle Tom rib tip eating coon. God Bless! (November 29, 2011)

or

> For all your inuendos and read-between President Obama's lines, there's nothing worse than a Black Republican talking black for whites who dare not to. He's the "houseboy bastard son of the slave master" trying to distance himself from the field slaves, so he continues getting porkchops while the field

slaves get chitterlings. Have you seen the price of chitterlings today, or the shares in chitterlings on the stock market? Republicans and conservatives have NOT taken a step forward, they're side stepping to protect institutional racism, and give you a spin on your "read-between-the-lines," bigoted opinion of what our President is really saying. (October 9, 2011)

or

Saw your lying ass on the *Ed Show.* Hey, uncle tom, house negro, as [former vice president Dick] Cheney's slave, do you know if you'll be freed in his will, when he soon dies and drops dead, and burns in hell? (October 1, 2010)

Comparatively speaking, what Mr. Belafonte said in regards to Herman Cain being a conservative and seeking the most powerful job in the world appears relatively mild to the sampling from my in-box, but it was telling that Mr. Cain was granted protection by the U.S. Secret Service early in his bid for the presidency; I suspect his e-mail and phone lines received worse commentary than my own.

Let's return now to the discussion of Tavis Smiley's freedom to offer his thoughts on Mr. Obama's leadership and his efforts to hold him accountable for results in his book, *Accountable: Making America as Good as Its Promise.* Why would blacks be so seemingly indifferent to the racism they perpetuate against those with the same skin color? Rather than celebrating and welcoming diverse views of thought, blacks such as Smiley—who are a break from the monolithic plantation of thought whereby blacks are viewed as members of a racial and/or ethnic community rather than individual citizens expressing their unique viewpoint—are vilified for doing so. I should know—this has been the reality I have encountered for my entire life for daring to express and espouse conservative views that are often different from what black Americans are supposed to think, act upon, or believe. One would have hoped that the election of our first black president of the United States would have put an end to racial-identity politics once and for all, but as we shall discuss momentarily, I believe racial polarization and isolation has become worse, rather than improved, since President Obama's election.

Regardless, Thompson's article from *The Washington Post* referenced above quotes a black blogger who exemplifies the belief that disagreement of President Obama is akin to pulling a crab back down into the barrel:

> Glen Ford, who co-edits the left-leaning *Black Agenda Report,* says the pull to support Obama is powerful for blacks. When Obama ran for the U.S. Senate in 2004, Ford recalls, editors at the online publication endorsed him even though he was too middle-of-the-road for their tastes. "We did not want to be perceived as the proverbial crabs in a barrel trying to bring a brother down," Ford says.[6]

Even though Mr. Ford's thoughts expressed above related to Mr. Obama's run for the Senate in 2004, I believe they are all too representative of the views of many blacks in the United States today: I might not agree with his views but I don't want to bring a brother down, *because he's black.* This discouraging view is wrong on so many levels I don't know quite where to begin.

I believe it is the height of naiveté when considering the domestic and international challenges facing the United States today to vote for, and support, a candidate based strictly on the color of their skin. Like nearly every American, I celebrated President Obama's inauguration and assumption of duties as president of the United States because I believed then, as I do now, that he and his family have done more to change our impression of who we are as a people at home as well as impressions foreign nations will hold of us as Americans. At the same time that we celebrate our ability to support and elect a candidate based on their ideas, vision, and leadership, we lose ground as a nation by failing to hold that leader accountable for his actions or by persisting in supporting that individual strictly on racial grounds.

Is it any less racist to vote for a particular candidate because they are black than to vote for a candidate because they are white? In 2008 Americans nominated and subsequently elected the first president of the United States who also happened to be black. Didn't that fact alone signal that the American populace had evolved to look beyond skin color and assess a candidate for their leadership ability, persuasiveness, and political/policy agenda? I can safely hazard that 95 percent of whites would never blindly vote for a candidate because he or she was white; that alarm bells aren't going off in many of the black households that provided President Obama with 95 percent of the black vote (and did so because he was black) should be troubling. What about his views on foreign policy? A plan to reform Social Security and curb entitlement spending? A strong path forward to return America to economic and fiscal health? No. The cult of ethnicity we have discussed throughout apparently dominated critical analysis of Mr. Obama's candidacy to the extent that for many blacks it sufficed to pull the lever for a presidential candidate due to the color of his skin rather than the core of their convictions.

As I was quick to discover in 2009 and continue to observe as we head into the 2012 presidential election cycle, the charge of racism would extend far beyond blacks accusing other blacks not supporting President Obama of being sellouts or Uncle Toms; opponents of the president's political and policy agenda would soon be tarred with the same epithet should they articulate disagreements with the president's vision or agenda.

After pressing Congress to move quickly on his plan to revitalize the economy, President Obama signed the American Recovery and Reinvestment Act on February 17, 2009. Dubbed by the media as the "stimulus bill," President Obama pledged that the $787 billion package[7] would stunt job losses, put Americans back to work by undertaking "shovel ready" jobs at the state and local level, and provide tax relief for many Americans.

In January 2009, two advisers who were set to join President Obama's economic team, Christina Romer and Jared Bernstein, warned that failure to pass the stimulus bill would cause American unemployment rates to soar beyond 8 percent. In January 2009, the nation's unemployment rate stood at 7.6 percent; it would rise to 8.1 percent the following month despite the claims by the Obama administration that the stimulus bill would keep rates beneath 8 percent.

For the first time, many Americans found themselves in the position to judge the president not based on his historic arc to attain the presidency or the fluency of his words; citizens could ascertain whether Obama's veracity regarding his policies would affect them and the country had borne out against a demonstrable yardstick. In the present case, President Obama had pledged that unemployment would not rise higher than 8 percent if Congress presented him with his $787 billion stimulus bill—now Americans could assess the figures released by the Department of Labor's Bureau of Labor Statistics and see if the president's deeds matched his words. In the months following passage of the stimulus bill, the unemployment rate would rise to 8.1 percent in February 2009, 8.5 percent in March 2009, 8.9 percent in April 2009, and 9.4 percent in May 2009. One can match the president's statements about the unemployment rate to the actual rate increases reported since enactment of the stimulus package and conclude that perhaps more had been promised than was feasible to deliver.

Unfortunately, the discussion about the stimulus bill had taken a dark racial overtone just one day after President Obama signed the package into law. On February 18, 2009, the *New York Post* printed a cartoon depicting two police officers with guns smoking and standing over a chimpanzee they had just presumably shot with the caption reading: "They'll have to find someone else to write the next stimulus bill." I should point out that police officers in Connecticut had been forced to shoot and kill a chimpanzee that had violently attacked a woman the previous day. The immediate reaction, which would soon reverberate across the Internet and the mainstream media, to the *New York Post* cartoon was remarkable: a vicious and racist attack had just been launched against President Obama.

Having observed the *Post* cartoon in the newspaper myself that morning, I had barely given it a second glance; my main concern was over the poor woman the chimpanzee had mauled in Connecticut—

both of her hands had apparently been bitten off and her face would be brutally disfigured for the rest of her life.

Soon my telephone line would begin to ring with requests to appear on cable news television to offer my thoughts on the cartoon. I was flabbergasted at the time: everyone knew that President Obama had nothing to do with the drafting of the stimulus bill. In fact, the president had been rather roundly criticized for allowing the Congress to bulk up the package with the usual earmarks, bridges to nowhere, and other pet projects they include to fleece the taxpayers but look good to their constituents by bringing home money to their congressional districts.

But President Obama as being the chimpanzee in the cartoon? The thought had never once crossed my mind until others repeatedly brought that point of view to my attention. The following evening I was invited to appear on the *Anderson Cooper 360* television program on CNN to discuss the cartoon that had suddenly gripped the American consciousness and captivated many water cooler conversations across the country. Here is a brief exchange of the fireworks that had erupted around me:

COOPER: Ron, is there any other explanation to it for you?
CHRISTIE: I think there is. And here's where I think I might disagree with my two colleagues on this subject.

As a proud black man, I don't look at a chimpanzee as an African American. I don't look at it as a reflection of who I am and who African Americans are in this country.

And frankly, if it's supposed to be a portrayal of President Obama, the president didn't write the stimulus bill. The bill was written by Speaker Pelosi in the House and by Senate Majority Leader Harry Reid. For goodness' sake, we just had a chimpanzee who went nuts yesterday. The speaker of the House and the majority leader wrote the bill. The president didn't write the bill. The president probably hasn't had time to read the bill from the time [it was] sent to him in the White House until he signed it. So I don't think this is an indictment of President Obama. Let's just not try to find everything to be a racially insensitive matter. . . . .

[CNN Contributor Roland] MARTIN: Ron, can you not see the reality and the history in this now? Are you talking about—in terms of what was there. There was no chimpanzee with a sign underneath it that said "Congress" or said "Pelosi" or said "House Democrats." And so to sit here and to say that you can't equate the two, we understand that there's a history and a legacy . . . There's a history there. There's a legacy there. That's the whole point . . .

CHRISTIE: I also read the comments of the cartoonist who said that was not his intent. Let's give people the benefit of the doubt, as opposed to always finding racial problems in every situation.

[CNN Senior Political Analyst David] GERGEN: But Ron . . . but Ron, I hope—do you agree that a lot of people would look at that and say chimpanzee, baboon, Obama, they're trying to link all those together? Don't you think—do you not think it's open to that interpretation?

CHRISTIE: David, I think if you look at what happened with the chimpanzee who went berserk in Connecticut yesterday, that's how I looked at it. That's how I interpreted it. It was a very timely news event.[8]

Apparently, a raw nerve was still very much exposed and present on matters of race even as President Obama enjoyed a strong showing of popularity one month into his term in office. When I appeared on CNN that evening in February 2009, I was very much aware of the use of chimpanzees and monkeys to depict blacks throughout American history. As a frequent television political commentator myself, I had an even greater familiarity with the concept as the Internet is filled with identical descriptions of those animals as being representative of me. At the same time, what I said on air to Anderson Cooper and his guests was as true then as it is for me today: I never once considered such a cartoon or a depiction to have been analogous to President Obama. If I had, I would have led the charge on television and radio to denounce it, regardless of party affiliation.

And yet, I was repeatedly attacked personally on television and in the blogosphere for being delusional, a racist, and even a chimp myself. Fine. You put yourself in the public light and there are those who will disrespect you and the views you express. I understand that.

What I found most troubling, however, was the immediate rush to judgment that the *New York Post* had attacked Obama because he was a black president, not merely the president of the United States. No matter that a chimpanzee had gone berserk the day before in Connecticut and had been headline news in New York City for the manner in which it had maimed an innocent woman and ultimately had to be shot by police. I was just stunned by the ferocity of those that wanted the *Post* cartoon to be racist despite the fact that both the cartoonist and the newspaper itself said they had not intended any racial overtones with their errant attempt at satire. What did a chimpanzee filled with holes in a cartoon have to do with the president? If someone had said that had been a spoof on then Speaker of the House Nancy Pelosi or Senate majority leader Harry Reid I would have understood the allegorical connection more clearly: both leaders were widely credited with writing and shepherding the stimulus bill through the Congress.

But in this instance, the cartoon set the stage for what would be an all-too-familiar charge during the first term of the Obama presidency: If you disagree with the president based on policy or politics, you must be a racist. A cartoon depicting a bullet-riddled chimpanzee with a caption asking who will write the next stimulus bill? It could only be a racist media depiction of black people from days long ago, implying that America's first black president had been equated with a chimpanzee and not treated with respect.

When I tried to rebut this notion on CNN, I was called "delusional" by their political commentator Roland Martin. This was a phrase that would be repeated often of me over the airwaves and in the blogosphere. Was I delusional for thinking that the cartoon was an attempt at satire that had nothing to do with President Obama? Or were they delusional for thinking that racism lurked behind every corner and that any criticism of the president was rooted in racism?

The day I appeared on CNN on February 18, 2009, the headlines in newspapers and the banners on cable news outlets led with the narrative they had hoped or believed to be true. Here is one representative sample from *ChicagoTribune.com:* "Rev. Al Sharpton denounces *New York Post* editorial cartoon as racist—Civil rights leader says chimpanzee-stimulus bill depiction is a clear insult at President Barack Obama."[9] While Reverend Sharpton and I have been friendly over the years, the minute I heard he was out in front protesting the cartoon I knew that the issue wouldn't be covered with the objectivity it deserved. Sharpton equals controversy and controversy sells newspapers and pays for advertisements on cable news television programs— the media was certain to run with the story of "Obama as chimp equals racism toward our first black president" and run with it they did. Consider the following statement by Reverend Sharpton, which was widely disseminated both here in the United States and around the world:

> Being that the stimulus bill has been the first legislative victory of President Barack Obama (the first African-American president) and has become synonymous with him, it is not a reach to wonder are they inferring that a monkey wrote it?[10]

For its part, the *New York Post*'s statement in defense of their publication of the cartoon went largely unnoticed as Sharpton's voice was the one many in the mainstream media wanted to hear, not the editor in chief of the embattled newspaper. Lest both sides not be fairly represented, here is Col Allan's response to Reverend Sharpton as reported by the U.K. *Guardian:*

> "The cartoon is a clear parody of a current news event, to wit the shooting of a violent chimpanzee in Connecticut," he said. "It broadly mocks Washington's efforts to revive the economy.

Again, Al Sharpton reveals himself as nothing more than a publicity opportunist."[11]

We need not revisit the fact that I do not believe that the stimulus bill was synonymous with President Obama or that the depiction of a fallen ape was meant to represent the president. What I did find of interest was an article from *Mother Jones* magazine, certainly not a conservative- or right-leaning publication, in their analysis of the chimpanzee incident. Consider the following:

I'll leave Sharpton's motivation alone, but this whole thing seems a little puzzling. Consider three recent events.

1. January 20: A black man is inaugurated president of the United States.
2. February 16: Police shoot and kill a chimpanzee after it attacks his owner's friend.
3. February 17: President Obama signs the $787 billion stimulus package into law. It is widely seen, particularly by Republicans, as a gigantic boondoggle.

Guess which one of these is irrelevant to the cartoon? If you picked #1, you're right. This cartoon has nothing to do with the ethnicity of Obama's father and everything to do with the fact that the stimulus bill is messy. So messy, in fact, that it could have been written by a chimpanzee.[12]

Before we leave this discussion, I would encourage you to open your Internet search engine of choice and type "George W. Bush Chimpanzee." I was amazed to see numerous altered pictures and drawings depicting America's forty-third president as a primate. Oddly, I don't recall a media frenzy when those images were posted about Mr. Bush. Just a passing thought as we move along.

Certainly, February 18, 2009, brought unwanted attention to the president and his administration on matters of race. The *New York Post* published the chimpanzee stimulus bill cartoon and later that day Attorney General Eric Holder would deliver his now infamous "nation of cowards" speech at the Department of Justice. As we leave the chimpanzee incident behind, it is remarkable to think that President Obama had been elected on an optimistic campaign pledge to bring hope and change to America and had vowed repeatedly to set aside the petty grievances that had marked our political discourse and pull together as American citizens united by our love of country.

What this incident demonstrated more than anything else for me was the fact there were people across the country that had bought into the cult of ethnicity logic that refused to hail Obama's accomplishment of being elected president as emblematic of his political and oratorical skills and instead viewed him as an African American president, rather than a president of the United States who happened to be black. The net result of this mentality would be that any criticism of the president would be seen through the prism of racism rather than the viewpoint of a politician being assessed by his constituents for his legislative, foreign policy, and other achievements.

THE RACE CARD AS A WEAPON AGAINST DETRACTORS OF PRESIDENT OBAMA

What I didn't know then and am startled to know today is the extent to which supporters of President Obama—and even Mr. Obama himself—would equate criticism of his policies as being rooted in racism. And I believe that February 18, 2009—less than one month after he had been sworn in as president—was the day certain Americans started to lose faith in Obama's invocation of the motto of the United States of "Out of Many, One" to instead focus on the cult of ethnicity and identify their fellow citizens by the color of their skin and/or ethnic affiliation. This, of course, was the day Attorney General Eric Holder delivered his now infamous "nation of cowards" speech at the Department of Justice.

A presidency predicated on the theme of hope and change would soon devolve into an acrimonious and bitter campaign with partisans supporting the president resorting to calling his political and ideological opponents racist for failure to support either Mr. Obama or his policies. That many of these wounds were brought about by the vocal charges of racism from the president's supporters and even the president himself is the biggest travesty of all that we shall now discuss in greater detail.

With the president and congressional Democrats having passed and signed the stimulus bill into law, they next turned their attention to overhauling the nation's health care delivery system. Universal access and coverage for health care has been a priority of the Democratic Party for more than fifty years. At the same time, the American economy in the spring of 2009 could have been best described as anemic. People were concerned about keeping their job, a roof over their head, and enough resources to put food on the table.

As winter gave way to spring and early summer, the president and congressional Democrats were almost singularly focused on enacting a health care bill by year's end. A statement issued by the White House on June 6, 2009, revealed Mr. Obama's three key goals for a health reform bill:

> In his weekly address, President Barack Obama described his goals for fixing our broken health care system. With skyrocketing costs threatening fiscal collapse, real reform that provides quality, affordable health care for every American is a necessity that cannot wait. To do this, reform must be built on lowering costs, improving quality, and protecting consumer choice so people who are happy with their coverage can keep it.[13]

In short, President Obama promised that his health reform bill (yet to be written by the Congress) would lower the costs of health care, allow people to keep their current health coverage if they were happy with it, while also improving the quality of care delivered. All three goals of the president's reform package were laudable, but many skeptics across the entire political spectrum wondered aloud whether the president could expand access to coverage for some thirty million people, lower costs, improve quality of care, and still allow those pleased with their present insurance to maintain it without penalty. For a government several trillion dollars in debt, with archaic safety nets such as Social Security and Medicare seemingly headed toward insolvency, the president's promises on health reform seemed to many too good to be true.

Unfortunately, the myopic drive to push health care reform at the expense of strengthening the economy and reducing the size of government awakened the sleeping giant known as the American taxpayer. After projections of the cost of the stimulus bill rose to more than $800 billion and Congress rushed to pass a 2,700-page health care bill that would cost just under $1 trillion, people began to react angrily once they heard the president's package would add to the deficit rather than reduce health care costs, limit rather than expand coverage, and that many people content with their plans would either lose their health insurance or see their premiums rise dramatically.

These factors led to the rise of a political force that would realign the political landscape in Washington, D.C., and end the dominance of the Democrats running the government on either side of Pennsylvania Avenue from the Congress to the White House. The force had an innocuous sounding name—the TEA (Taxed Enough Already) Party—but soon charges would reverberate that its opposition to President Obama's health care reform efforts was thinly disguised racism. These serious allegations and the relatively miniscule proof offered to demonstrate a racist mind-set behind policy disagreements with the president would lead to a significant degree of anger toward President Obama and a steady erosion of white voters disillusioned with his use of the race card.

On April 15, 2009, thousands of self-identified Tea Party members took to state capitals across the United States in a symbolic gesture of the patriots who lined Boston Harbor 235 years ago to protest against high government taxation. What made the Tea Party protests against high taxes and government natural was the organic nature in which the demonstrations would mobilize. Unlike an established political party like the Republican or Democrat parties with extensive e-mail lists and connections to state political party structures, the Tea Party protestors mobilized via e-mail chains, Internet, and blog postings, and word-of-mouth encouragement.

Despite the efforts of certain media outlets and Democrat operatives that sought to characterize the Tea Party as an extension of the Republican Party, it became readily apparent that this was an independent group of citizens that was disgusted by the business-as-usual political climate in Washington, D.C. While the crowds were small at first, hundreds became thousands in cities across the country, all of whom were tired of the prospect of increased taxes, feared government control of health care, and skyrocketing federal budget deficits.

This narrative is important as it sets the stage for the volatile political mood facing President Obama as he stumped across America during the summer of 2009 to promote his health care reform bill as well as his pledge to reduce taxes for 95 percent of Americans. The Tea Partyers suspected that 95 percent of Americans did not mean 95 percent of American *taxpayers* given that half of the U.S. population does not pay federal income taxes; they feared that President Obama was attempting to "spread the wealth around," as he famously said on the campaign trail, from those that paid federal income taxes to those that did not.

The nation was embroiled in a serious discussion about the direction of the country as well as the legitimate size and scope of the federal government. While most opponents to the president's public policy agenda had their ire rooted in genuine and fundamental policy agreements, opponents to the Tea Party in the media and in the Democratic Party had quietly grumbled that opposition to the president was based on racism. On September 9, 2009, the strain between the two sides would explode in the open and dominate the political and national discourse for months following a speech President Obama had delivered to a joint session of Congress that evening.

The summer of 2009 had not treated President Obama kindly. When he began his town hall conversations about health reform in early June, his job approval ratings stood at a respectable 63 percent. The more the president discussed his health agenda, the lower his job approval ratings dipped in the polls. By September 1, 2009, according to Rasmussen polling data, the president's overall job approval ratings had slid at least 19 percent since the beginning of the year. According to a *U.S. News & World Report* article on his decline in the polls, 46 percent of Americans approved of the president's performance while 53 percent disapproved—the lowest level of support during the Obama presidency to date.[14] Columnist Bonnie Erbe of *U.S. News* captured the essence of the decline in President Obama's support when she observed:

> Why is the public losing confidence so quickly? My set of predominant reasons would differ from most others. First, he's a piker who's learning on the job and it shows. His stimulus package was not designed to have an immediate effect on the economy and he is not being credited with any improvement as a result. His laissez-faire approach to health care reform has fizzled.
>
> Top that with the fact he's made a number of tactical errors such as reaching out too much and too often to his opponents and they're not listening. But his liberal base is, and it's fuming on a number of fronts, including most recently his decision to increase troops in Afghanistan.
>
> Does that mean he won't win a second term? At this point I would say no. The disheveled GOP has yet to mount a candidate who can beat him. Maybe in a second term Mr. Obama will learn how to lead.[15]

While certainly a stinging indictment of the Obama presidency to date, I think Erbe's criticism mirrored what many conservatives and Tea Party activists truly believed: the president was learning to govern the United States while undergoing on-the-job training at a time when promised benefits from the stimulus package had failed to materialize and many were concerned about the enormous breadth and scope of his proposed health care reform.

As members of Congress returned to the nation's capital following fiery but peaceful town hall discussions in which their constituents had vented their frustration with the expanding size and scope of government, President Obama was urged to reverse the pendulum of public opinion, which had swung heavily against enacting health care reform. Seeking to put an end to this erosion of support among the American people as well as members of his own party, the president elected to address the nation during a joint session of Congress on September 9, 2009, to regain the initiative and press for passage of the health care bill by year's end.

As I watched the president deliver his remarks live from the well of the House of Representatives, I was struck by the feisty if not combative murmurs and body language as the cameras swept through the Republican side of the aisle. As one who worked on Capitol Hill and had personally attended nearly every State of the Union address for seven years, I was struck by the tone and the behavior of the assembled legislators: Republicans seemed to take issue and exception with all of what President Obama had to say, while Democrats were almost comically enthusiastic and boisterous in their attempts to show pleasure with Obama's push to complete work on the comprehensive health care package.

Of particular angst to Republicans was the sense that the legislation as written would permit illegal aliens to qualify for the benefits contained within the package. Over the summer, conservative members of the House and Senate had been outspoken in their opposition to providing such benefits to illegal aliens, and the president and his congressional allies sought to assuage such concerns by saying that only U.S. citizens and those in the country legally would qualify for the new health provisions once passed. As the Republicans fidgeted and murmured under their breath while their Democrat colleagues clapped and whistled along with Obama's remarks, the president took a moment to dispel the illegal alien receipt of services under the proposed health law:

THE PRESIDENT: Some of people's concerns have grown out of bogus claims spread by those whose only agenda is to kill reform at any cost. The best example is the claim made not just by radio and cable talk show hosts, but by prominent politicians, that we plan to set up panels of bureaucrats with the power to kill off senior citizens. Now, such a charge would be laughable if it weren't so cynical and irresponsible. It is a lie, plain and simple. (Applause.)

There are also those who claim that our reform efforts would insure illegal immigrants. This, too, is false. The reforms—the reforms I'm proposing would not apply to those who are here illegally.

AUDIENCE MEMBER: You lie! (Boos.)

THE PRESIDENT: It's not true. And one more misunderstanding I want to clear up—under our plan, no federal dollars will be used to fund abortions, and federal conscience laws will remain in place. (Applause.)[16]

And with just two words, previously unknown South Carolina Representative Joe Wilson (R-SC) would garner worldwide attention for the manner in which he interrupted President Obama's assertion that illegal immigrants would not be covered under the bill when he exclaimed "You lie!" As a stunned Speaker of the House and vice president looked to see who had shouted out to interrupt the president's remarks, Obama himself took a second to collect his thoughts before continuing on with his speech.

While I thought at the time that Wilson's conduct was unbecoming for a member of the House of Representatives to upbraid the president in such a manner, I also thought Wilson had given voice to the frustrations many conservatives and Tea Party activists felt about President Obama and his promises. After all, before passage of the stimulus bill Americans were told that unemployment would not spike higher than 8 percent; the unemployment rate for August 2009 was pegged at 9.7 percent in data released by the Department of Labor just five days prior to the president's remarks of September 9. Many companies had warned that the health bill in its present form would cause them either to drop employees or dramatically reduce coverage options. Trust with Washington and trust in President Obama's words versus action, was at a pretty low level among conservatives at the time he took to the well to address the nation on the benefits of health care reform.

That being said, while I believed Representative Wilson was wrong to have interrupted the president in the manner that he had, I believed him when he said he was frustrated and reacted spontaneously to the words President Obama had just uttered. Having met the congressman several times and spoken with him personally since his election to Congress, I thought the outburst was very much out of character for a man I believed was rather mild mannered and soft spoken. I thought at the time that he should immediately apologize to the president as well as his colleagues and put the matter behind him.

Unbeknownst to me, Representative Wilson had provided the president's supporters the opening they had been clearly looking for: expressing loud and vocal opposition to President Obama and his policies was racism, plain and simple. While I had watched the swelling ranks of the Tea Party with interest, I never had the sense that they were motivated by anything other than a fundamental disapproval with the direction President Obama sought to take the country. But racist? The thought hadn't crossed my mind. That is, until Representative Wilson provided the spark that lit a fuse beneath the president's supporters to allege racism was behind the growing and vocal opposition to Mr. Obama's policies.

Maureen Dowd, the caustic columnist for *The New York Times,* wrote an op-ed on September 13, 2009, entitled "Boy, Oh, Boy" regarding Representative Wilson and his outburst. While we discussed this column in *Acting White,* our present discussion is focused strictly on the manner in which people sympathetic to President Obama charged opposition to him, his policies, or his politics was grounded in racism. Dowd, perhaps seeking to be perceived as whimsical or clever, instead helped continue a destructive narrative in which not only was America a nation of cowards on race, many in the country were *still* racist despite the election of the first president who happened to be black. Consider the opening from her column:

> Surrounded by middle-aged white guys—a sepia snapshot of the days when such pols ran Washington like their own men's club—Joe Wilson yelled "You lie!" at a president who didn't.
>
> But fair or not, what I heard was an unspoken word in the air: You lie, boy! . . .
>
> I've been loath to admit that the shrieking lunacy of the summer—the frantic efforts to paint our first black president as the Other, a foreigner, socialist, fascist, Marxist, racist, Commie, Nazi; a cad who would snuff old people; a snake who would indoctrinate kids—had much to do with race.[17]

First, it is important to point out that Dowd was the one who inserted "boy" after "You lie." Congressman Wilson never uttered the term "boy," a pejorative toward blacks. Instead, rather than acknowledge the progress and the strides the country has made to increase the number of blacks serving in the Congress (presently 41 Democrats and 2 Republicans), Dowd exclaimed that President Obama was "surrounded by middle-aged white guys"—no matter that the House of Representatives that evening had nearly a hundred black, Latino, and Asian American members present. The more inflammatory insinuation was to suggest that the black president on the podium was surrounded by the middle-aged racists who felt his place was in the kitchen or with a tray on his hand than dictating policy. So in Dowd's world, a shout of "You lie!" translates to "You lie, boy!" because Obama was surrounded by a majority of whites?

Also notice how she grouped Representative Wilson in with the Tea Party rallies that had swelled in city after city throughout the summer across the United States. There will always be racists in America, and there were isolated reports that some fringe elements had carried signs that were racially offensive. But to brand an entire group of peaceful citizens making their voices heard by their elected officials as "shrieking lunacy" only reinforced the impression of many that Dowd represented an elitist and privileged disdain toward those who live in "fly over" states rather than the enlightened climes of the Upper West Side or San Francisco.

But Dowd wasn't finished with her attempt to paint those who were concerned by the expansion of government, increased taxes, and disapproval of President Obama's polices as racists. Undeterred, she pushed on by declaring:

> But Wilson's shocking disrespect for the office of the president . . . convinced me: Some people just can't believe a black man is president and will never accept it . . . Now [Obama's] at the center of a period of racial turbulence sparked by his ascension. Even if he and the coterie of white male advisers around him don't choose to openly acknowledge it, this president is the ultimate civil rights figure—a black man whose legitimacy is constantly challenged by a loco fringe.[18]

I would agree with Dowd that Wilson had shown disrespect to the office of the president. No question about it. I even agree that some people cannot believe a black man is president and will never accept it. But to suggest that President Obama was in the midst of a period of racial turbulence sparked by his ascension, Dowd demeans his very accomplishment of having been elected president in the first place. Both during the primary and general elections for the presidency, Mr. Obama prevailed in numerous states across the South as well as in rural areas in New England and across the Midwest. To suggest now that the country was in a racially turbulent period due to Obama's ascension to become America's first president of color does not square with the facts. Why?

During the presidency of Obama's immediate predecessor, George W. Bush and his administration were accused of being racially insensitive for insufficient efforts to help people in New Orleans following Hurricane Katrina. During "A Concert for Hurricane Relief" broadcast on the NBC network on September 2, 2005, to help residents of the Gulf Coast rebuild their lives following the crippling disaster, thirty-three-year-old rapper Kanye West infamously asserted, "George Bush doesn't care about black people."[19]

West's remarks served as a catalyst for other black leaders who had been frustrated by President Bush and his leadership to accuse him of racism—a charge that would reverberate throughout the country and spark heated debates. Consider Congressman Charlie Rangel's remarks during a Congressional Black Caucus town hall meeting several weeks after West's assertion that President Bush didn't care about black people, recounted in the following editorial from the *New York Sun:*

> "George Bush is our Bull Connor."
>
> Mr. Rangel's metaphoric linkage of Mr. Bush to the late Theophilus "Bull" Connor—who in 1963 turned fire hoses and attack dogs on blacks, including Martin Luther King Jr., demonstrating in favor of equal rights—met with wild applause and cheering at a Congressional Black Caucus town hall meeting, part of the organization's 35th Annual Legislative Conference. . . .
>
> The storm, he said, showed that "if you're black in this country, and you're poor in this country, it's not an inconvenience—it's a death sentence . . ." Mr. Rangel left his audience with a parting thought.
>
> "If there's one thing that George Bush has done that we should never forget, it's that for us and for our children, he has shattered the myth of white supremacy once and for all," the congressman said. [20]

Interesting. At a town hall meeting sponsored by the Congressional Black Caucus, a member of the "conscience of the Congress" asserted that the current president of the United States was of equal notoriety to Bull Connor, one of the most heinous figures and personification of evil from the civil rights era—a man who ordered violence and dogs to be set upon peaceful black demonstrators in Birmingham, Alabama.

In this vein, despite assertions from Ms. Dowd from *The New York*

Times, that the country had been placed in a racially turbulent climate due to the ascension of Mr. Obama to the presidency is demonstrably false. Black cultural and political figures such as Mr. West and Congressman Rangel were quick to play the race card when they deemed it would suit their political advantage to suggest that blacks were victims at the hands of white oppressors.

One final note about Congressman Rangel's remarks is appropriate at this juncture. Beyond the observation that he equated President George W. Bush to Bull Connor during a Congressional Black Caucus town hall meeting, it is important to know who was standing alongside the Congressman when he uttered his racist remarks: Senators Barack Obama and Hillary Clinton, Reverend Al Sharpton, and former congressman and NAACP head Kweisi Mfume. Their silence and acquiescence to Congressman Rangel's outrageous outburst was particularly deafening—a vivid illustration of the culture of revenge by self-appointed black leaders who do not seek equality and inclusiveness in America but instead perpetuate a culture of revenge by lashing out at what they deem to be white society.

Returning to our discussion of the Obama administration and their inflammation of race as a topic that divided the country along racial and ethnic lines rather than stress our shared citizenship, recall that it was Attorney General Eric Holder who first stepped into the national spotlight in February 2009 by declaring America to be a nation of cowards on matters of race. Next, it was Mr. Holder's Department of Justice that dismissed a case in which the department had prevailed in bringing charges against the New Black Panther Party for violating the Voting Rights Act of 1965 by intimidating voters.

Enablers of President Obama such as *New York Times* columnist Maureen Dowd conveniently ignore situations where the administration could have applied the law equally to prosecute violations of the Voting Rights Act against black defendants (Black Panthers) or make insensitive comments that inflamed racial tensions, such as the attorney general's remarks regarding America being "a nation of cowards" on matters of race. Instead, Dowd and certain black leaders were all too willing to play the race card to lash out against their political opponents in order to stifle legitimate conversations about the leadership and direction President Obama's administration sought to take the country. To this end, Dowd found a willing accomplice in the form of then House majority whip Jim Clyburn (D-SC), whom she cited in her piece. Of his colleague's outburst toward President Obama, Mr. Clyburn remarked:

> A lot of these outbursts have to do with delegitimizing him as a president. . . . In South Carolina politics, I learned that the olive branch works very seldom . . . You have to come at these things from a position of strength. My father used to say, "Son, always remember that silence gives consent."[21]

Remarkable. Now the dean of the South Carolina congressional delegation, a gentleman who happened to be black, was accusing Representative Wilson (and ostensibly the Tea Party) of outbursts seeking to delegitimize President Obama and that the olive branch should be ignored to resolve disputes in favor of a more militant response. Shouldn't Wilson's apology to the president have been enough to settle the matter since the professed outrage revolved around Wilson's alleged demeaning of Obama in the chamber of the House of Representatives?

I suspect it never occurred to people like Maureen Dowd and Representative Clyburn that frustrated citizens across the country had felt their government had delegitimized *them* by defiantly insisting on passing a health care reform measure that was losing popularity by the day amid concerns that the bill would cost too much, cover too few, and take away insurance coverage from patients who were happy with their existing plans. By instead accusing legitimate disagreements with President Obama's public policy agenda of racism, this line of attack only hardened racial resentment and created an increase of resentment based on race that remains to the present day.

Sadly, Maureen Dowd's column with its incendiary charges of racism in the aftermath of the Joe Wilson incident only accelerated efforts by others to speak out in a similar vein rather than acknowledge that legitimate policy disagreements with President Obama did not equal racism. Just two days later, Representative Hank Johnson (D-GA) went a step further by suggesting that Representative Wilson's outburst, if not addressed with a strict censure by the full House of Representatives (one step shy of expulsion), could trigger a reemergence of the Ku Klux Klan. I was stunned when I read the following report of Representative Johnson's statement:

> "He [Representative Joe Wilson (R-SC)] did not help the cause of diversity and tolerance with his remarks—if I were a betting man I would say it instigated more racist sentiment," [Representative] Johnson said Tuesday. "And so I guess we'll probably have folks putting on white hoods and white uniforms again and riding through the countryside intimidating people. . . . That's the logical conclusion if this kind of attitude is not rebuked, and Congressman Wilson represents it. He's the face of it."[22]

Once again, many black leaders have become all too comfortable utilizing race and perpetuating a culture of revenge by speaking in terms that do not promote equality and inclusiveness but instead lash out at what they deem to be demons in white society. Did Representative Johnson really believe that his colleague uttering "You lie!" to the president of the United States would return America to the days of the KKK donning hoods and intimidating people in the countryside? I would submit that Representative Johnson's own words were far more inflammatory and did not help the cause of diversity and tolerance—facts conveniently ignored by a media all too willing to perpetuate the myth that blacks are victims, in need of special, rather than equal, rights.

And while the forty-fourth president of the United States was unwilling to confront the rising racial tensions that were being fanned by those eager to score political points as they silenced legitimate policy disputes by alleging racism, America's thirty-ninth president was eager to enter the fray.

From September 15 to 16, 2009, as the country grappled with the "You lie!" remark and the accompanying charges of racism or racist sentiment, former President Jimmy Carter entered the debate. Appearing on *NBC Nightly News* with anchor Brian Williams, Carter only inflamed a volatile subject:

> In an interview with NBC's Brian Williams, former Democratic president Jimmy Carter attributed much of the conservative opposition that President Obama is receiving to the issue of race.
>
> "I think an overwhelming portion of the intensely demonstrated animosity toward President Barack Obama is based on the fact that he is a black man," Carter said. "I live in the South, and I've seen the South come a long way, and I've seen the rest of the country that share the South's attitude toward minority groups at that time, particularly African Americans."
>
> Carter continued, "And that racism inclination still exists. And I think it's bubbled up to the surface because of the belief among many white people, not just in the South but around the country, that African-Americans are not qualified to lead this great country. It's an abominable circumstance, and it grieves me and concerns me very deeply."[23]

So an organic, loosely organized network of citizens troubled by the rapid expansion of federal power emanating from Washington, D.C. has in Carter's view done nothing more than demonstrate animosity toward President Obama because he's a black man? I was insulted by this arrogant, simplistic explanation, as I think it is demeaning to blacks, since in Carter's myopic view people are unable to assess a black president based on his views and policies. The short and simple explanation for Carter was best intended as "If you don't like President Obama's views and stance on issues, you must be a racist." Period.

Interestingly, many people reacted with anger and passion when

President Bush elected to initiate military action against the governments of Iraq and Afghanistan during his presidency, but no one was accused of basing their displeasure with his decision to go to war on Mr. Bush's ethnicity. Yet President Carter was unable or unwilling to entertain the notion that not all disagreement with a president that happened to be black was based on race and racism.

President Carter continued down this line of misguided thinking when he shared with Brian Williams his belief that racist inclinations had bubbled up to the surface not just in the South but across the United States where people did not believe an African American was qualified to lead the country and that he, Carter, was greatly concerned about this unfortunate turn of events.

Again, do I believe some of the opposition generated toward President Obama is rooted in racism? Of course I do. But the notion that President Obama was not qualified to run the nation based on skin color alone is ludicrous. Quite to the contrary, there was nothing in then Senator Obama's background when he announced his decision to run for the Democratic nomination that led me to believe he was qualified to become the president of the United States and commander in chief of the armed forces and my rationale had nothing to do with the fact he was black.

Sadly, Mr. Carter wasn't finished with his racially tinged political analysis of the rising opposition to President Obama's politics and policies. The following day, while addressing students at Emory University, President Carter continued his assault on those who disagreed with President Obama as motivated by his skin color rather than his words and deeds in office. As CNN would report on the former president's exchange:

Former President Jimmy Carter reiterated Wednesday that he believes racism is an issue for President Obama in trying to lead the country.

"When a radical fringe element of demonstrators and others begin to attack the president of the United States as an animal or as a reincarnation of Adolf Hitler or when they wave signs in the air that said we should have buried Obama with Kennedy, those kinds of things are beyond the bounds," the Democrat who served from 1977–1981 told students at Emory University.[24]

While former President Carter undoubtedly felt he was offering both comfort and moral support from the thirty-ninth to the forty-fourth president, his counsel had the unintended impact of angering many people, myself included, who found his assessment to be racist, counterproductive, and more destructive rather than conciliatory on matters dealing with President Obama's policies and his ethnicity.

First, the Tea Party activists that gathered across the United States and in Washington, D.C., could not fairly be characterized as all being part of a "radical fringe element." But a majority of the Tea Party as being representative of a fringe element of disruptive people? Not very likely.

If only President Carter had applied the same logic and rationale to the treatment given to President Bush during his eight years in office. Signs of the former president depicted as Hitler and an animal (even a chimpanzee) and Bush's face being burned in effigy didn't seem to bother President Carter. To say nothing of Code Pink, an antiwar protest group seeking to attack Secretary of State Condoleezza Rice with hands dyed red to mimic blood as she testified in a hearing on Capitol Hill.

As I noted a few moments ago, this depiction of President Obama as the poor, hapless African American victim of racism rather than being the leader of the free world and subject to intense scrutiny did little to assuage the impression that Obama was due special consideration and dispensation for being black and thus off-limits for the harsh criticism suffered by his predecessors in office. Which makes President Obama's failure to address the issue head-on when Maureen Dowd, Representative Johnson, and former President Carter joined the chorus of Al Sharpton and others to declare that opposition to his policies was rooted in racism all the more regrettable. That truly would have been a teachable moment on race had the president told everyone to knock off the chatter of racism and brought a level of propriety and responsibility back to the political dialogue.

There was a reason why President Obama's approval ratings tumbled from nearly 70 percent to 45 percent in less than eight months in 2009. Were more than 20 percent of Americans now racist but they hadn't been several months prior? An analysis by Obama's own presidential campaign staff revealed that Obama had performed best during the primary election in states with the smallest percentage of black voters. Clearly, in the fall of 2009 racism was not the cause of Obama's rapidly declining popularity.[25]

Perhaps the government had not met the promises made to its constituents, as the unemployment rate continued to soar despite a massive infusion of taxpayer dollars designed to strengthen the economy and stem job losses. Perhaps President Obama could have better listened to the legitimate concerns articulated by those of opposing political parties and ideologies when they were concerned by stimulus spending, auto company bailouts, and a proposed health care overhaul that would have dramatically changed the relationship patients currently maintained with their health care provider with a brand of insurance they feared they would lose under the new system. As conservative columnist Kathleen Parker noted in her column "Playing the Racial Deck" in September 2009:

It is the height (or depth) of racism to suggest that any opposition to Obama's policies is race-based . . . Where racism appears, it needs to be exposed and expunged. But, let's be equally brutal about reverse racial sensitivity, the kind that obscures or hinders the search for truth . . .

Sources close to [Senator John] McCain's 2008 campaign say that he was so concerned about appearing racist that he was reluctant to emphasize his resume as a war hero vs. that of community organizer. He also had a list of words including "risky," that he refused to use for fear of connoting something racially negative about his opponent.

All of these are reasons enough to be sensitive to race but to also be wary of the racist epithet. Our racially divided past, and hoped-for unified future, is too important to be coopted for political purposes—by either side.[26]

If only more journalists, politicians, and partisan supporters of President Obama had had the opportunity to read and reflect upon Parker's words above. Given the powerful legacy and impact slavery and racism have had upon the fabric of the society in the United States, hurling the charge of racism to make a political statement only diminishes the impact and importance of such an allegation where the facts are warranted for doing so.

And so the pattern would continue as 2009 drew to a close and 2010 began. The American public remained deeply skeptical of the claims of President Obama, Speaker Nancy Pelosi, and Senate majority leader Harry Reid as they implored their colleagues to complete work on the health care bill and then move along to address jobs and economic empowerment issues. While polls varied on the president's job approval, CBS News reported in early January 2010 that Obama's approval rating had slipped to the lowest level of his presidency at 46 percent.[27]

Another CBS News poll taken the same day on January 11, 2010, had even more ominous news for President Obama: just 36 percent of Americans believed Obama was doing a good job shepherding health care reform, while 54 percent disapproved of the job he was doing to reform the American health care delivery system.[28] President Obama and his congressional leadership had a long road ahead of them to ensure passage of their landmark goal. Before we close our discussion of the utilization of the race card by supporters of President Obama—and eventually the occupant of the Oval Office himself—to dismiss legitimate criticism of his legislative and political goals, there are two key incidents that occurred in 2010 that bear brief mention at this juncture.

First, as poll numbers on the president's personal approval ratings and stewardship of heath care reform continued to decline, the executive director of the Virginia State Conference of the NAACP opined in the *Richmond Times-Dispatch* on March 22, 2010, that passage of the health reform bill would directly lead to a backlash against President Obama. Consider the following account as reported in the newspaper that morning:

> As landmark health care legislation cleared the house yesterday and makes its way to President Barack Obama, Virginia NAACP leaders predicted there would be a "blacklash" against it from opponents.
>
> King Salim Khalfani, in a news conference this morning, said that African Americans including the president still face racism and discrimination.
>
> "I am expecting more of a blacklash because it's affecting African people first and foremost," he said. Khalfani referenced Obama depicted as the Joker in whiteface, a witch doctor, and Hitler, and said that discrimination against people of color continues.[29]

I had honestly hoped that the beginning of a new year would usher in a new perspective among supporters of the president—with a full year in office, would they now regard criticism of Mr. Obama as a criticism of his leadership rather than always looking at him as America's black president? Yes, racism still existed in America at the start of 2010, but I had hoped that by President Obama following through on his promises to reform health care and to revitalize the economy that his supporters—and detractors—would assess him as a leader and not as a member of a particular racial and/or ethnic group. Substantive policy disagreements with Obama should have been analyzed, accepted, rejected, or refuted, but such a blanket forecast of impending resentment against the president only discredited their analysis as being the familiar "African Americans as victims" meme rather than an honest and intellectual assessment of the facts.

Just as Senator John McCain was afraid of using certain words or themes during his campaign against Obama for fear of being accused of being racist; now American citizens harboring no ill will toward their president but increasingly concerned about the direction the country was heading were now being equated to being members of the Ku Klux Klan.

And so it was that on March 20, 2010, the ultimate use of the race card was employed against members of the Tea Party during a demonstration on Capitol Hill as members of the House of Representatives were set to vote on the health reform bill. Hundreds had gathered to urge members to vote against the bill and there were loud, but respectful chants of "Kill the bill," which could be heard inside the congressional office buildings. I say this from a perspective of firsthand knowledge; I had been in the Cannon House Office Building for several hours that day to deliver political commentary for MSNBC on the looming vote.

As the story would develop, several members of the Congressional Black Caucus had emerged from their offices to walk across the street to the Capitol to vote on the bill. This is how the McClatchy Newspapers reported what allegedly took place:

Demonstrators outside the U.S. Capitol, angry over the proposed health care bill, shouted "nigger" Saturday at U.S. Rep. John Lewis, a Georgia congressman and civil rights icon who was nearly beaten to death during an Alabama march in the 1960s . . .

"They were shouting, sort of harassing," Lewis said. "But, it's okay, I've faced this before. It reminded me of the sixties. It was a lot of downright hate and anger and people being downright mean."

Lewis said he was leaving the Cannon office building to walk to the Capitol to vote when protesters shouted "Kill the bill, kill the bill," Lewis said. "I said 'I'm for the bill, I support the bill, I'm voting for the bill'," Lewis said.

A colleague who was accompanying Lewis said people in the crowd responded by saying "Kill the bill, then the n-word." "It surprised me that people are so mean and we can't engage in a civil dialogue and debate," Lewis said.[30]

The McClatchy article and accompanying quotations above were written as fact. What disturbs me is the manner in which the mainstream media immediately assumed Congressman Lewis and other members of the Congressional Black Caucus were assaulted with the *n*-word when there was actually no proof that such an incident took place other than from a member of Congress, Representative Emanuel Cleaver (D-MO), who had accompanied John Lewis and allegedly heard the slur being hurled.

While Congressman Lewis said that people were yelling at him as he walked to the House chamber, *he* never claimed that the *n*-word had been used against him. In numerous press accounts of the alleged event, readers were led to believe this racial epithet had been hurled at Lewis. Despite numerous attempts by those attempting to get at the heart of the story in the media, Congressman Lewis's office not only wouldn't provide the congressman to comment for the story, but they would neither confirm nor deny events as described in other outlets.

Moreover, there were numerous congressional staff members and others participating in the demonstration with cellular phones videotaping the event and no racial slurs were heard on contemporaneous coverage of the event that were posted on YouTube and other Internet outlets. If such a racially tinged event had occurred, why was there no video footage or others present who could corroborate the use of the *n*-word toward Congressman Lewis?

In an effort to dispel the notion that the Tea Party demonstrators were racist and had used offensive language during their demonstration on Capitol Hill, conservative columnist Andrew Breitbart posted a $100,000 reward to anyone who could provide indisputable proof that the *n*-word had been hurled at Representative Lewis and others as they walked outside of the Capitol that day in March. For all the certainty that the incident took place, I find it rather ironic that no one has come forward to claim the reward. Recall that the $100,000 would have been donated in the name of the person with corroborating evidence to the United Negro College Fund. One would assume that if such an event had occurred as described, a truth teller as well as a philanthropist would step forward to help a deserving student attend college.

The reason no one would come forward, of course, is the fact that I don't think the events as described ever took place. I was there the day of the protests and to a person, everyone I spoke to or saw was respectful yet passionate in being present to urge their representatives to vote against the health care bill. No one shouted a racial slur at me and I never felt uncomfortable. In fact, I had rather enjoyed myself as I spoke with people from across the country united in their respectful disagreement with what the House of Representatives was about to do by passing the president's health care bill.

In the weeks that followed the alleged *n*-word incident on Capitol Hill, many conservative columnists and concerned individuals sought to get to the truth of the matter. On April 24, 2010, Mark Skoda, founding member of the National Tea Party Federation, sent a letter to Representative Barbara Lee in her capacity as chair of the Congressional Black Caucus in an effort to find evidence that Representative Lewis had been assailed with the *n*-word. In part, Skoda wrote:

> The National Tea Party Federation (the "Federation") is comprised of approximately seventy-five local and national tea party groups, which collectively represent over 500,000 individual members. The Federation was formed primarily to create a unified message and media response amongst key leadership and their affiliates.
>
> The Federation does not and will not tolerate any form of racism, violence, or hate speech; in fact, its charter expressly re-

jects the same, and its membership rules specifically require that each member and its leadership comport themselves accordingly. It will not surprise you, therefore, that we treat each and every allegation of racism lodged against the Tea Party with the utmost concern, which is the reason we write you today.

As you are no doubt aware, on March 20, 2010, the Tea Party held a "Code Red Healthcare Rally" (the "Rally") on and around Capitol grounds in Washington, D.C. Both during and subsequent to the Rally, members of your Caucus, including Congressmen John Lewis, Andre Carson, and Emanuel Cleaver, but in particular Congressmen Carson and Lewis, alleged that members of the assembled Tea Party crowd hurled racial epithets at them multiple times, i.e., the N-word, fifteen times.

We believe to our core that racism and hate speech have no place in civil political discourse and debate—and, we are sure you agree. So, it is no doubt in our mutual interest to drill down on this incident and identify those persons alleged to have used the N-word at the Rally, so that they can be appropriately isolated and personally condemned.

Unfortunately, despite weeks of searching, we have been unable to find any evidence corroborating Mr. Lewis' and Mr. Carson's allegations.

We therefore turn to you, and respectfully request that you provide us with any and all evidence—video, audio, interviews, first-hand accounts, etc.—of the N-word being hurled against your members (or anyone else) during the Rally.[31]

As of this writing, there has been no response from Congresswoman Lee to the National Tea Party Federation's effort to find proof corroborating the use of racially offensive language. It is interesting to note, however, that *The New York Times* did offer a limited retraction due to Andrew Breitbart's repeated requests for proof of audio, video, or other information that would prove the truth of the allegations asserted.

On August 3, 2010, Breitbart posted the following on his Web site regarding the *New York Times*'s muted retraction:

> Buried at the bottom of a story published the other day, the *New York Times* printed a curious little correction:
> The Political Times column last Sunday, about a generational divide over racial attitudes, erroneously linked one example of a racially charged statement to the Tea Party movement. While Tea Party supporters have been connected to a number of such statements, there is no evidence that epithets reportedly directed in March at Representative John Lewis, Democrat of Georgia, outside the Capitol, came from Tea Party members.[32]

But in many ways, the damage had already been done. The media had reported from March 20, 2010, on that Lewis had been verbally assaulted with the *n*-word and liberal columnists, television commentators, along with various newspapers and magazines printed an ugly scenario as fact rather than determining whether the story had been embellished at best and fabricated at worst. Simply put, a false charge of racism is nothing less than racist itself. To suit their political narrative, opponents of the Tea Party turned to the race card and allegations of racism to thwart a sizable movement that threatened to wrest control of the House of Representatives and the U.S. Senate from the Democrats and put a brake on President Obama's ambitious agenda.

Not only did these allegations of racism hurt the reputation of those who recklessly hurled them, but also, I believe, they harmed the standing of President Obama among the constituents he was elected to serve—regardless of their skin color. After his repeated promises of a postracial America and his calls for reconciliation and unity during the campaign, the president's silence on an issue that divided the country, brought back painful memories from the violence employed against blacks during the civil rights era. That it appeared motivated by partisan politics rather than the truth only hurt the president's standing and reputation. His silence and lack of a visible presence reminding people to respectfully agree to disagree on sensitive matters in general and to be particularly careful not to inflame debates with allegations of race and racism was deafening. Quick to defend Professor Gates and admonish America to have a teachable moment on race on one hand and absent and steadfastly avoiding the difficult task of stepping in between two groups of people who were engaged in an ideological conflict that suddenly had racial overtones was a missed opportunity to lead the country and bring her citizens closer together was not missed by those looking for America's first president who happened to be black to be relevant at a key juncture.

As the drumbeat of "Tea Party is racist" continued rather than subsided, a subtle shift in perspective took hold between President Obama and many of his constituents and those who had pulled the lever for him in 2008. Disillusioned voters began to move away from the party of hope and change to seek leadership from the Republicans or to become independent of either political party. The hostility generated by being constantly accused of being a racist while government continued to expand its size, scope, and reach would take its toll on President Obama and the Democratic Party later that year. Consider this remarkably prescient column written by David Paul Kuhn in the *Los Angeles Times,* entitled "Why Democrats Are Losing White Men," written just days after the Lewis/Tea Party confrontation, on March 22, 2010:

> Millions of white men are walking away from the Democratic Party. In November, their departure could well lead to a GOP landslide on a scale not seen since 1994 . . . Today, among whites, only 35 percent of men and 43 percent of women say they'll back Democrats in the fall . . . White men have moved away from Obama as well. Only 38 percent approve of the president, which means that millions of white men who voted for Obama have now lost faith in him.

Kuhn was nearly clairvoyant in his prediction. Republicans would gain sixty-three seats during the November 2010 midterm elections and wrest control of the House of Representatives from the Democrats—

winning the highest total House victory for a single party since 1948 and the Republicans' largest midterm election victory since 1938.

Despite the optimism and enthusiasm over President Obama and the Democrats' control of the federal government in 2009 after eight years of Republican leadership, passions cooled and cynicism mounted once the president was forced to govern rather than campaign. An unpopular health care bill, a dramatic increase in federal spending, and the sense that Washington, D.C., remained out of touch on key pocketbook issues caused many voters to turn away, disillusioned by what had taken place during Obama's first two years in office.

I further believe the incessant charges of racism and other inflammatory rhetoric emanating from the supporters of the president that were largely uncorroborated exacted a significant toll against Mr. Obama in both his popularity and people's perception of him as a leader. President Obama's deeds did not match his actions on bringing the country together on key policy issues in general, and he and his administration either inflamed racial conflict through their actions or remained curiously silent when a strong voice and leadership were desperately needed.

As we will discuss in our final chapter in the following pages, President Obama has the opportunity to quell the racial disharmony that has crippled his presidency and made him vulnerable to defeat in his bid for reelection later this year. Only by speaking with a strong voice and with clear moral conviction can the president calm the tempests that roil his presidency. From Attorney General Holder's nation of cowards comment to the teachable moment on race with Professor Gates and countless other incidents of alleged or perceived racism, President Obama's silence where a calming voice was necessary to subdue supporters of his presidency and policy agenda who hurled charges of racism in the face of scant evidence will present him with a difficult challenge to prove that he is the leader of all of the citizens in the United States not just a selected few based on skin color and/or ethnicity.

As mentioned previously, to charge racism in the absence of proof of such allegations is racist in and of itself, but in a more insidious form. Seeking to asphyxiate the will and desire of those in opposition to the president's agenda with charges of racism is not only morally wrong but also corrosive to the fabric that holds our society together. Barack Obama's failure to personally intercede and lead the country forward and past this cowardly attempt to stifle legitimate opposition to his policies, had little or nothing to do with him as a person or the color of his skin but tarnished his legitimacy when he failed to speak out and remind voters he had been elected as the leader of all the citizens of the United States, not just those who shared his policy goals or the skin color.

THE HYPOCRITICAL PARADOX OF THE REVEREND AL SHARPTON/ PRESIDENT OBAMA ALLIANCE

A serious discussion regarding the crass manner in which the race card has been used as a weapon by so-called black leaders advocating for special, rather than equal, rights while seeking to destroy legitimate debate would not be complete without a special examination of one of the most infamous practitioners of this most destructive trade: the Reverend Al Sharpton. Sharpton, as of this writing, is the daily talk show host of MSNBC's *PoliticsNation* television program. Though he is billed by MSNBC as "the civil rights activist and minister," I suspect many Americans under the age of forty have little idea to the extent Mr. Sharpton made a name for himself by perpetuating a culture of revenge in which those who stood in his path were tarred with the charge of being racist as he sought his own personal fame, fortune, and recognition in the name of being a civil rights activist and a minister.

Sharpton rose to national prominence in 1987 after the shocking rape allegations of Tawana Brawley were brought to light. Brawley, then a fifteen-year-old girl from suburban New York City, had transfixed the nation with her claim that she had been abducted and repeatedly raped in the woods of upstate New York. What made her allegations all the more troubling is that Brawley, when found several days later, was in a bag covered with dog feces, with racial slurs written upon her body. Brawley, a young black girl, had claimed that at least two white men, possibly as many as six, some of whom were police, had committed these terrible deeds.

As news of the story broke across the country, the Reverend Al Sharpton stood before the microphones and cameras as Brawley's adviser and spokesman. As the police investigated the matter more closely, inconsistencies in the young girl's story began to emerge. Rather than cooperate with the police and grand jury investigating the charges, Sharpton advised Brawley not to testify.

New York governor Mario Cuomo (D-NY) asked the attorney general of the state of New York to investigate; Sharpton infamously noted that asking Brawley to cooperate and speak with the attorney general looking into the matter would be like "asking someone who watched someone killed in the gas chamber to sit down with Mr. Hitler."[33]

By late 1988, the grand jury had concluded that the story Brawley told had been concocted; she was not the victim of kidnapping, rape, or sexual assault. It was a cruel hoax that had needlessly inflamed racial tensions in the United States, but one which firmly placed Sharpton's larger-than-life personality within the context of the national dialogue. Some ten years later, one of the defendants in the case successfully brought a defamation lawsuit against Sharpton in which Sharpton was ordered to pay $65,000. Proclaiming his innocence in light of two court decisions in which Brawley's deceits were successfully prosecuted—and for which she ultimately recanted and admitted perjury—Sharpton would proclaim statements such as: "Apologize for what? For believing a young lady," or "When people around the country know that I stood up for a young lady . . . I think it will help me."[34]

What this story, tragic for the innocent people caught up in the lies and deceit of Brawley and Sharpton, illustrates is that the civil rights activist and minister was never about reaching the truth. He was more interested in the ends justifying the means—Sharpton *believed* Brawley's story even after it had been proven to be demonstrably false . . .

so why should he apologize for something that wasn't true when he believed it to be so?

This is important as linguist John McWhorter noted in his seminal work *Winning the Race: Beyond the Crisis in Black America,* since Sharpton was integral in ushering in a new era in which America looked at so-called black leaders not based on their qualifications for office or influence, but instead, because they "acted out" and sought special treatment based on race, rather than equality itself.

> Before long, black "leaders" committed to acting up over action were accepted as normal on the black political scene. Al Sharpton rose to prominence in the 1980s refusing to recant his support of an arrantly mendacious rape accusation by a teenage black woman . . . The idea of this as progressive is senseless unless we see that theatrics was the point. Sharpton has since done nothing to indicate otherwise: He has spearheaded no legislation and given no sign of wanting to, and his National Action Network has only made *gestures* toward his stated goal of registering black voters. Yet there has been no nationally influential body of black leaders directly and sustainedly decrying Sharpton's tactics and freezing him out of all substantial discussion of blacks' plight.[35]

The gulf between the career trajectories of the Reverend Al Sharpton and President Obama could not be any wider—Sharpton made a name for himself on the national scene by playing the race card, while Obama assiduously avoided doing so. Yet, as President Obama faced increasing pressure from members of the Congressional Black Caucus and many in black media outlets for not pursuing a sufficiently black agenda, it was the Reverend Al Sharpton to whom the White House turned for help to help quell the political squall from the so-called black community. Once a man castigated for being kerosene on the American political landscape for nakedly pursuing an agenda for blacks to receive special, rather than equal, treatment in society, Sharpton was quick to embrace his new role and the perception of legitimacy afforded him by President Obama.

According to an August 3, 2010, cover story in *Newsweek* magazine entitled "The Reinvention of the Reverend Al," President Obama often seeks the counsel of Sharpton, a man who in his own words in the article notes: "My mission, my message, and everything else about me is the same . . . The country may have changed, but I haven't."[36] Judging from Sharpton's recently articulated views, it is clear that he still sees America as a country divided between blacks and whites—a country where blacks are entitled to special, rather than equal, rights.

Consider, for example, the following offered by Sharpton in comparing former president Bill Clinton to President Obama regarding their support in the so-called black community:

> [Bill] Clinton passed laws like welfare reform that really hurt us, and all these people were willing to give him a pass. We get the first black president and we're ready to knock him down before he's in there fourteen months. What has he done to hurt us?

A short review of the facts shows that both of Sharpton's above assertions are demonstrably false; yet Sharpton must have known that the reporters covering him and his statements would never delve deeper to ascertain the truth. Instead, his comments fit a narrative that the mainstream media is comfortable with—blacks needing special, rather than equal, treatment in current American society—and the issue is left unaddressed.

The Personal Responsibility and Work Opportunity Reconciliation Act (aka, "welfare reform") enacted in 1996 set forth three very important legislative goals: (1) reduce dependence on government assistance; (2) reduce child poverty, and (3) reduce rates of illegitimacy, while strengthening marriage.[37] A five-year assessment of the dramatic overhaul of the welfare delivery system conducted in 2001 showed that all three key areas of reform had been met.

First, in the five-year period after enactment of welfare reform, the number of Americans receiving Aid to Families with Dependent Children (AFDC) and Temporary Assistance for Needy Families (TANF) dropped by more than 50 percent. Next, the levels of child poverty in the United States dropped from 20.8 percent when the welfare reform bill passed in 1996 to 16.9 percent in 1999. More directly, during that time frame, the black child rates had dropped to the lowest points in U.S. history.[38]

Finally, beginning with the new tone set in Washington, aimed at limiting, for the first time in U.S. history, both the amount of time and assistance an individual could receive from the welfare program, illegitimate birth rates declined in the United States. According to a study entitled "The Effects of Welfare Reform," written by Heritage Foundation scholar Robert Rector, black illegitimacy rates continued to decline and that:

> The unique and dramatic slowdown in the growth of illegitimacy clearly coincided with Welfare reform. The slowdown is undoubtedly the result of changes in the social messages surrounding Welfare, particularly the new emphasis on limited aid and personal responsibility.[39]

This brief discussion is critical; immediately following passage of welfare reform legislation signed into law by President Clinton, the three main goals of the statute were not only met, but had paid particularly good dividends on black households across the country by lowering dependence on the government while lowering child poverty and illegitimacy rates. How, then, could Mr. Sharpton claim that such a law "really hurt us"? Because he knew that he would never be challenged to put forth facts to prove his assertion. Ironically, the color-blind welfare reform bill did more to help all Americans regardless of the color of their skin by treating them equally—cash payment and time limits would be applied to those who qualified for such programs based on their income, rather than skin color.

Next, Mr. Sharpton claimed that President Obama was being

unfairly criticized by some in the black community despite his limited time in office—"what has he done to hurt us," Sharpton asks. Presumably, the "us" is members of the so-called black community in America. In 2009, following President Obama's first full year in office, black unemployment in the United States stood at 15.6 percent—a marked contrast between Hispanic unemployment at the end of 2009 (12.7%), whites (9.3%), and Asians (7.3%).[40]

By June 2011, the unemployment rates for blacks in the United States had gone from bad to dire—16.2 percent overall, with 17.5 percent of black males unemployed.[41] In Sharpton's home of New York City, black unemployment stood at 34 percent for young black men aged 19 to 24.[42] By September 2011, black unemployment had spiked to 16.7 percent—the worst level for blacks in the United States since 1984—some twenty-seven years.[43] An objective review of the number of black Americans working in the United States had declined since President Obama had taken office, while the number of people seeking employment in the same demographic had significantly increased.

When Sharpton asked the subjective question during the summer of 2010 "What had President Obama done to hurt 'us,'" an objective observer might have noted that the president's stimulus package and other measures had not had the intended effect of reducing unemployment in America in general and that African American communities in particular were hardest hit.

This is just one telling example of how Al Sharpton elected to present himself as a leader of black people rather than a leader of those Americans whose voices deserve to be heard—regardless of the color of their skin. An objective observation of the impact on President Clinton's efforts to forge compromise with congressional Republicans in 1996 demonstrates that many Americans who were previously enrolled in federal welfare were able to wean themselves from government assistance while child poverty and out of wedlock birth rates decreased.

Similarly, unemployment rates steadily increased during the first term of the Obama administration, despite assurances that passage of the president's stimulus and other economic reform measures would keep unemployment beneath 8 percent. A more objective evaluation of the president's performance might well conclude that his stated objectives did not match their desired outcomes. Instead, as we will discuss momentarily in how best to move past the rising backlash in America in chapter 8, supporters of President Obama must ground their support for him as an individual and a politician, rather than assessing his success or failure based on the color of his skin.

Let me offer a few final observations regarding the double standard Sharpton employs to demand for special, rather than equal, rights for blacks. First, Sharpton joined radio talk show host Tom Joyner's call for blacks to stick together in support of President Obama because of his race rather than his performance in office. As *The Washington Post* would note:

> For several months, [Joyner] has pleaded with his 8 million listeners to get in line behind the first black president. "Stick together, black people," says Joyner, whose R&B show reaches one in four African American adults. The Rev. Al Sharpton, an ally of President Obama who has a daily radio show and hosts a nightly cable television program, recently told the president's black critics, "I'm not telling you to shut up. I'm telling you: Don't make some of us have to speak up."[44]

Sharpton's line is particularly telling, and also a sad commentary that so-called black leaders have used with increasing regularity against those who dare to articulate thoughts or a viewpoint different than their own. In a thinly veiled threat, Sharpton is telling blacks who would publicly disagree with America's first black president that they should proceed carefully lest Sharpton and his ilk attempt to silence their opposition by "speaking up." Yet another vivid example of how these so-called black leaders would use their position to lash out against those they deemed either to be a threat or offer a differing viewpoint than what the self-anointed black leaders characterize what purports to be mainstream black thinking.

As for Mr. Joyner, he appealed to the emotion and sensibilities of blacks rather than threaten suppression like Mr. Sharpton, when he elaborated:

> We have the chance to reelect the first African-American president, and that's what we ought to be doing. And I'm not afraid or ashamed to say that as black people, we should do it because he's a black man.[45]

Although the manner in which each man sought to deliver his appeal was different, the message they both delivered was equally saddening to me: support President Obama based on the color of his skin rather than the totality of his accomplishments and/or failures. In other words, cast your ballot to reelect Obama and perpetuate the notion that America's first black president must be treated differently—with special consideration—because he's black rather than an American politician seeking to be rehired despite the fact that such special treatment of Obama is detrimental to our cohesiveness as a society based on individual citizens rather than differing groups of racial and ethnic members.

Sharpton was quick to race to a microphone to allege racism and discrimination by Republicans in light of the move by several states to tighten up the electoral process to prevent fraud by requiring citizens to show a valid ID before receiving their ballot. As discussed previously, the notion that to apply a law in a racially neutral manner to require such identification as racist is troubling. This perpetuates a myth that blacks are inferior, in need of special, rather than equal, treatment before the law, and otherwise feeble and ignorant. Not to Mr. Sharpton, though—he alleged in an op-ed written for *The Huffington Post* that the old days of Jim Crow have returned in the twenty-first century with the first African American to occupy the Oval Office.

> [T]he federal Voting Rights Act superseded individual state's attempts at bigotry and marginalization. Now, more than forty

years after the historic success of this historic legislation, many
Republicans would like to slowly and covertly repeal the practice by establishing voter ID requirements in an effort to re-
strict individuals participating in the process. My message to
them: don't think you're fooling anyone; we see your attempts
at stealing the 2012 election and you will not get away with it.[46]

Never one to let facts get in the way of a good narrative he's interested
in telling, Sharpton's statement is revealing in regards to who is racist
and who is not in our society today. What facts does he offer to show
that Republicans would like to "slowly and covertly repeal" the success
of the Voting Rights Act of 1965? Are there specific Republicans he
can point to? Are there specific comments in which Republicans have
indicated that they seek to nullify the right of blacks to vote in the
2012 election? If so, let's have that discussion. If not, Sharpton's pan-
dering for special, rather than equal, treatment for blacks under the
law belittles the cause of people he claims to want to help. Are blacks
so ignorant, inferior, and incapable of obtaining an identification card
to navigate in today's society? If Sharpton's view is correct, is it any
less racist to require identification for purchasing allergy medication
and alcohol, or obtaining a driver's license to operate a car? Few would
dare challenge Sharpton on his assertions lest he brand them as a racist
or use his position to lash out against his political opponents—I reject
the notion that blacks cannot themselves be racist and the hurling of
what I believe to be scurrilous and baseless accusations by Sharpton
above is simply racist and inflammatory language without proof to
shed light on his allegations.

Finally, I should note one final hypocritical pose by Mr. Sharpton
before moving on. During late 2011, Sharpton was particularly outspoken against Republican opposition to extending a payroll tax
holiday for American workers—despite legitimate criticism that such
an extension would not promote strong economic growth. On the
December 5, 2011, broadcast of his show on MSNBC, Sharpton
would thunder: "[T]he fight to keep money in the pockets of 160 million Americans continues, but Republicans are fighting against it."[47]

There was only one motive for that statement—Sharpton wanted his viewers to believe that Republicans were mean-spirited by not allowing taxpayers to keep more of their hard-earned money. What was truly mean-spirited and hypocritical was the behavior displayed by Mr. Sharpton himself—one who in late 2011 owed the federal government more than $880,000 in payroll taxes!

According to the December 12, 2011, edition of the *New York Post,* Sharpton's National Action Network advocacy group and two for-profit companies were $5.3 million in debt and owed $2.6 million in federal taxes, nearly $900,000 in state taxes, and $883,503 in payroll taxes—even though Sharpton was kind enough to pay himself a salary of $241,732.[48] For Sharpton to assert that Republicans were fighting against keeping money in the pockets of 160 million Americans while he himself had failed to pay nearly one million dollars in taxes owed to the federal government is beyond the height of hypocrisy. I believe this is the embodiment of self-anointed black leaders preaching one level of piety others should follow while they elect to follow their own separate and inherently unequal rules. Apparently, President Obama, in his zeal for reelection, did not feel compelled to remind his friend to pay nearly one million dollars in federal payroll taxes while he and Mr. Sharpton railed against their political opponents.

For a president who sought to heal the racial rifts that have challenged American citizens since our founding more than two hundred years ago, the choice of Al Sharpton to become one of President Obama's confidants is a puzzling one. A man who has largely made a name and a career for himself by being involved in controversial matters of race is hardly the first person one would expect the president to lean upon. There are some, like Todd Boyd, a professor of critical studies at the University of Southern California, who "see a cynical ploy by Obama to use Sharpton as a foil to [Jesse] Jackson, embracing, as he puts it, 'the lesser of two evils.'"[49]

Perhaps there is a more simple, yet discouraging explanation. Heading into a presidential reelection just months away, President Obama has seen his support among high school–educated whites and Hispanics erode, while African Americans overwhelmingly embraced

Mr. Obama's candidacy four years ago and seem all but certain to cast more than 90 percent of their ballots for his reelection bid.

After the hope and change promised in his original campaign, Mr. Obama appears to have now abandoned that pledge to mount a reelection campaign based not only on blaming Republicans for the difficult economic environment in America, but also on rallying African Americans and other ethnic minorities to his side to eke out a narrow victory. The president who labored assiduously not to be the next "black" candidate seeking the Oval Office in 2008 today sees his potential return to office paved with a specific strategic approach in which blacks are motivated to reelect him *because* he is black. A winning strategy perhaps for President Obama's political fortunes—but a significant step back for race relations in the United States and her citizens as a whole by the deliberate and cynical choice of our first black president choosing to court support based on the color of his skin rather than on his ideas and record leads to an ethnically and racially divided America.

8. THE PATH AHEAD TO STOP HEADING BLACKWARDS

||||||||||||||||||||||||||||||||||||||||||||||||||||||||

THE UNITED STATES OF AMERICA HAS UNDERGONE A DRAMATIC TRANSformation over the past ten years. What once seemed impossible—the election of a black man to become president of the United States—has become reality. A country that has struggled over equality since its founding 225 years ago has seen blacks assume some of the most prominent positions in government, finance, academia, and the arts due to their hard work, intellect, and ambition. As a society, America has in many ways become stronger by following the motto: "Out of Many, One."

And yet, the election of the first black man to the presidency has also confronted America with unforeseen challenges. While most people thought America may have entered a new, "postracial" era, there were many others who believed that President Obama would confer special, rather than equal, rights on people of color because their race and ethnicity were the same as his. As the Obama administration settled into the routine of running the nation, some citizens were unable to view Mr. Obama as the first president who happened to be black rather than as America's first black president. This would lead to charges of racism and/or discrimination against those with legitimate policy or legislative disagreements with the president and elected representatives in Washington, D.C. Many Americans became disillusioned when the hope and change promise dissolved into business and politics as usual. Even worse, however, was the sense that President Obama and his administration were playing the race card to demonize their opponents.

Consider, for example, the interview President Obama conducted with *Rolling Stone* magazine in October 2010. When asked for his views on the Tea Party movement, the president replied:

> There are strains in the Tea Patty that are troubled by what they saw as a series of instances in which the middle-class and working-class people have been abused or hurt by special interests and Washington, but their anger is misdirected.
>
> And then there are probably some aspects of the Tea Party that are a little darker, that have to do with anti-immigrant sentiment or are troubled by what I represent as president.[1]

The president's exchange above is particularly surprising to me in that there is a calculus in Mr. Obama's thinking that automatically gravitates to the "opposition of Obama as racist" mind-set. Having attended several Tea Party rallies myself, the unifying message I have encountered is that there are a large majority of citizens who believe that their elected representatives in the White House and in the U.S. Congress have dramatically increased the size, scope, and influence of the federal government. These rallies were intended to be a rallying cry not unlike the original Boston Tea Party of America's revolutionary days, when the tyranny and power of the throne proved too much to America's earliest colonists. Two hundred and thirty-six years later, a new group of citizen discontent predicated on the conviction that they have been "Taxed Enough Already" (TEA) spurred many citizens to peaceful yet vocal demonstrations against the direction their leaders in Washington, D.C., sought for the country.

Rather than brushing off such criticism as being misguided, President Obama and the Congress added $5 trillion to the national deficit through increased spending, causing many more Americans to question the wisdom of adding a new health care entitlement program in the midst of difficult economic times. Misguided or not, Americans are allowed to harbor legitimate policy disagreements with their president and are further permitted to show their displeasure through anger. More telling, however, was the president's view that there were "some aspects of the Tea Party" that were "a little darker," or were troubled by what Obama represented as president. His line of reasoning is danger-ous and reveals why the president has lost a significant number of inde-pendent and white male voters since the 2008 election cycle.

Moving beyond his hope and change theme, intertwined with the notion of "Obama as Lincoln" and uniter of America in times of con-flict, citizens were able to reflect upon the president's actions once it became time to govern rather than campaign. I can't think of a presi-dent, Republican or Democrat, in the last thirty years who has done more to single out people for harboring ulterior racial motives as they went about their daily lives. Cambridge Police Department? Acting stupidly based on race. Tea Party protests? Misguided, angry people motivated by darker motives based on what Obama represents as presi-dent. Not only does this line of behavior belittle the office of the presi-dent but it diminishes the present occupant of the Oval Office as well.

It is not the president's job to openly speculate about the racial moti-vations of his constituents. Yes, racism remains in America today but to openly opine about what moves people to action based on race is improper and goes against what the president himself had said moti-vated him while on the campaign trail. Consider the following of what then Candidate Obama spoke of in his admiration for President Lincoln:

> But the second thing I admire most in Lincoln is that there is just a deep-rooted honesty and empathy to the man that al-lowed him to always be able to see the other person's point of view and always sought to find that truth in the gap between you and me. Right? That truth is out there somewhere and I don't fully possess it and you don't fully possess it and our job then is to listen and learn and imagine enough to be able to get to that truth.

If you look at his presidency, he never lost that . . . And
Lincoln just found a way to shape public opinion and shape
people around him and guide them without tricking them or
bullying them, but just through the force of what I just talked
about—that way of helping to illuminate the truth. I just find
that to be a very compelling style of leadership.[2]

If Candidate Obama really admired President Lincoln's ability to em-
pathize with another person's point of view in seeking the truth, then
President Obama must have left behind these same attributes in Chicago, for he did not display the same character traits while dealing with
political dissent from the Oval Office.

Often during the first three years of his first term in office President Obama publicly took sides to praise political supporters and allies
while also seeking to demonize his opponents. That he would further
do so in terms of race, I believe, has led to a tangible erosion of support
that could hamper his reelection efforts later this year. Why? Despite
repeated attempts to publicly appear neutral on the issue of race,
President Obama has repeatedly signaled otherwise in private and
unguarded moments, such as the *Rolling Stone* interview, that he believes race to be behind those who disagree with his leadership or
public policy priorities.

Consider the following excerpt from Kenneth T. Walsh's book
Family of Freedom: Presidents and African Americans in the White House
regarding President Obama's thoughts on his political opponents:

But Obama, in his most candid moments, acknowledged that
race was still a problem. In May 2010, he told guests at a private
White House dinner that race was probably a key component in
the rising opposition to his presidency from conservatives, especially right-wing activists in the anti-incumbent "tea party"
movement that was surging across the country. Many middle-
class and working-class whites felt aggrieved and resentful the
federal government was helping other groups, including bank-
ers, automakers, irresponsible people who had defaulted on their

mortgages, and the poor, but wasn't helping them nearly enough, he said.

A guest suggested that when tea party activists said they wanted to "take back" their country, their real motivation was to stir up anger and anxiety at having a black president and Obama didn't dispute the idea. He agreed that there was a "subterranean agenda" in the anti-Obama movement—a racially biased one—that was unfortunate. But he sadly conceded that there was little he could do about it.[3]

If Walsh's account is truly reflective of President Obama's thinking, it reveals an arrogant, dismissive demeanor toward several million of the citizens he was elected to lead. While race might motivate a minority of citizens to disapprove of Obama regardless of what he said or did in office, to characterize a wider effort by conservatives and Tea Party activists of having a racially biased subterranean agenda is very troubling.

As we discussed earlier, there were thousands of people who reacted angrily to President Bush's decision to initiate military activities to topple governments in Iraq and Afghanistan in the aftermath of the 9/11 attacks on America. However, President Bush never accused his political opponents of having a bias against him or attacked them for their opposition. He would generally note that while people could tend to agree to disagree, he had hoped the American people trusted him and the decisions he had made on their behalf.

The exchange cited from Kenneth Walsh's book further disturbs me because it implies that Obama had written off a segment of society on a strictly racial basis: "If they don't like me, it is because they are racially motivated." Has the former constitutional law professor and now president posited that significant opposition to his public policy agenda is based on his race and concluded that is the case? If so, did President Obama and his like-minded supporters decide this on fact or conjecture?

And finally, could President Obama have angered many of his fellow citizens when he demonized Republicans during the 2010 election cycle by declaring the following, transcribed by the White House from a campaign rally in Rhode Island on October 25, 2010:

> Finally, we get this car out of the ditch, and it's banged up. It needs some body work, needs a tune-up. But it's pointing in the right direction. The engine is turning and it's ready to go. And we suddenly get this tap on our shoulders. We look back, who is it? The Republicans. And they're saying, "Excuse me, we want the keys back." You can't have the keys back. You don't know how to drive! (Applause.) You can't have them back. Can't do it. (Applause.) Not after we've worked this hard.
>
> We can't have special interests sitting shotgun. (Laughter.) You know, we got to have middle-class families up in front. (Applause.) We can't—we don't mind the Republicans joining us. They can come for the ride, but they got to sit in back. (Laughter.)[4]

The implied reference to Rosa Parks's brave defiance in refusing to move to the back of the bus on December 1, 1955, in Montgomery, Alabama versus a divisive political pep rally held on October 25, 2010, on the eve of a midterm election with Democrats and President Obama fighting to keep Democratic control of the Congress was at best beneath the dignity of the office of the president. That President Obama would feel comfortable trying to play to the crowd by suggesting that Republicans were inferior and needed to ride in the back of the vehicle of state as blacks had had to do during Jim Crow as a sign of their inferiority is appalling.

And on the *same day* that the president had chortled that Republican should ride in the back of the car, consider what he told Latinos during an interview that was broadcast on the Univision Network:

> If Latinos sit out the election instead of saying, "We're going to punish our enemies and we're gonna reward our friends who stand with us on issues that are important to us," if they don't see that kind of upsurge in voting in this election, then I think

it's going to be harder and that's why I think it's so important that people focus on voting on November 2.[5]

E Pluribus Unum. "Out of Many, One." The president of the United States is elected to represent all of the citizens in the country he leads be they black or white, Jewish or Christian, rich or poor. To openly encourage Latinos to "punish our enemies and we're gonna reward our friends who stand with us on issues of importance to us" is not only beneath the dignity of the office Mr. Obama was elected to lead, but dangerously close to the cult of ethnicity brand of politics Arthur Schlesinger warned against. President Obama is not in a position to pick winners or losers—enemies or friends. The oath of office each president-elect must take before assuming the office of the presidency is prescribed by Article II, Section 1 of the United States Constitution:

> I do solemnly swear (or affirm) that I will faithfully execute the office of President of the United States, and will to the best of my ability, preserve, protect and defend the Constitution of the United States.[6]

The faithful execution of the office of the president of the United States does not permit President Obama the luxury to encourage people to punish their friends and reward their enemies—particularly not when Obama could be accused of picking winners and losers based on racial and/or ethnic traits.

In the days following October 25, 2010, leading up to the November 2nd election day, the Internet and blogosphere were filled with posts written by people who were enraged by President Obama's apparent racist remarks. The criticism had nothing to do with the president's skin color but rather with his urging that based on party affiliation one group of citizens should ride in the back of the bus and that Latinos should reward their friends and punish their enemies at the ballot box. One can only imagine how the mainstream media would have covered the story had President McCain been the author of those words, rather than the actual president, Barack Obama. Was Obama given a pass by the media in uttering these remarks because he was black? I will let the reader draw his or her own conclusion.

Rather than seeking to demonize his political opponents, President Obama would have been wise to have reflected on the words of the president he most sought to emulate: Abraham Lincoln. In Lincoln's second inaugural address the president told the nation:

> With malice toward none, with charity for all, with firmness in the right as God gives us to see the right, let us strive on to finish the work we are in, to bind up the nation's wounds, to care for him who shall have borne the battle and for his widow and his orphan, to do all which may achieve and cherish a just and lasting peace among ourselves and with all nations.[7]

Perhaps in the days to come President Obama will remember the words of his predecessor in office from Illinois and draw true inspiration from them rather than from the political wordsmiths that help him craft his public remarks to win pyrrhic victories in which some American citizens are labeled the winners and others political losers.

This will require Obama to speak more persuasively as to why his prescription is the proper medicine for the maladies that ail the country: a stagnant economy, looming short falls in the Social Security and Medicare programs, and the lack of a coherent vision for American foreign policy in an increasingly turbulent world as authoritarian governments fall or remain locked in a struggle for power across the Middle East and the African continent.

THE PATH AHEAD TO KEEP AMERICA FROM HEADING BLACKWARDS

While we have reflected on a number of indicators that show the United States of America to be increasingly divisive on matters of race, there are several steps I believe we must take together as a society if we are truly going to embrace the notion that our diversity is our strength and our strength is our diversity rather than become balkanized in communities segregated by race/ethnicity rather than citizens of the United States drawn together by our common bond.

(1) Embrace the American motto: *E Pluribus Unum*—"Out of Many, One"

In the last several decades we have made several significant strides forward as a nation. People of color seized the opportunity to obtain an education once government-sanctioned separate-but-equal discrimination was struck down in the historic *Brown v. Board of Education* decision before the Supreme Court in 1954. From the financial services sector to the field of academia, in the halls of Congress and the Supreme Court as well as the Oval Office itself, people of color have shattered glass ceilings that once seemed impenetrable. And yet with the historic election of the nation's first black president, the country has become polarized along racial lines in ways that could never have been entirely predicted on January 20, 2009.

As members of the Congressional Black Caucus and political commentators like Tavis Smiley fault President Obama for not pursuing a "black agenda," the country is forced to confront leaders who openly advocate a public policy agenda based on skin color/ethnic identification rather than best course for America as a whole. Most Americans can trace their ancestry to faraway lands; some of our forefathers immigrated here to chase the American dream while others were involuntarily brought to our shores to help build it for others. Regardless of our past, we all share one unique aspect in common regardless of our skin color and/or ethnic heritage: we are American citizens.

We have been blessed in the twenty-first century with an equal opportunity to achieve the American dream through hard work, perseverance, and ingenuity. Balkanization based on race or ethnicity serves only to pull our society further apart rather than bring us closer together. We don't need a black agenda, a white agenda, or a Latino agenda to fulfill our destiny. We need an American agenda that harnesses our strengths and talents regardless of the color of our skin.

We must not form racial and/or ethnic enclaves that, whatever they contribute to multiculturalism, promote isolated and segregated rather than inclusive communities. The pioneers of the civil rights era would be appalled that the legacy of their brave work to eliminate segregation in the United States was instead used as a wedge to demand special, rather than equal, rights based solely on race or ethnicity from their fellow citizens.

(2) End, Not Mend Affirmative Action Programs Based on Race

For us truly to embrace the notion that out of many we are one, we must end government-sanctioned programs that discriminate based on racial and/or ethnic characteristics. The march for equality is over in most respects. Yes, there remains in certain communities a disparity between wealth between blacks and whites. This can be overcome via hard work, children being brought into the world with loving two-parent households, and students going to school to learn the skills they need to compete in an increasingly competitive global economy. Affirmative action programs that treat one group of citizens under the color of law differently than others are not only wrong, but immoral.

We can take an honest look in the mirror and recognize that there are many steps we can take as a society to narrow the wealth and opportunity gap that exists in America today. I believe education is the civil rights issue of the twenty-first century. If we seek to avenge past discrimination with discrimination in the present, we have hardly addressed the true underlying issues that hinder advancement of people of color.

For too long we have tolerated schools that have little to do with teaching children and more to do with preserving the rights of teachers to accrue seniority and job security, while failing in their mission of preparing the next generation of leaders. By taking affirmative action to ensure our most at-risk students are taught and nurtured in schools conducive to learning rather than serving as a repository to shuffle students from one grade to the next, we will address deficiencies in learning and ensure that children are prepared for college through the knowledge gained in classroom instruction from nursery school to their final year in high school.

Gradually and over a period of time, blacks and other students of color will not be eyed with the suspicion that they were admitted to fill minority quotas, with one standard of admission requirements for whites and a lower standard for people of color. Similar suspicions will be eased in the workplace when the goal of a diverse workplace does not discriminate against candidates based on the color of their skin. The best and the brightest will be motivated to work for the best bank, school, law firm, or advertising agency, and well-prepared and qualified candidates will be selected based on their merit rather than skin color.

Over time, the lingering doubts of whether a promotion was denied or an opportunity to advance thwarted due to affirmative action to place less qualified individuals in desired positions once a new culture slowly evolves that values hard work and intellect to attract, recruit, and hire the best qualified people regardless of the color of their skin, but rather based on the content of their character and ability.

Moreover, if we still seek to take affirmative steps to reach a hand up, rather than a handout, to those most in need, shouldn't a person's economic and educational status be examined rather than strictly administering such programs based on skin color?

(3) The March for Civil Rights Is Over

As Americans, we have overcome much of the dark stain slavery has inflicted upon our society and our history. The marches for equality during the civil rights era have resulted in an America where people are free to learn, live, and work as equals with their fellow citizens. The barriers that once blocked blacks from entry into America's finest public and private institutions of higher learning have been removed, but the new opportunities will remain useless unless children are prepared to learn and compete at an early age.

Groups such as the NAACP and the Congressional Black Caucus need to examine their role and purpose in the twenty-first century. Do we really need a National Association for the Advancement of Colored People when the very term itself is offensive? Is such segregation wise when a young black man has been elected president of the United States? Shouldn't we be seeking to advance *all* Americans regardless of the color of their skin?

As for the Congressional Black Caucus, why are they permitted as a government-sanctioned organization to segregate based on race and ethnic lines and prohibit the inclusion of whites, Asians, and Latinos who have been eager to join in the past? Our elected leaders in the local, state, and federal levels have an obligation to promote the best interests of all the constituents they were elected to serve, not just those of a particular ethnic hue. What should be good for the goose should be good for the gander—if whites aren't permitted to form a legislative caucus and exclude blacks, then blacks should not be permitted to do the same toward whites.

Similarly, there is no such thing as black leaders in America anymore. Gone are the days where charismatic young men such as Dr. Martin Luther King and Malcolm X could purport to speak singularly and convincingly for the needs of the black community. Our country has evolved from a time in which blacks were marginalized and largely living in the Southern part of the United States to one in which blacks live in all fifty states and receive the protections and safeguards of the Constitution that once only applied to whites. At the time the Voting Rights Act of 1965 was passed, there were only three hundred African American officials elected across the country. Today there are more than nine thousand, including forty-three members of Congress.[8]

Also, many of the strong leaders from the civil rights era in the 1960s emerged from the pulpits of their local churches; today, blacks serve as CEOs of Fortune 500 companies, as four-star generals in the United States military, and of course, as president. Thankfully, the days of being black and excluded from American society are over.

Despite many attempts by the mainstream media to coronate the Reverends Jesse Jackson Sr. and Al Sharpton as national leaders of the "black community," I would contend no such community exists.

Just like every other racial/ethnic group in the United States there are blacks who are wealthy, while others are poor. Blacks who live in urban cities while others who live in rural communities; blacks with Ivy League educations while others have yet to graduate from high school.

In other words, seeking to define a community by color or ethnicity and then allowing one or two individuals to speak for an entire race is not reflective of where we are as an American society today. This attempt to neatly define a group of people, to put them in convenient boxes, is nothing more than a divisive, racist attempt to marginalize one group of people in society at the expense of others. The Reverends Jackson and Sharpton are quite content to perpetuate this fictitious black vs. the rest of America narrative because it allows them to call for special, rather than equal, rights based on race in which they can determine who the winners and losers are on a given issue. Have you ever wondered where the millions of dollars of grants and gifts that have been donated to ostensible charitable organizations under the control of these two men have gone? I have. What tangible ends or accomplishments have they achieved as a result?

Once we move away from defining people based on their skin color and focus on an individual's given strengths and weaknesses, we can then move away from a cult of ethnicity mind-set that rewards an entire group based on their ethnicity rather than rewarding individuals based on their unique merit. Just as one leader cannot purport to speak for all white people, no one man or several individuals can lay claim to speak for an entire group of people brought together only based on the color of their skin.

(4) We Must Eliminate Race as a Wedge Issue in Politics

January 20, 2009, will be a day long remembered in American history: for one of the last barriers had been shattered that many had never dreamed possible. On that day, Barack Hussein Obama took the oath of office and became the forty-fourth president of the United States. Unfortunately, after campaigning on a theme of unity and inclusiveness, President Obama and his supporters would inject race into substantive discussions of public policy and government in a way that proved corrosive to our national cohesiveness.

From telling us that America has been a nation of cowards, claiming that white police officers had acted stupidly in arresting a black professor, or branding the Tea Party movement as racist, what should have been three years of an Obama presidency that spoke to the unity of our society has instead been marked by a level of racial tension that has not been seen in years.

We must remind our elected officials that they are not given the distinct privilege of public service to then discriminate against their constituents on racial/ethnic lines. The steady erosion of support from white voters President Obama has witnessed during his first term in office may well inhibit his ability to occupy the Oval Office for another four years. What remains to be seen is whether President Obama can recalibrate his presidency to freely administer the laws of the American justice system to ensure all citizens are treated fairly under the color of law rather than press or deny prosecution based on the skin color of the victim or alleged perpetrator.

President Obama would go a long way to eliminate the suspicion that his administration favors blacks and other ethnic minorities by offering a full explanation as to why a case won by the Department of Justice against the New Black Panther Party was dropped. At the same time, Attorney General Holder should have been fired for his nation of cowards comments, his reference during a congressional hearing to blacks as "my people," and for not thoroughly investigating whether the Department of Justice Civil Rights Division declines to prosecute crimes against alleged black discrimination under the law in cases where the victim is white versus vigorous prosecutions of white defendants when the alleged victims are black.

As President Kennedy once famously remarked that race has no place in American law and life, President Obama would be well served to remind those who serve in his administration of this cornerstone principle. We can vigorously debate issues, discuss the best course ahead for the United States, and politely agree to disagree with our fellow citizens. But branding one group of citizens as our friends and others as enemies is not only destructive, but particularly divisive, when done so on the basis of race.

I would implore all participants in public service to set an honorable example for their fellow citizens to follow by refraining from hurling allegations of racism against political opponents to muzzle their legitimate right to speak. Instead, by limiting charges of racism to disturbing events that warrant swift repudiation, if not legal action, we can restore a more civil discourse in every aspect of our life in society.

Finally, America's first black president has an obligation to all of the citizens he is honored to represent regardless of their skin color. President Obama movingly spoke of setting aside past grievances and bringing the country together once he was elected and inaugurated as president. Unfortunately, his deeds have not matched the lofty goals he set for himself and for the country. Unlike some of my conservative brethren, I do not want the Obama presidency to be a failure. I may want many of his domestic and foreign policy initiatives to be defeated on their merits, as I believe the United States remains a center-right country and many of the president's priorities to expand government have troubled many people as being too much government, too much debt, and too many barriers for the private sector to create jobs that will stem the tide of America's perilous economy.

At the same time, I believe President Obama's election has forever changed the perception of the United States at home and abroad. No longer will children, when asked what they would like to be when they grow up, receive a wry chuckle from a grandparent when the child responds "president of the United States." With his election, Obama shattered a barrier I thought I would never see broken during the course of my life.

Whether he likes it or not, President Obama has an obligation to all of the citizens he represents to lead convincingly, without bias toward any favored constituency, and to inspire confidence in his leadership. Thus far in his administration, Obama has largely failed in these key areas. He is no longer in the Illinois State Senate: voting "present" has ceased to be an option for the most powerful chief executive in the world. As we have seen over the course of the first three years of the Obama presidency, he has shown a willingness, intentional or not, to allow members of his administration to show a bias based on race that has fueled the perception that Obama in certain situations favors blacks over whites, believes millions of his constituents are racist because they are conservative or self-affiliated with the Tea Party, and controls a Department of Justice that apparently favors discrimination over one group of people based on their race at the expense of others because of their race.

President Obama's failure to lead convincingly on many matters has failed to inspire confidence. Yet nothing the president has done has undermined Americans' trust in his leadership more than the perception that he is racially partisan. Whether the president and those closest to him can take corrective measures this late in his term to inspire voters to reward him with another term in office remains uncertain.

What is certain, however, is that President Obama can project to his fellow citizens that he sees America not in terms of black and white, but in terms of red, white, and blue. That we truly are a diverse melting pot that does not require multiculturalism or the cult of ethnicity to divide us based on skin color or national origin but instead draw strength from our singular status as American citizens. Most important, President Obama can set an example for all Americans to follow that will put an end to the acrimony that has dominated our political landscape since his election to office: putting an end to special, rather than equal, rights based on the color of skin of a group of people and celebrating the strength each individual brings as a unique American citizen.

APPENDIX

IIIIIIIIIIIIIIIIIIIIIIIIIIIIIIIIIIIIIIIIIIIIIIIIIIIIII

DECLARATION OF BARTLE BULL FROM: RACE NEUTRAL ENFORCEMENT OF THE LAW? THE U.S. DEPARTMENT OF JUSTICE AND THE NEW BLACK PANTHER LITIGATION—AN INTERIM REPORT. NOVEMBER 19, 2010.

Similar testimony was provided by Bartle Bull, who was serving on that date as part of a roving legal team on behalf of Senator John McCain's presidential campaign. Mr. Bull has extensive experience in political campaigns and a record of supporting the voting rights of minorities. Among his past activities, Mr. Bull indicated that he had served on the Lawyers' Committee for Civil Rights Under Law in Mississippi in the 1960s; was the publisher of the *Village Voice;* was the New York campaign manager for Senator Robert Kennedy's presidential campaign in 1968; was a campaign worker on behalf of Charles Evers's campaign for governor of Mississippi; was the 1976 New York State campaign manager for Jimmy Carter's presidential campaign; was the 1980 chairman for the New York Democrats for Edward Kennedy; was the chairman of New York Democrats for both Mario Cuomo and Hugh Carey; and that he worked for Ramsey Clark's Senate campaign. As to the 2008 election, Mr. Bull indicated that he was chairman of New York Democrats for John McCain.

Mr. Bull was interviewed by Department of Justice personnel on

Election Day, as well as in preparation for the lawsuit eventually filed by the Department. In a declaration prepared for use in the lawsuit he stated, in part:

> I watched the two uniformed men confront voters, and attempt to intimidate voters. They were positioned in a location that forced every voter to pass in close proximity to them. The weapon [a nightstick] was openly displayed and brandished in sight of voters.
>
> I watched the two uniformed men attempt to intimidate, and interfere with the work of other poll observers whom the uniformed men apparently believed did not share their preferences politically.
>
> In my opinion, the men created an intimidating presence at the entrance to a poll. In all of my experience in politics, in civil rights litigation, and in my efforts in the 1960's to secure the right to vote in Mississippi through participation with civil rights leaders and the Lawyers Committee for Civil Rights Under Law, I have never encountered or heard of another instance in the United States where armed and uniformed men blocked the entrance to a polling location. Their clear purpose and intent was to intimidate voters with whom they did not agree. Their views were, in part, made apparent by the uniform of the organization the two men wore and the racially charged statements they made. For example, I have heard the shorter man make a statement directed toward white poll observers that "you are about to be ruled by the black man, cracker." To me, the presence and behavior of the two uniformed men was an outrageous affront to American democracy and the rights of voters to participate in an election without fear. It would qualify as the most blatant form of voter intimidation I have encountered in my life in political campaigns in many states, even going back to the work I did in Mississippi in the 1960s. I considered their presence to be a racially motivated effort to

intimidate both poll watchers aiding voters, as well as voters with whom the men did not agree.

Declaration of Bartle Bull at 2-3, United States v. New Black Panther Party for Self-Defense et al., No. 09-0065 SD (E.D. Pa., executed Apr. 7, 2009) (not filed), available at http://michellemalkin.cachefly.net/michellemalkin.com/wp/wp-content/uploads/2009/05/bull-declaration_04-07-20092.pdf (last visited October 21, 2010).

NOTES

IIIIIIIIIIIIIIIIIIIIIIIIIIIIIIIIIIIIIIIIIIIIIIIIIIIIIIII

PROLOGUE

1. Arthur M. Schlesinger Jr., *The Disuniting of America: Reflections on a Multicultural Society* (New York: W. W. Norton & Company, 1998), 17.
2. "MLK Speech Before the Youth March for Integrated Schools," *Peacework* Magazine (December 1998–January 1999), accessed March 21, 2011, http://www.peaceworkmagazine.org/pwork/1298 /declead4.htm.

CHAPTER ONE

1. *Scott v. Sandford,* 60 U.S. 393, 405 (1857).
2. *The Oxford Companion to the Supreme Court,* Kermit L. Hall, ed. (New York: Oxford University Press, 1992), 761.
3. U.S. Constitution. amend. XIV, sec. 1, cl. 1.
4. Schlesinger, *The Disuniting of America,* 20–21.
5. Sarah Song, "Multiculturalism," *The Stanford Encyclopedia of Philosophy (Winter 2010 Edition),* Edward N. Zalta, ed., URL =

<http://plato.stanford.edu/archives/win2010/entries/multicultur
alism/>.

6. President John F. Kennedy's inaugural address, January 20, 1961,
American Rhetoric: Top 100 Speeches, www.americanrhetoric
.com/speeches/jfkinaugural.htm.

7. General George Washington, letter to the members of the Volun-
teer Association and other Inhabitants of the Kingdom of Ireland
who have lately arrived in the City of New York, December 2,
1783. The Writings of George Washington, ed. John C. Fitzpat-
rick, vol. 27, p. 254. http://quotationsbook.com/quote/45543
/#axzz1BPg5pRNs.

8. "Would Democrats Please Drop the Race Baiting?," Gregory
Kane, Washington Examiner, August 31, 2011, http://washington
examiner.com/opinion/columnists/2011/08/would-democrats
-please-drop-race-baiting.

9. "Population Bulletin Update: Latinos in the United States 2010,"
Population Reference Board, December 2010, http://www.prb.org
/Publications/PopulationBulletins/2010/latinosupdate1.aspx.

10. National Center for Educational Studies, U.S. Department of Education, http://nces.ed.gov/whatsnew/commissioner/remarks2010
/11_18_2010.asp.

11. Richard D. Lamm, "I Have a Plan to Destroy America and Many
Parts of It Are Underway," The Social Contract, Spring 2004, 180–
181.

12. Schlesinger, The Disuniting of America, 23.

13. Columbia Journal of American Studies, quoting a speech given by
President Franklin D. Roosevelt on February 1, 1943, authorizing
Japanese Americans to serve in World War II. From "Internment
to Containment: Cold War Imaginings of Japanese Americans,"
in Go for Broke by Edward Tang, http://www.columbia.edu/cu
/cjas/tang-4.html.

14. "PM's Speech from Munich Security Conference," www.num
ber10.gov.uk., February 5, 2011, http://www.number10.gov.uk
/news/speeches-and-transcripts/2011/02/pms-speech-at-munich
-security-conference-60293.

15. Noam Chomsky, U.S. activist/linguist (1928–), Quotations Page, http://www.quotationspage.com/quote/37179.html.

16. "PM's Speech from Munich Security Conference."

CHAPTER TWO

1. Executive Order 10925 (March 6, 1961).

2. Ibid.

3. John F. Kennedy, "Radio and Television Report to the American People on Civil Rights," White House, June 11, 1963, John F. Kennedy Presidential Library and Museum, http://www.jfkli brary.org/Research/Ready-Reference/JFK-Speeches/Radio-and -Television-Report-to-the-American-People-on-Civil-Rights-June -11-1963.aspx.

4. Martin Luther King Jr., *Trumpet of Conscience* (New York: Harper & Row, 1968), 10 and 15.

5. Kai Wright, ed., "Learning to Talk of Race: The Modern Era," in *The African American Experience: Black History and Culture Through Speeches, Letters, Editorials, Poems, Songs, and Stories* (New York: Black Dog and Leventhal Publishers, 2009), 697.

6. *Adarand Constructors, Inc. v. Pena,* 515 U.S. 200 (1995), Clarence Thomas, concurring opinion.

7. Ibid.

8. *Hopwood v. Texas* 78, F.3rd 932 (1996).

9. Ibid.

10. Calif. Const. http://www.leginfo.ca.gov/.const/.article_1.

11. "California Students Protest Attack on Affirmative Action," *Militant* 60:43, December 2, 1996, http://www.themilitant.com/1996 /6043/6043_4.html.

12. Ibid.

13. "Jesse Jackson Leads Protest of California's Affirmative Action Ban on 34th Anniversary of King's 'Dream' Speech," *Jet,* September 15, 1997, 4.

14. Ibid.

15. Michael Eric Dyson, "Myths, Distortions, and History: Affirmative Action, with Ward Connerly, Moderated by Yvonne Scruggs-Leftwich," in *Debating Race with Michael Eric Dyson* (New York: Basic Civitas Books, 2007), 64.

16. Ibid., 66.

17. Ibid., 80.

18. Ibid., 81.

19. Ibid., 81–82.

20. *Abigail Noel Fisher v. University of Texas at Austin et al.*, "Brief *Amicus Curiae* of Gail Heriot, Peter Kirsanow & Todd Gaziano, Members of the United States Commission on Civil Rights, in Support of the Petitioner," U.S. (5th Ct. App., October 19, 2011).

21. *Grutter v. Bollinger,* 539 U.S. 306 (2003).

22. Ibid.

23. David A. Lehrer and Joe R. Hicks, "UC Proves Prop. 209's Point," *Los Angeles Times,* July 12, 2010, http://articles.latimes.com/2010/jul/12/opinion/la-oe-lehrer-affirmativeaction-20100712.

24. *Grutter v. Bollinger,* 539 U.S. 306 (2003); Frederick Douglass, "What the Black Man Wants: An Address Delivered in Boston Massachusetts, on 26 January 1865," in *The Frederick Douglass Papers,* J. Blassingame and J. McKivigan, eds. (New Haven: Yale University Press, 1991), 59 and 68.

25. "SMU Shuts Down Bake Sale to Protest Affirmative Action," Beaumont Enterprise.com, September 24, 2003, http://www.beaumontenterprise.com/default/article/SMU-shuts-down-bake-sale-to-protest-affirmative-749518.php.

26. Jennifer Styles, "Whites-Only Scholarship Generates Controversy," CNN.com, February 20, 2004, http://www.cnn.com/2004/EDUCATION/02/18/whites.only.scholars/.

27. "Texas Organization Offering Scholarships for White Males Only," Cleveland Leader.com, February 28, 2011, http://www.clevelandleader.com/node/16067.

28. Ibid.

29. John H. Bunzel, *Race Relations on Campus: Stanford Students Speak* (Stanford, Calif.: Stanford Alumni Association, 1992), xvi.

30. Ibid., 23–24.

31. Ibid., 41–42.

32. Michael Meyers, "Stop the Black-Only Treatment," *Washington Post,* May 26, 2006, A21.

33. Ibid.

34. Michael Meyers, "Stop the Black-Only Treatment," Washingtonpost.com, May 26, 2006, http://www.washingtonpost.com/wp-dyn/content/article/2006/05/25/AR2006052501985.html.

35. Ibid.

CHAPTER THREE

1. "Leader," Dictionary.com, March 14, 2011, http://dictionary.reference.com/browse/leader.

2. "Statement to the President of the United States by the Congressional Black Caucus," March 25, 1971, pp. 1 and 3, accessed March 14, 2011, http://www.house.gov/cleaver/cbc/pdf/CBC1971.pdf.

3. "Pres. Nixon, Late in Reply, but Tells Black Caucus; 'Our Goals Are Same,'" *Jet,* June 3, 1971, 5.

4. "Congressional Black Caucus (1971–), BlackPast.com, accessed March 14, 2011, http://www.blackpast.org/?q=aah/congressional-black-caucus-1971.

5. "Vision and Mission," Congressional Black Caucus Foundation, Inc., accessed March 18, 2011, http://www.cbcfinc.org/about-cbcf/visionmissiongoals.html.

6. Jake Sherman, "Rangel: Still Working to Avoid Hearing," *Politico,* July 27, 2010, http://www.politico.com/news/stories/0710/40301.html.

7. Formally known as the House Committee on Standards of Official Conduct.

8. Sally Goldenberg, "Desperate Rangel Wraps Self in Civil Rights," *New York Post,* August 30, 2010, 2.

9. Meghan Clyne, "President Bush Is 'Our Bull Connor,' Harlem's Rep. Charlie Rangel Claims," *New York Sun,* September 23,

2005, http://www.nysun.com/national/president-bush-is-our-bull -connor-harlems-rep/20495/.

10. Jonathan Allen and John Bresnahan, "Black Caucus Whips for Charlie Rangel Reprimand," *Politico*, December 2, 2010, http:// www.politico.com/news/stories/1210/45877.html.

11. Jonathan Allen and John Bresnahan, "House Censures a Defiant Charles Rangel by Overwhelming Vote," *Politico*, December 2, 2010, March 15, 2011, http://www.politico.com/news/stories/1210 /45883.html.

12. Star Parker, "Charlie Rangel, the Congressional Black Caucus and 'Free' Elections," Americans for Constitutional Government Reform, November 22, 2010. http://a4cgr.wordpress.com/2010/11 /24/08-415/.

13. Ron Christie, "Sorry, Charlie," *Huffington Post*, December 10, 2010, http://www.huffingtonpost.com/ron-christie/sorry-charlie _b_783839.html.

14. Ibid.

15. John Bresnahan, "For CBC, the Joy Is Tempered by Worry," *Politico*, September 23, 2009, 24.

16. Mary Katharine Ham, "Eyewitness to St. Louis Scuffle: 'SEIU Representative Punched Him in the Face.'" *The Blog*, in *Weekly Standard*, August 7, 2009, http://www.weeklystandard.com/we blogs/TWSFP/2009/08/eye_witness_to_st_louis_scuffl.asp.

17. David Freddoso, "Will N.A.A.C.P. Repudiate Their Own Racist Comments About Kenneth Gladney, Caught on Tape?" *Washington Examiner*, July 12, 2010, http://washingtonexam iner.com/blogs/beltway-confidential/will-naacp-repudiate-their -own-racist-comments-about-kenneth-gladney-caugh#ixzz1G m9gWKQJ.

18. Emanuel Cleaver, II, "A Letter to America from the New Chairman of the Congressional Black Caucus," Congressional Black Caucus, accessed February 17, 2012, http://www.house.gov/cleaver /cbc/letter.html.

19. Josephine Hearn, "Black Caucus: Whites Not Allowed," *Politico*,

January 22, 2007, http://www.politico.com/news/stories/0107/2389.html.

20. The House Ethics Committee is comprised of an equal number of Republicans and Democrats. The committee may investigate alleged ethical transgressions by members of the House of Representatives and either drop the charges due to lack of evidence, or offer a series of sanctions on which the full House may vote. These sanctions might consist of a reprimand, a censure in which a member must stand in the well of the House where the charges are read to the member after a vote of censure occurs, or expulsion for violating the rules of the House.

21. Alexander Laska, "Congressional Black Caucus Continues to Block Cao," Scoop Daily, May 14, 2009, accessed on Georgia Heritage Council, February 17, 2012, http://georgiaheritagecouncil.org/site2/commentary/dean-racist-black-caucus042710.phtml.

22. Lisa Lerer and Nia-Malika Henderson, "Tension Between CBC, Obama," Politico, March 11, 2010, 1.

23. "Bush Deficit Vs. Obama Deficit in Pictures," in Foundry, a blog in the Heritage Foundation, March 24, 2009, http://blog.heritage.org/2009/03/24/bush-deficit-vs-obama-deficit-in-pictures/.

24. Lerer and Henderson, 20.

25. Hamil R. Harris and Krissah Thompson, "Obama to Meet at the White House with Black Church Leaders," Washington Post, April 6, 2010, http://www.washingtonpost.com/wp-dyn/content/article/2010/04/05/AR2010040505745.html.

26. "Only for the Privileged Few? Members of Congress Value School Choice—for Themselves," Washington Post, April 20, 2009, A14.

27. Ibid.

28. "AFC Praises Recent Passage of D.C. Scholarship Bill from Key Committee," PR Newswire, March 10, 2011, http://www.prnewswire.com/news-releases/afc-praises-passage-of-dc-scholarship-bill-from-key-committee-117759763.html.

29. Robin Shulman, "Harlem Program Singled Out as Model," Washington Post, August 2, 2009, A3.

30. Ibid.

31. The Congressional Budget Act of 1974 prescribes that the president of the United States must deliver to the Congress a budget submission no later than the first week in February while Congress is mandated to complete their budget for the upcoming fiscal year no later than April 15. In 2010, for the first time since the adoption of the Congressional Budget Act in 1974, Congress did not even consider a budget resolution outlining the manner in which federal funds were to be spent for the upcoming fiscal year.

CHAPTER FOUR

1. Quotes attributed to the Reverend Jeremiah Wright taken from the Web site BumpShack, http://bumpshack.com/2008/03/18/pastor-jeremiah-wright-controversy-quotes/.

2. Barack Obama's Speech on Race, *New York Times,* March 18, 2008, http://www.nytimes.com/2008/03/18/us/politics/18text-obama.html?_r=1.

3. Ibid.

4. Ibid.

5. Ibid.

6. Daniel Patrick Moynihan, "The Deterioration of the Negro Family," in Kai Wright, *The African American Experience* (chap. 2, n. 5), 568–69.

7. Colbert King, "Celebrating Black History as the Black Family Disintegrates," *Washington Post,* February 5, 2011, http://www.washingtonpost.com/wp-dyn/content/article/2011/02/04/AR2011020404934.html.

8. Taken from a report issued by the New York City Department of Health and Mental Hygiene, http://www.nyc.gov/html/doh/html/vs/vs.shtml.

9. "41% of NYC Pregnancies End in Abortion," 7online.com, Janu-

ary 9, 2011, http://abclocal.go.com/wabc/story?section=news/lo
cal/new_york&id=7883827.

10. King, "Celebrating Black History as the Black Family Disintegrates."

11. "Barack Obama's Speech on Race."

12. Ibid.

13. *Carpe Diem,* economics blog by Mark. J. Perry, February 20,
2010, http://mjperry.blogspot.com/2010/02/dc-public-schools-129
-trillion-28170.html.

14. Ibid.

15. Ibid.

16. Ibid.

17. Will Dobbie and Roland Fryer, Jr., "Getting Beneath the Veil
of Effective Schools: Evidence from New York City," Harvard
University, November 2011, 1, http://www.economics.harvard
.edu/faculty/fryer/files/effective_schools.pdf.

18. Ibid.

19. Geoffrey Dickens, "Chris Matthews Hails Obama Speech as
'Worthy of Abraham Lincoln,'" *Newsbusters,* a blog in Tell the
Truth!, March 18, 2008, http://newsbusters.org/blogs/geoffrey
-dickens/2008/03/18/chris-matthews-hails-obama-speech-wor
thy-abraham-lincoln.

20. "Mr. Obama's Profile in Courage," *New York Times,* March 19,
2008, http://www.nytimes.com/2008/03/19/opinion/19wed1.html
?_r=1&ref=opinion.

21. Pearl S. Buck, "Obama Evokes Lincoln to Launch 2008 Bid,"
BookRags, February 10, 2007, http://www.bookrags.com/news
/obama-evokes-lincoln-to-launch-2008-moc/.

22. Recall that Chief Justice Roger Taney wrote the infamous opinion in the *Dred Scott* decision that ruled blacks were not afforded
citizenship protections nor were they American citizens under the
Constitution.

23. Abraham Lincoln, "First Inaugural Address," March 4, 1861,
http://www.bartleby.com/124/pres31.html.

24. Lauren Collins, "The Other Obama: Michelle Obama and the Politics of Candor," *New Yorker,* March 10, 2008, http://www .newyorker.com/reporting/2008/03/10/080310fa_fact_collins #ixzz1Etuay8ft.

CHAPTER FIVE

1. "Barack Obama's Acceptance Speech," *New York Times,* August 28, 2008, http://www.nytimes.com/2008/08/28/us/politics/28text -obama.html.
2. Ibid.
3. "Obama Victory Speech," *Huffington Post,* November 5, 2008, http://www.huffingtonpost.com/2008/11/04/obama-victory -speech_n_141194.html.
4. "Barack Obama's Acceptance Speech."
5. John Blake, "Obama's Victory Caps Struggles of Previous Generations," CNN.com, November 5, 2008, http://edition.cnn.com /2008/POLITICS/11/04/obama.history/index.html.
6. David Paul Kuhn, "That Huge Voter Turnout? Didn't Happen," *Politico,* November 8, 2008, http://www.politico.com/news/sto ries/1108/15422.html.
7. Ibid.
8. Jeff Zeleny, "Obama Arrives in Washington After Train Trip," *New York Times,* January 17, 2009, http://www.nytimes.com/2009 /01/18/us/politics/18obama.html.
9. "President Barack Obama's Inaugural Address," *White House Blog* on the White House Web site, January 20, 2008, http:// www.whitehouse.gov/blog/inaugural-address/.
10. Michael Eden, "Reflecting on Obama's 'Just Words' Speech," *Start Thinking Right Blog,* June 3, 2008, http://startthinkingright.word press.com/2008/06/03/reflecting-on-obamas-just-words-speech/.
11. Proclamation by President Barack Obama on a National Day of Renewal and Reconciliation, January 20, 2009, White House,

http://www.whitehouse.gov/the-press-office/national-day-renewal
-and-reconciliation-2009.

12. "Attorney General Eric Holder at the Department of Justice African American History Program," United States Department of
Justice, February 18, 2009, http://www.justice.gov/ag/speeches
/2009/ag-speech-090218.html.

13. Terry Frieden, "Holder: U.S. a 'Nation of Cowards' on Race Discussions" CNN.com, February 18, 2009, http://articles.cnn.com
/2009-02-18/politics/holder.race.relations_1_holder-affirmative
-action-black-history-month?_s=PM:POLITICS.

14. Walter E. Williams, "A Nation of Cowards," Townhall.com, February 25, 2009, http://townhall.com/columnists/walterewilliams
/2009/02/25/a_nation_of_cowards.

15. "President Barack Obama's Inaugural Address."

16. Ibid.

17. David Mamet, *The Secret Knowledge: On the Dismantling of
American Culture* (New York: Sentinel, 2011), 35.

18. "Press Briefing by Press Secretary Robert Gibbs," White House,
February 20, 2009, http://www.whitehouse.gov/the_press_office
/Briefing-by-White-House-Press-Secretary-Robert-Gibbs-2-20
-2009/.

19. Helene Cooper, "Attorney General Chided for Language on
Race," *New York Times,* March 7, 2009, http://www.nytimes.com
/2009/03/08/us/politics/08race.html?_r=1.

20. Ibid.

21. Ibid.

CHAPTER SIX

1. "Memorandum: Recommended Lawsuit Against the New Black
Panther Party for Self-Defense and Three Individual Members for
Violations of Section 11(b) of the Voting Rights Act., Department
of Justice #166-62-22," December 22, 2008. Written to Grace

Chung Becker, Acting Assistant Attorney General, from Christopher Coates, Chief, Voting Section; Robert Popper, Deputy Chief; J. Christian Adams, Trial Attorney; and Spencer R. Fisher, Law Clerk, United States Department of Justice.

2. Ibid., 4.

3. Ibid., 6.

4. Ibid., 7.

5. "'Security' Patrols Stationed at Polling Places in Philly," http://www.youtube.com/watch?v=neGbKHyGuHU.

6. "Memorandum: Remedial Memorandum Concerning Proposed Injunction Order, DJ #166-62-62," May 6, 2009. Written to Loretta King, Acting Assistant Attorney General, from Christopher Coates, Chief, Voting Section; Robert Popper, Deputy Chief; and J. Christian Adams and Spencer R. Fisher, Trial Attorneys, United States Department of Justice.

7. United States Commission on Civil Rights, Hearing on the U.S. Department of Justice and the New Black Panther Party Litigation, July 6, 2010, unnumbered hearing materials.

8. Ibid.

9. Jerry Seper, "Career Lawyers Overruled on Voting Case," *Washington Times,* May 29, 2009, http://www.washingtontimes.com/news/2009/may/29/career-lawyers-overruled-on-voting-case/?feat=home_cube_position1.

10. "Intimidate the CIA, Clear the Black Panthers?" *Washington Examiner,* August 16, 2009, http://washingtonexaminer.com/opinion/2009/08/intimidate-cia-clear-black-panthers/93162.

11. Testimony of the Honorable Barack Obama, a U.S. Senator from Illinois, "Protecting the Right to Vote: Election Deception and Irregularities in Recent Federal Elections." Hearing Before the Committee on the Judiciary, U.S. House of Representatives, March 7, 2007, Pgs. 5-6., http://judiciary.house.gov/hearings/printers/110th/33810.PDF.

12. Krissah Thompson, "Harvard Professor Arrested at Home," *Washington Post,* July 21, 2009, http://www.washingtonpost.com/wp-dyn/content/article/2009/07/20/AR2009072001358.html.

13. "News Conference by the President," White House, July 22, 2009, http://www.whitehouse.gov/the-press-office/news-conference -president-july-22-2009.

14. "Obama Seeks to Clarify 'Stupidly' Comment, Praises White Policeman," Fox News.com, July 24, 2009, http://www.foxnews .com/politics/2009/07/24/obama-seeks-clarify-stupidly-comment -praises-white-policeman/.

15. Ibid.

16. "Statement by the President," White House, July 24, 2009, http:// www.whitehouse.gov/the-press-office/statement-president-james-s -brady-briefing-room.

17. "Toplines—Gates Arrest—July 28–29, 2009," Rasmussen Reports, http://www.rasmussenreports.com/public_content/politics /questions/pt_survey_questions/july_2009/toplines_gates_arrest_ july_28_29_2009.

18. Associated Press, "Cop, Scholar to Meet Again after Obama Chat," MSNBC.com, July 31, 2009, http://www.msnbc.msn.com /id/32210408/ns/politics-white_house/.

19. J. Christian Adams, "Adams, Inside the Black Panther Case Anger, Ignorance and Lies," *Washington Times,* June 25, 2010, http:// 222.washingtontimes.com/news/2010/jun/25/inside-the-black -panther-case-anger-ignorance-and-/.

20. U.S. Commission on Civil Rights, "Race Neutral Enforcement of the Law? DOJ and the New Black Panther Party Litigation: An Interim Report," November 19, 2010, 74.

21. Ibid., 75.

22. Ibid., 58.

23. Ibid.

24. Ibid.; Jerry Markon & Krissah Thompson, "Dispute over New Black Panthers Case Causes Deep Divisions," *Washington Post,* October 22, 2010, http://www.washingtonpost.com/wp-dyn/con tent/article/2010/10/22/AR2010102203982.html. (According to the writers, "Legal experts have called the reversal exceedingly rare, especially because the defendants had not contested the charges.")

25. David Mamet, *The Secret Knowledge: On the Dismantling of American Culture,* 185.

26. "A Third Former DOJ Official Steps Forward to Support J. Christian Adams," PJ Media, July 6, 2010, http://pjmedia.com/blog/breaking-former-doj-officials-stepping-forward-to-support-j-christian-adams/.

27. U.S. Commission on Civil Rights, "Race Neutral Enforcement of the Law?," i.

28. "Debbie Wasserman Schultz Compares GOP-Backed Voting Bills to Jim Crow," *PolitiFact,* a blog in *Tampa Bay Times,* June 9, 2011, http://www.politifact.com/truth-o-meter/statements/2011/jun/09/debbie-wasserman-schultz/debbie-wasserman-schultz-compares-gop-backed-votin/.

29. Ibid.

30. Ibid.

31. James Taranto, "Eric Holder's People," *Wall Street Journal,* March 2, 2011, http://online.wsj.com/article/SB10001424052748703559604576176381487078812.html?mod=googlenews_wsj.

32. "Attorney General Eric Holder Speaks at the Lyndon Baines Johnson Library and Museum," Austin, TX, December 13, 2011. http://www.justice.gov/iso/opa/ag/speeches/2011/ag-speech-111213.html.

33. See full Bartle Bull Statement in Appendix. The titles associated with Bartle Bull come directly from page 6 of the Civil Rights Commission's report on the New Black Panther Party. http://www.usccr.gov/NBPH/USCCR_NBPP_report.pdf.

34. Ibid.

CHAPTER SEVEN

1. Ben Pershing, "Moran: GOP Won in 2010 Because 'A Lot of People' Don't Want Black President," *Virginia Politics,* a blog in *Washington Post,* January 27, 2011, http://voices.washingtonpost.com/virginiapolitics/2011/01/moran_2010_gop_victories_happe.html.

2. Jeffrey M. Jones, "Obama Approval Rating Stable, Polarized," Gallup, April 7, 2009, http://www.gallup.com/poll/117355/obama -approval-rating-stable-polarized.aspx.

3. Krissah Thompson, "Blacks at Odds over Scrutiny of President," *Washington Post,* April 6, 2009, A01.

4. Ibid.

5. "Harry Belafonte Calls Herman Cain a 'Bad Apple,'" *Click,* a blog in *Politico,* October 10, 2011, http://www.politico.com/blogs /click/1011/Harry_Belafonte_calls_Herman_Cain_a_bad_apple .html.

6. Ibid.

7. This figure was subsequently revised to $812 billion.

8. Transcript of CNN's *Anderson 360,* February 19, 2009, http:// www.freerepublic.com/focus/f-news/2188981/posts.

9. James Janega, "Rev. Al Sharpton Denounces New York Post Editorial Cartoon as Racist," *Chicago Tribune,* February 19, 2009, http://www.chicagotribune.com/news/nationworld/chi-talk-new -york-post-cartoonfeb19,0,3058822.story.

10. Ibid.

11. Oliver Burkeman, "New York Post in Racism Row over Chimpanzee Cartoon," February 18, 2009, *Guardian,* March 10, 2011, http://www.guardian.co.uk/world/2009/feb/18/new-york-post -cartoon-race.

12. Daniel Luzer, "Al Sharpton Is Wrong About Monkey Cartoon," *Mother Jones,* February 18, 2009, http://motherjones.com/riff/2009 /02/al-sharpton-is-wrong-about-monkey-cartoon.

13. "Weekly Address: President Obama Outlines Goals for Health Care Reform," White House, June 6, 2009, http://www.white house.gov/the_press_office/WEEKLY-ADDRESS-President -Obama-Outlines-Goals-for-Health-Care-Reform/.

14. Bonnie Erbe, "Obama's Approval Rating Tumbles as He Learns on the Job," *U.S. News and World Report,* September 1, 2009, http://www.usnews.com/opinion/blogs/erbe/2009/09/01/obamas -approval-rating-tumbles-as-he-learns-on-the-job.

15. Ibid.

16. "Remarks by the President to a Joint Session of Congress on Health Care," White House, September 9, 2009, http://www.whitehouse.gov/the-press-office/remarks-president-a-joint-session-congress-health-care.

17. Maureen Dowd, "Boy, Oh, Boy," *New York Times,* September 13, 2009, http://www.nytimes.com/2009/09/13/opinion/13dowd.html.

18. Ibid.

19. Lisa Flam, "George W. Bush: Kanye West Katrina Comment Was 'Disgusting,'" AOL News, November 3, 2010, http://www.aolnews.com/2010/11/03/bush-kayne-west-katrina-comment-disgusting-moment/.

20. Meghan Clyne, "President Bush Is 'Our Bull Connor' Harlem's Rep. Charles Rangel Claims," *New York Sun,* September 23, 2005, http://www.nysun.com/national/president-bush-is-our-bull-connor-harlems-rep/20495/.

21. Maureen Dowd, "Boy, Oh, Boy," *New York Times,* September 13, 2009, http://www.nytimes.com/2009/09/13/opinion/13dowd.html.

22. "Congressman Suggests People Will Don 'White Hoods' If Wilson Not Rebuked," FoxNews.com, September 15, 2009, http://www.foxnews.com/politics/2009/09/15/congressman-suggests-people-don-white-hoods-wilson-rebuked/.

23. Mark Murray, "Carter: Race Plays Role in Obama Dislike," NBC-News.com, September 15, 2009, http://firstread.msnbc.msn.com/_news/2009/09/15/4431383-carter-race-plays-role-in-obama-dislikes.

24. "Carter Again Cites Racism as Factor in Obama's Treatment," CNN.com, September 15, 2009, http://articles.cnn.com/2009-09-15/politics/carter.obama_1_president-jimmy-carter-president-obama-health-care-plan?_s=PM:POLITICS.

25. Marc Ambinder, "Race Over," *Atlantic,* January/February 2009, 65.

26. Kathleen Parker, "Playing the Racial Deck," *Washington Post,* September 20, 2009, A21.

27. Kevin Hectkopf, "Obama's Approval Rating Dips to New Low," CBSNews.com, January 11, 2010, http://www.cbsnews.com/8301 -503544_162-6084818-503544.html.

28. Stephanie Condon, "Poll: Obama Health Care Marks Hit New Low," CBSNews.com, January 11, 2010, www.cbsnews.com/8301 -503544_162-6084856-503544.html?tag=contentMain%3bcon tentBody.

29. Chris I. Young, "NAACP's Khalfani: Expect 'Blacklash' on Health Care," *Richmond Times-Dispatch,* March 22, 2010, http://www2 .timesdispatch.com/news/2010/mar/22/naac22gat_20100322 -120801-ar-8273/.

30. William Douglas, "Tea Party Protestors Scream 'Nigger' at Black Congressman," McClatchy, March 20, 2010, http://www.mc clatchydc.com/2010/03/20/90772/rep-john-lewis-charges-protest ers.html.

31. Letter from the National Tea Party Federation to Congressional Black Caucus Chair Barbara Lee, April 24, 2010.

32. Andrew Breitbart, "I Got My Correction Thanks to the *New York Times,* Now Who's Next?" Big Journalism, August 3, 2010, http:// bigjournalism.com/abreitbart/2010/08/03/i-got-my-correction -thanks-to-the-the-new-york-times/.

33. William Saletan, Ben Jacobs, and Avi Zenilman, "A Troubling Story About Al Sharpton," *Slate,* September 8, 2003, http://www .slate.com/articles/news_and_politics/ballot_box/2003/09/the_ worst_of_al_sharpton.html.

34. Ibid.

35. John McWhorter, *Winning the Race: Beyond the Crisis in Black America* (New York: Gotham Books, 2006), 158–59.

36. Allison Samuels and Jerry Adler, "The Reinvention of the Reverend Al," *Newsweek,* August 3, 2010, 34.

37. Robert Rector, "The Effects of Welfare Reform," Heritage Foundation, March 15, 2001, http://www.heritage.org/research/testimony /the-effects-of-welfare-reform.

38. Ibid.

39. Ibid.

40. David Goldman, "Black Unemployment Keeps Trending Higher," CNNMoney.com, December 4, 2009, http://money.cnn.com/2009/12/04/news/economy/black_unemployment/.

41. Michelle Miller, "African-American Unemployment at 16 Percent," CBSNews.com, June 19, 2011, http://www.cbsnews.com/stories/2011/06/19/eveningnews/main20072425.shtml.

42. Ibid.

43. Annalyn Censky, "Black Unemployment: Highest in 27 Years," CNNMoney.com, September 2, 2011, http://money.cnn.com/2011/09/02/news/economy/black_unemployment_rate/index.htm.

44. Guy Benson, "Black Influencers Urge 'Racial Loyalty' to Obama," Townhall.com, October 18, 2011, http://townhall.com/tipsheet/guybenson/2011/10/18/black_influencers_urge_racial_loyalty_to_obama.

45. Krissah Thompson, "Can Obama Hold On to African American Voters in 2012?," *Washington Post,* October 17, 2011, http://www.washingtonpost.com/politics/can-obama-hold-on-to-african-american-voters-in-2012/2011/09/30/gIQA1IeisL_print.html.

46. Reverend Al Sharpton, "Eric Holder Is Correct: Let the Federal Government Stop the Racism of Individual States," *Huffington Post,* December 15, 2011, http://www.huffingtonpost.com/rev-al-sharpton/eric-holder-voter-id_b_1151175.html?ref=latino-voices&ir=Latino%20Voices.

47. Transcript, *PoliticsNation,* MSNBC.com, http://www.msnbc.msn.com/id/45568664/ns/msnbc_tv-politicsnation/#.TuuNDZj7UfE.

48. "Rev. Al Deep in the Red," Isabel Vincent and Melissa Klein, *New York Post,* December 10, 2011, http://www.nypost.com/p/news/local/manhattan/rev_al_deep_in_the_red_FFFX2IRlXVlP0sh79dWyxL.

49. Allison Samuels and Jerry Adler, "The Reinvention of the Reverend Al," *Newsweek,* August 3, 2010, 37.

CHAPTER EIGHT

1. Jann S. Wenner, "Obama in Command," *Rolling Stone,* October 14, 2010, 39.
2. Dan Balz and Haynes Johnson, "A Political Odyssey: How Obama's Team Forged a Path That Surprised Everyone, Including the Candidate," *Washington Post,* August 2, 2009, A11, cited in Kenneth T. Walsh, *Family of Freedom: Presidents and African Americans in the White House* (Boulder, Colo.: Paradigm Publishers, 2011), 184.
3. Walsh, *Family of Freedom,* 223.
4. "Remarks by the President at DCCC General Reception, Rhode Island Convention Center, Providence, Rhode Island," White House, October 25, 2010, http://www.whitehouse.gov/the-press -office/2010/10/25/remarks-president-dccc-general-reception.
5. Ashley Southall, "Obama Vows to Push Immigration Changes," *Caucus,* a blog in *New York Times,* October 25, 2010, http://the caucus.blogs.nytimes.com/2010/10/25/in-appeal-to-hispanics -obama-promises-to-push-immigration-reform/.
6. U.S. Constitution. art. II, sec. 1.
7. Abraham Lincoln, "Second Inaugural Address," March 4, 1865, http://www.bartleby.com/124/pres32.html.
8. John Lewis, "A Poll Tax by Another Name," *New York Times,* August 26, 2011, http://www.nytimes.com/2011/08/27/opinion/a -poll-tax-by-another-name.html?_r=1.

Index

||||||||||||||||||||||||||||||||||||||||||||||||||||||||||

AUTHOR'S NOTE AND ACKNOWLEDGMENTS

||||||||||||||||||||||||||||||||||||||||||||||||||||||

March 2012. New York, NY

What I sought to undertake with *Blackwards* was a contemporary yet historical look at the destructiveness that seeking special, rather than equal, rights has done and is doing to the United States of America. The guiding principle of our country says it all: "Out of many, one." Chances are we have all hailed from a distant shore at some point in our not too distant past and arrived at America's shores either voluntarily or under servitude. What we have built together, in spite of the dark legacy of slavery and discrimination, is the true beacon of hope and democracy that is the envy of the world.

Yet the struggles fought in the Civil Rights era are now threatened by a mentality that celebrates an identification along racial and ethnic lines that will destroy the very essence of who we are as a country. More than anything, I wanted to stress the importance of American unity as citizens of a diverse and rich society rather than falling prey to the myopic notion that one group of people should be treated under the color of law any different than any other citizen. We are not comprised of African Americans or black leaders in the twenty-first century; we are comprised of more than 300 million American citizens.

As I have found throughout the book-writing process, there are far too many people for me to thank individually for their endless patience in me as I undertook this task. I remain grateful to my publisher Thomas Dunne for his belief in this project. Thanks again to senior editor Rob Kirkpatrick for his patience and counsel, along with my agent and friend Eric Lupfer from William Morris Endeavor for helping connect the dots.

To my colleagues and dear friends Andy Hartsfield and Peter Kaylid, your generosity of spirit and kindness over the years means so very much to me. I also wish to thank my magnificent colleagues from the John F. Kennedy School of Government Institute of Politics at Harvard University. Many of the revisions of this book occurred during my time as a resident fellow in the fall of 2011. To my fellow Fellows, staff, and students at the IOP, I am grateful for your unwavering patience and energy as I juggled writing this book while leading my Washington Political Ecosystem study group. I particularly wish to acknowledge IOP Director Trey Grayson, Cathy McLaughlin, Eric Andersen, Cathey Park, and Kerri Collins for their support and encouragement. And Diane Casey-Landry, Christina Bellantoni, Tad Devine, Steve Grand, and Linda Moore Forbes, my fall 2011 Fellows, will be friends for life.

And as always, I remain in love and awe of my amazing wife, Jennifer Kay Christie. Your love, patience, consideration, and support are endless. Our life together is the best gift I could have ever hoped for.

9-12

MK